Sociology, Work and Industry

Sociology, Work and Industry

Dr. Lalita Sharma

RANDOM

RANDOM PUBLICATIONS
NEW DELHI (INDIA)

Sociology, Work and Industry

ISBN 978-93-5111-414-7

Published in 2014 in India by

RANDOM PUBLICATIONS

Reprint : 2015

4376-A/4B, Gali Murari Lal, Ansari Road
New Delhi-110 002
Phone : +91-11-43580356, +91-11-23289044
e-mail: randomexports@gmail.com, sales@randompublications.com, info@randompublications.com

Type Setting by : Keystoneprintads, Delhi-110051
Digitally Printed at : Replika Press Pvt. Ltd.

Preface

Work, in sociology, is defined as the carrying out of tasks, which involves the expenditure of mental and physical effort, and its objective is the production of goods and services that cater to human needs. An occupation, or job, is work that is done in exchange for a regular wage or salary. In all cultures, work is the basis of the economy, or economic system. The economic system for any given culture is made up of the institutions that provide for the production and distribution of goods and services. These institutions may vary from culture to culture, particular in traditional societies versus modern societies.

The sociology of work goes back to the classical sociological theorists. Karl Marx, Emile Durkheim, and Max Weber all considered the analysis of modern work to be central to the field of sociology. Marx was the first social theorist to really examine the conditions of work in factories that were popping up during the industrial revolution, looking at how the transition from independent craftwork to working for a boss in a factory resulted in alienation and deskilling.

Durkheim, on the other hand, was concerned with how societies achieved stability through norms, customs, and traditions as work and industry changed during the industrial revolution. Weber focused on the development of new types of authority that emerged in modern bureaucratic organizations.

The study of work, industry, and economic institutions is a major part of sociology because the economy influences all other parts of society and therefore social reproduction in general. It doesn't matter if we are talking about a hunter-gatherer society, pastoral society, agricultural society, or industrial society; all are centered around an economic system that affects all parts of society, not just personal identities and daily activities. Work is closely intertwined with social structures, social processes, and especially social inequality.

This book is part of a recent and very exciting development. To the layperson it might seem obvious enough that the work and industrial sociology is part of the social world and not isolated from the rest of society.

I thank all members of my team who have helped in the preparation of the book. My special thanks go to "Random Publications" who have published the book.

– Dr. Lalita Sharma

Contents

1

Sociological Perspectives on the City

GLOBALISATION AND THE CITY

Globalisation has given major cities a role of hitherto unprecedented importance. It may be that consolidation of the solid web of economic, financial, political, cultural and tourist ties which today connects the world's major conurbations has helped to strengthen this position. The current dynamic places cities in a situation of great responsibility to the extent that economic development, technological innovation, scientific advances and artistic creation are born out of the major urban conglomerations, and spread from there to the rest of civilization. Europe is a fine example of this. A comparative analysis of the regions which make up the European Union reveals that there exists a clear correlation between urban identity and development. It is the capital regions, and those which contain major conurbations, which occupy the leading positions in terms of economic prosperity.

However, this status as leader, positioning cities centre stage, also implies a wide range of shared challenges. In the same way that major cities take on a common, collective protagonism, based on this great network which connects them and which seems to drive everything, it is also clear that, today, large conurbations face the same challenges, and are confronted with the same threats. There are many demands to which the city is subjected in the modern world. Migratory processes, the saturation of urban spaces, the obsolescence of infrastructure, the need to introduce technological innovation, industrial relocation... these are all challenges on a large scale which, to a greater or lesser extent, define the agenda of every major city.

They are issues requiring an effective, committed and responsible answer from local authorities. They are all trials to be overcome, challenges to the sustainment of the current model of global development, so clearly based on urban progress. We must come up with formulas which will allow cities to find an effective and convincing responses to all these questions. Having come this far, it would seem wise to stop and think about the desirability of considering a new urban policy, as certain states seem to be doing these days. It may be that the current distribution of responsibilities among the various administrative levels and the corresponding financial dependencies and balance, are obsolete. This is hardly surprising since they date from earlier times in which the prominence of the city was by no means comparable to the situation today.

This is a complex task, a transformation which is necessary but, given its scope, will not be simple and will demand the involvement of all. In this regard, it is striking how in modern times "competitivity" is commonplace in literature dealing with regional and urban spaces whereas references to "cooperation" are few and far between. There can be no doubt that our system feeds on competition and that the rivalry among the world's main cities to attract qualified inhabitants, manufacturing investment or tourist flows is creating the possibility for change, adaptation, innovation and, ultimately, progress.

However, it is no less true that, to the extent that major cities face the same challenges, to the extent that their future is defined by the same phenomena, there also exists a huge capacity for cooperation. There would seem to be enormous possibilities for urban collaboration on a global scale. Major cities must be capable of establishing and developing the mechanisms needed to guarantee a leading position in the allocation of public administration in line with their key role in our societies.

In this whole context, it would seem necessary to convince the other agents involved that major cities are today suffering the consequences of a clear imbalance which is threatening the sustainability of the model itself. There is no correlation between the scale and complexity of the role they have played over recent years and the financial and administrative resources on which they are able to draw in order to put this into practice. Hence, the need to seek out new perspectives and imaginative solutions to bring balance to the situation.

EFFECTS OF GLOBALIZATION ON CITIES IN DEVELOPING COUNTRIES

Studies on urban land use shows that urban areas are of enormous political, social, economic and cultural importance to the various regions in which they are located. Cities of more influences are those that could be classified in "world and regional cities", of which Lagos the case study is striving to belong. Lagos is about the third largest and economically active city in Africa after Cairo in Egypt and Johannesburg in South Africa.

These cities have population of over 10 million people. Lagos is located in West Africa, Egypt in North Africa and Johannesburg in South Africa. Thus these cities can be described as the "Africa Triangle Cities Network". They are strategically positioned to influence and determine the socioeconomic destiny of Africa. These cities have the tendencies to be among the largest and most fast-growing among cities in developing countries. These cities serve simultaneously as national and regional engines of growth, centres of technological and cultural creativity, houses of the poor and deprived, the sites and sources of environmental pollution. These are the most sensitive settlements in Africa to global economic policies and technological development. Thus, they transmit development impulses to the hinterlands of the areas in which they are located.

Lagos in particular is essentially the loci of Nigeria and the West Africa economic activities. The city is linked both to the economies of the hinterland in Nigeria at the national scale and to the wider regional and global economy through trade, investment, culture and technology. Like in cities throughout the world, Lagos has the history of earlier responses to global reforms in organisation of production, economic policies with significant spatial effects than any other city in the West African sub-region. This could be traced to the rate of responses of cities in Nigeria to recent global economic policies in Africa at the dawn of the twenty-first century.

Three recent global socio-economic policies are discussed in this paper in order to bring to focus the trends of socio-economic development attempts in Africa in general and Nigeria in particular. In Nigeria in the recent times, these policies are the Structural Adjustment Programme, the New Partnership for Africa Development and the concept of privatisation. The paper touched on the influence of the World Bank and the International Monetary Fund in particular as they attempt at improving the economic fortune of developing countries. It discusses indepth of the contemporary economic phenomenon "globalisa-tion", its contextual basis, advantages and the likely problems it could create for developing countries as these countries are not in any advantageous position to reap the full benefits of globalisation.

Conceptual Issues

Three key economic transformation concepts are discussed in this paper as examples of attempts at achieving sustainable economic development in Nigeria. These concepts are the SAP, NEPAD and the issue of privatisation. The Structural Adjustment Programme was introduced into Nigeria as a response to the International Monetary Fund technical advice as a response to the recognition of the structural distortion in the Nigeria economy in 1986. The SAP was also designed to restore medium term viability to the balance of payment options of Nigeria. Adedeji stated that it may have been necessitated by the devastations of irresponsible domestic economic policies. However it requires policy action by deficit and surplus countries. This is necessary for the policy to produce the desired effects especially for developing economies. Specifically SAP was introduced into Nigeria when it became evident that the ad-hoc policies of the past could not bring about the desired change in the economy. It was aimed to achieve the following restructuring and diversification of the productive base of the economy, to achieve fiscal and balance of payment, to lay the basis for a sustainable non-inflationary or minimal inflationary growth, to lessen the dominance of unproductive investments in the public sector and to improve the sector's efficiency and intensify the growth potential of the private sector.

Despite the comprehensive breath, and the radical determination which characterised the programme, SAP was confronted with many problems during implementation some of which include substantial increases in prices of goods and services. Since its implementation relied on market forces to dictate the direction of the economy in an environment of insufficient government bureaucracy, relatively narrow and weak private entrepreneurship, high dependence on foreign input, it failed to produce the desired or optional solutions envisaged. It led to the collapse of the industrial sector as most industries could not cope with the high cost of imported raw materials and machinery. The housing and building materials sector also collapsed and a temporary stagnation was experienced in the construction and sustainable urban development sectors of the economy.

The New Partnership for Africa Development formulated by African leaders as a roadmap to Africa's development in the new millennium is worth mentioning. The thrust of NEPAD is that Africa's development strategy must be experimental and not imposed. It is also aimed at new partnership that is both credible and capable of reversing Africa protracted economic and political backwardness and increasing marginalisation in the world economy. This new policy is based on the condition that African out of their own volition are ready to take their destiny in their hands. That development is about empowerment and self-reliance and that its sustenance has to rest on the people and not the foreign benevolent guardians. NEPAC is however a comprehensive document on Africa future and position relative to global development. It comprises of policies on peace, security, democracy, politics, governance, infrastructure, human resource development, agriculture, environment, culture, science and technology, capital flow and market access.

Each theme has a programme of action. For example under infrastructure, it highlights vision on roads and highways, airports, seaports, railways, waterways and telecommunications. It states the need to increase investment in infrastructure and establishment of African institutions that will train and produce highly skilled technicians and engineers. Similarly under information and communication technology sub-theme, it stresses the need to work with regional agencies such as the African Telecommunication Union to design model policy legislation for telecommunication reform, regulatory capacity, establishment of a network of training and research institutions to built high-level manpower. Despite the impressive aim of NEPAD many scholars on Africa political economy are skeptical about its prospect, as the restructuring of the World Order has had many painfully consequences for Africa. With the mutation of GATT to WTO, for example, Africa forfeited a fairly reliable platform for tabling her grievances relating to multilateral trade agreement. Also, the greatest strength of Africa in world trade which is export of primary products have been eroded by biotechnology through the development of synthetic alternatives to primary commodities.

This definitely places Africa in a poor position in the WTO, thus positioning Africa in a largely unfavourable trading position in a global context. This situation Aderemi, noted places Africa in a peripheral position in the world economy as it has increasingly declining demand of her products in the world market. The option for survival is to make her market open, its policies structured to accommodate market signals with limited negotiating strength to dictate market prices. For NEPAC to survive therefore Africa will have to pool her resources together in order to place herself in a better position of negotiation. This will entail a radical and combative approach to solving the economy dilemma of Africa.

The third global economic policy ravaging the world is the concept of privatisation, especially of the State owned enterprises, services and infrastructure. Generally it involve the selling or leasing on State assets to the private sector. Its merits include its ability to reduce financial burdens on strained government budgets, capacity to improve efficiency of services and potential for attracting investment to capital starved sectors. It has the capacity to offer the chance of improving both the livelihoods of individuals and the services which they depends on in their day to day lives. Presently in Nigeria and in most developing countries the State have over-extended themselves, suffocating private and community initiatives in the provision and management of municipal services such as waste management, rail transit, parks, parking, water supply, electricity, telephone, amongst others.

Privatisation might not be total withdrawal leaving everything to the private sector. Appropriate government intervention such as in policy formation and monitoring are always in the hands of government. This demand highly skilled public administrators capable of performing such complex technically difficult and politically sensitive tasks. These requirements are not presently well developed in many developing countries including Nigeria. This means that government will have to prepare for this new role of transition from providers to enablers.

Also government will not only make initial assessments on how services should be supplied but also to administer her role as supervisor once these establishments are taken over by the private sector. The capacity required should include ability to analyse and maintain market conditions, manage and enforce contracts, regulation of monopolists, coordinate, finance and support producers, enable community self provision and support consumers with information and alternatives. This can only be achieved with government institutions sufficiently equipped to maintain the delicate balance between supporting private and community efforts. Towards achieving these objectives the Nigeria government established the Bureau of Public Enterprises to facilitate the privatisation of many government agencies in various sectors which include the oil sector, power, telecommunication, cement, hospitals, hotels, steel, air lines amongst others.

Appreciable progress have been made by the BPE, however efforts towards privatisation in Nigeria has been confronted with many teething problems among which are underpricing, unattractive incentives, instability in policies and enforcement. Most of the implementation efforts have been unfriendly to the people.

Globalisation and Developing Countries

The issue of globalisation which seeks to integrate various parts of the world into a global economy and global finance system has increasingly been attracting considerable debate. The forging of a global economy is an intoxicating and momentous process, one of the major structural features of the contemporary age. The concept of globalisation views the global economy as one, which works as a unit on real time on a planetary scale. It is an economy concept where capital flows, labour and commodity markets, information, raw materials, management and organisation are internationalized and fully interdependent throughout the planet. It corresponds to an attempt at contraction of space and time through the development of new means of communication and information technologies across the planet. Globalisation perceives the world as a trade unit without socio-political barriers and constraints.

It is the process through which people, goods and services, trades, ideas and information flows across the borders of countries with ease. This has been enhanced greatly by technological breakthrough through the development of the computer and telecommunication. Globalisation is characterised by liberalization of the world economies and economic activities that are free from institutional control and which fosters and promotes free market mechanism, private enterprise, open competition, professionalism and excellence in corporate governance. It seeks to promote specialisation and the principle of comparative advantage in the production of goods and services on a global scale. It is aimed at creating a new world economic order, efficiency, competitiveness, efficient allocation of resources and speedy growth of the world economy.

Since economic factors are very strong among factors influencing the growth of cities, there is no doubt that this new phenomena, like the transportation and automobile revolution will have pronounced effects on how cities will develop. This will vary among different world economic regions *i.e.* developing countries and the developed countries. First it can be speculated that globalisation would generate greater disparity and increase poverty in developing countries as these regions are not at equal levels and positions to compete with developed countries. Also it could be an attempt to impose western standards, needs and values in developing countries as successfully done with SAP, all to the benefit of developed world through their multinational corporations.

This is in line with the view of Simon in his historical excursion of Africa economic path, Simon stated that over the past millennium, developing countries particularly in Africa have been subjected to dramatic external interventions and influences enmeshing them firmly within the emerging world system. He stated further that with successive conquest, colonizations and associated cultural imperialisms of Arab and European, Islam and Christianity and more recently the western imposed modernization and spread of capitalist ideology all have transformed and internationalized African culture in all areas of life include the use of land as land use concepts and standards adopted by many African countries are reflections of their colonial masters home standards.

Effects of Globalisation on Cities in Developing Countries

In most developing countries cities globalisation impact will vary greatly in extent and intensity over time, spatially, within and between cultures and social class. Due to the weak financial base and technology, developing countries will be at a disadvantage position in a world of globalised trading of industrial products. Though this may vary within and among regions in developing countries. In Africa and Lagos in particular it will result into paucity of inward foreign direct investment and export of secondary and tertiary products as the traditional strengths of these regions are production and export of primary products, while a high proportion of manufactured goods are imported. Therefore globalisation is likely to be of little advantage if any to developing countries as most of them will turn into consuming nations.

At the global seen the influence of global economic direction have been documented in Latin America, Asia and Caribbean. Their findings shows that significant regional and local differences exists. This reflect, the vulnerability of these regions to external policies and the level of their integration into the changing international economic order. In the recently independent nations such as in South Africa, strands of European colonial impact still exist and Zimbabwe is rigorously battling the aftermath of colonial land tenure policy.

Unfortunately for developing countries globalisation is gradually resulting into a new structure of global competition due to the appearance of "global" markets and "global" production complexes. This scenario has been influence greatly by many factors among which are new innovations in technology, such as micro-electronics, telecommunication, material science all of which exert profound impact on refashioning world production systems. There has been tremendous growth of transnational production and the increase openness and interdependence among national economies. Also there has been a great lip in global financial market, with varsity improved global telecommunication and infrastructure.

This can easily be noticed in the investment of transnational companies particularly in telecommunication and transportation in Nigeria especially in Lagos. These changes have been manifesting at both the national, the Lagos urban economy and individual enterprises levels. At the national level the impact has been on the intensification of international and local competition for markets and investments. It has also increase the rate of employment into these new sectors though at the detriment of the formal industrial sector which is on the downward side. At the enterprises level, it has opened up the need for adoption of new process technologies, flexible working system, and organisation and shifting towards flexible rather than mass production system.

The concept of "space of flows" emerged from the process of globalisation. Also the emergency of "global or world cities" is fast growing roots. These cities are the loci for new international division of labour in manufacturing, they are key hubs for the control and coordination of global finance and producer services. Due to the strategic positions of these cities as the optimal beneficiaries of new, dynamic, highincome growth sectors of the economy "global city status" is something to be coveted, defended and fought for.

The effects of globalisation on the city land use is disturbing as it has both positive and negative effects. However, since it is a global trend it is better for cities to be positioned as a player in the phenomena. Despite the fact that Lagos within the African and particularly West African sub-region context is a leading city it stands to benefit in the new competition process through efficiency and job creation. For many cities in developing countries they will be left out of the globalisation process as they are not in comparative positions when compared with the developed countries. This might be a clug in the process of comparative development of the less developed regions.

This new international division of labour characterised by export-processing manufacturing may bypass many cites in less developed world to the extent that the economic structure of such nations will include the gradual depletion of industrial and production land uses. These nations will turn into merely consuming nations, thus creating dangerous socio-economic crisis in the immediate future. Also, these regions lack basic conducive environment for globalisation to strive. Apart from their spatial locations, their geographical significance is uncertain coupled with nonexistence of strong, and reliable state apparatus. They also lack competitive technology and human resource infrastructure. For Lagos, as in the case of many cities in developing regions the preconditions for global competition are not in existence. Such condition include the capacity to develop "niche product" which require flexibility in the production process. This can only be acquired through appropriate organisational framework and human resource. Due to instability, unreliable policy framework, poor state of infrastructure and security in many developing countries, a situation of which Lagos is not an exception globalisation processes have been stolled, with corresponding severe consequences for urban economies and environment.

In terms of industrial investments and land use, Rakodi noted that large foreign enterprises have continuously shunned Africa, thus turning Africa to be the only large and populous continent without a true newly industrializing country. It is perhaps only the city of Johannesburg that is presently aiming at attaining "world city" status in this decade.

Towards this, the city has evolved strategies which include building up the financial and producer service sector, attracting the offices of international organisations and developing a cultural strategy to image the city better to foreign investors. The formal economic sector in many developing countries is gradually on the decline due to the impediments to growth generated by globalisation. This is a prominent feature in Lagos as the informal sector has invaded the city economic fabric. In many countries in sub-Saharan Africa, regular urban wage employment opportunities constitute between 5-10 per cent.

Recent studies shows a decline from this range with Central African Republic (33.6%) and Gambia (27%). Also the formal wage employment in the public sector of these countries have been on the increase with massive retrenchments accompanied by the declining absorptive capacity of the formal private sector. Abiodun noted that at least 70 per cent of the unemployed in Lagos are aged between 15-29, while in Kenya according to House, the mostly affected age group for unemployment comprises those aged 20-29, who represent 65 per cent of all those reported as unemployed.

The socio-economic and spatial consequences of retrenchment is increasingly growing of the informal sector. This sector is characterised by small-scale, mostly family-operated or individual activities. This is a common phenomena in cities of the developing countries. In Africa Rondinelli and Kasarda, documented that this sector provide jobs for about 63 per cent of total work force in urban Africa. ILO estimates that in the 1990s about 93 per cent of Africa urban labour force will be in the informal sector. Also this sector appear as survivalist and enterprises types. The survivalist are in form of people unable to secure regular wage employment or access to economic sector of their choice. The enterprises group appears as small businesses employing between one to four paid employees, they are predominantly in the trade related activities.

Despite the gloomy nature of the benefit derivable from globalisation by cities in developing countries it is important to note that these cities with Lagos as an example has benefited enormously from this process.

Among the notable gains of the city are:

- Emergency of new employment opportunities.
- Inflow of capital
- Improve telecommunications
- Improved city-scape
- Improved transport infrastructure
- Rapid changes in economic structure
- Cultural integration
- Generation of revenue to government
- Improved local capacity.

Recently with the liberalization of many aspects of Nigeria economy such as in the mass media in particular, the telecommunication sector particularly the telephone, inflow of computer networks such as internet services etc.; all these have opened up new employment opportunities in Nigerian cities in particular as most of these services have their operational bases in the cities where there is pool of consumers and skilled labour force. This is very prominent in Lagos.

These activities takes place in space and specific locations, thus they have contributed in opening up of hitherto undeveloped areas in the city. Inflow of capital into the country to support the establishment of these services have been majorly from foreign investors as they possess the technology and high valued currency which can easily be converted into the local currency with good values. This has greatly revigorate the domestic economy of town and cities in Nigeria particularly in Lagos.

The city landscape has been significantly transformed by the installation, erection and conversion of existing buildings to fit into the new use of these global enterprises. This is more pronounced in the telecommunication sectors where giant billboards are now corporate status symbols in the cityscape. This has generated bandwagon effects into other sectors sense of outdoor advertisement. This serves dual roles of income generation and improved cityscape.

There has been improvement in the transportation sector. This is presently more pronounced in the air transportation sector where the private sector consist of both local entrepreneur and foreign investors. This has improved greatly the nature of air traveling in the country. A rapid transformation of the national economy has been experienced. Unfortunately this has been to the detriment of the industrial sector as the economy is shifting towards the services sector and importation of industrial goods.

Cultural transformation is also on the increase as the opening-up of the economic system allows exposure to cultures of other regions of the world particularly those of the home origins of transitional enterprises of Europeans, Americans and Asian origins. Tremendous financial gains have been experienced by all levels of government in Nigeria generally especially in the areas of licencing, while state and local governments have also generated enormous revenues from the establishment of new enterprises brought into the countries and various cities due to globali-sation trend.

The need to reap the benefit of these new service industries brought by globalisation has been a source of challenge to Nigerians, who at various levels braced-up to improve their capacities to fit into the requirements of this transformation.

Recommendations and Conclusion

Unfortunately most developing countries of the world have been in the world trade system on unfavourable terms in which they are dependent on developed countries. Though attempts were made in the 1960s to achieve autonomous economic and political status by means of statecentred and interventionist strategies they have achieve very little. With this unsuccessful attempts, developing countries are always vulnerable to the policy dictates of the developed world and international agencies especially the International Monetary Fund and the World Bank.

The practical effects of globalisation phenomena embraces a wide range of issues at socioeconomic, geographical and political levels. This paper has examined the diverse rhythms and characteristics of effects of globalisation on the future of cities in developing countries, with emphasis on Lagos, Nigeria. Since globalisation involve the process of building a world market with the aim of integrating national economies into the world market and the transition from a high volume economy into a high value economy, it will therefore require high level of political commitment, good governance and policy stability.

Nations in developing regions will have to refocus themselves by development of appropriate manpower through high yield capacity building process. This will have the dual advantage of technological development which is critical in the world where biotechnology has made nonsense of the traditional raw material export advantage position of developing countries.

It is also necessary for developing country especially in Africa to incorporate her NEPAD in an advantageous position in the globalisation process. This might require the development of the hybrid version peculiar to Africa. There should be value added to export and increase in the level of domestic savings through which appreciable capital base can be derived in a world where there is internationalization of fund. The issue of corruption should be addressed and the provision of investment friendly infrastructural facilities should be of prime concern of developing countries. Effort should be made towards achieving acceptable investment security and security to life and property.

POLITICS AND URBAN PLANNING

THE PROLOGUE

Cities are probably the most complex things that human beings have ever created. They are the wellsprings of culture, technology, wealth and power. People have a love-hate relationship with cities.

We are torn between our needs for community and privacy and the conflicting attractions of urban and rural life. Urban Planning can be defined as the design and regulation of the uses of space that focus on the physical form, economic functions, and social impacts of the urban environment and on the location of different activities within it. The various fields that are encountered in urban planning are:-

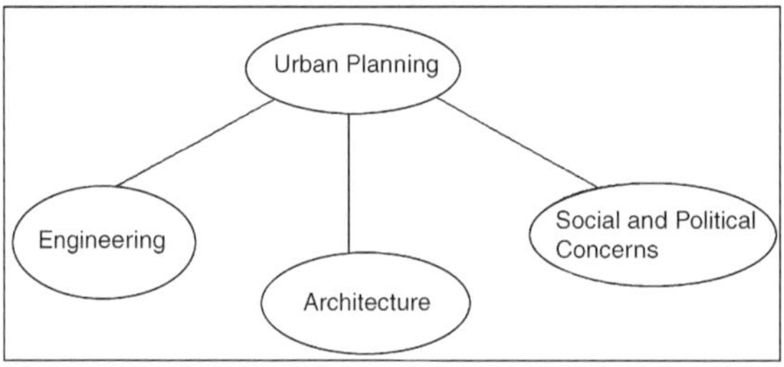

The need of the hour is sustainable development. With increasing population and growing pollution, we can't ignore the ill effects of planning on the environment.

Sustainable development refers to:

- Utilising the present resources keeping in mind the future needs of the society, so as not to exhaust the resources.
- It should not disturb the ecological cycle and hence preserve the environment.

History of Urban Planning

City planning has always been of chief concern since times immemorial. Evidence of planning has been unearthed in the ruins of cities in China, India, Egypt, Asia Minor, the Mediterranean world, and South and Central America. Early examples of efforts towards planned urban development include orderly street systems that are rectilinear and sometimes radial; division of a city into specialised functional quarters; development of commanding central sites for palaces, temples and civic buildings; and advanced systems of fortification, water supply, and drainage.

Most of the evidence is in smaller cities that were built in comparatively short periods as colonies. Often the central cities of ancient states grew to substantial size before they achieved governments capable of imposing controls.

Urban Planning in India

India has characteristically drifted with history, rising periodically to accomplish great things. In no field has this been truer than in town planning. From prehistoric Mohenjo Daro, to the imperial city of New Delhi, to Corbusier's Chandigarh, India has pioneered in town building.

The technique of diagnostic survey, commonplace in planning practice today, is the somewhat belated result of Patrick Geddes' work in India four decades ago: the City Improvement Trusts in existence since the 1800's are models of their kind.

Emerging Pattern of Urban Growth in India

The urban problems are not all of recent making. In India the urban situation had become serious because of the large increase in population since 1921.

While the percentage increase for the nation as a whole was 11%, 14%, 3% and 13.4% respectively, for the decennial periods 1921-1951, the urban areas increased by 21%, 32% and 54% respectively, during the same periods. The urban drift is continuing unabated. A comparison of the urban population in 1991 and 2001 is as follows:-

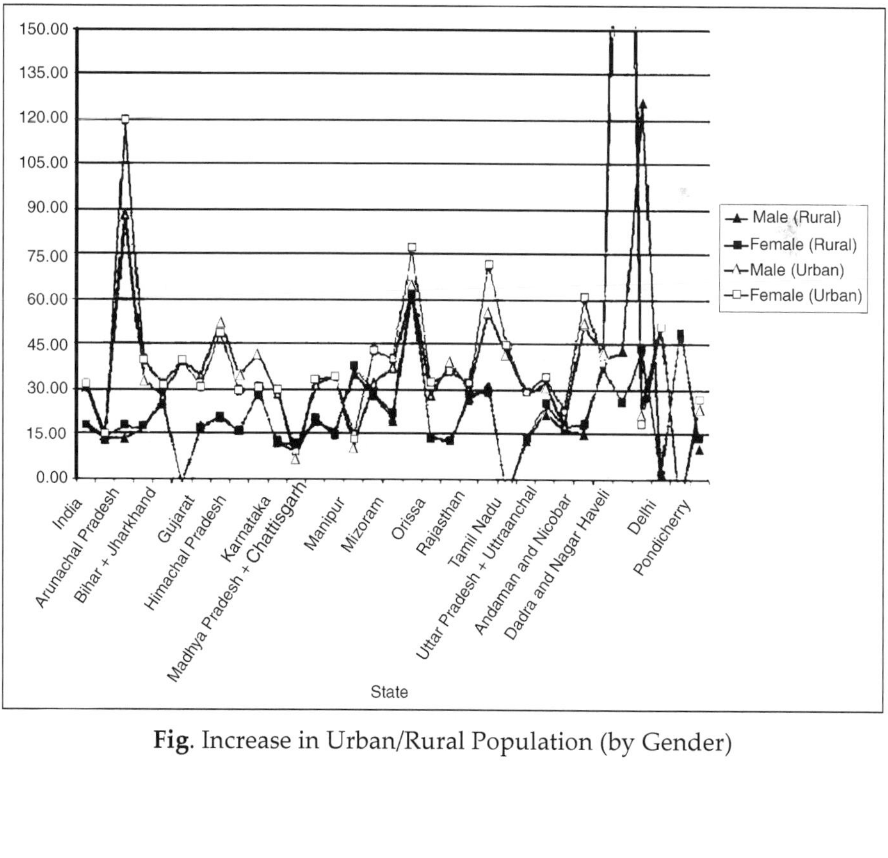

Fig. Increase in Urban/Rural Population (by Gender)

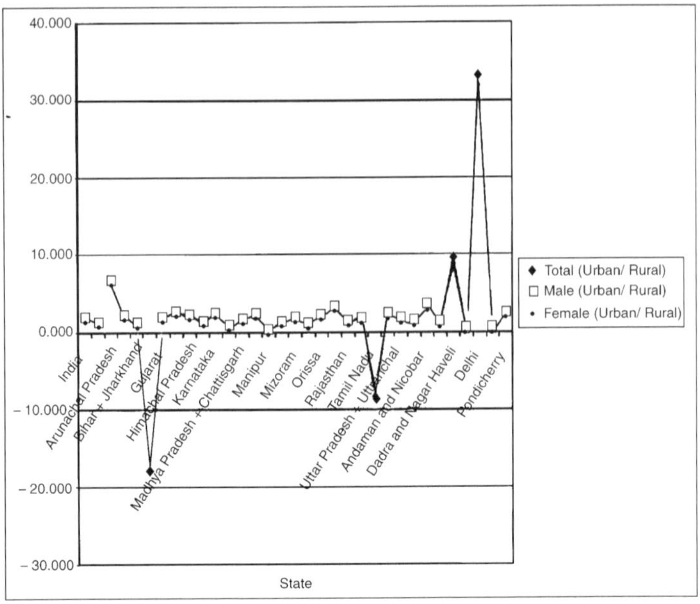

Fig. Ratio of Increase in Urban to Rural Population

The heavy shifts of population are the result of the lack of adequate employment opportunities in the villages and the attraction of relatively high wages and amenities in the towns. Unemployment and particularly underemployment in agriculture stimulates this tendency. Since 1947 when the country was partitioned, there has been a heavy influx of refugees into urban areas. The number of towns with populations in excess of 100,000 doubled in the twenty years prior to 1951. Today Greater Calcutta counts a population of about 5 million while Bombay and Delhi have populations of 3 and 1 million, respectively. Planning and development have not and perhaps could not keep pace. In contrast to the examples of New Delhi and Chandigarh most towns in India have grown haphazardly. They have a large proportion of substandard houses and huts of flimsy construction, poorly ventilated, over-congested and often lacking in the essential amenities.

On the state level some progress has been made in enacting planning legislation and setting up planning agencies. The results have not all been entirely satisfactory. In several cases efforts were made by some states to abolish or merge planning departments with the public works department. Nevertheless, the Second Plan largely places the onus of planning on the states. If planned urban development is to be undertaken, said the Planning Commission, "each state should have a phased programme for the survey and preparation of Master Plans for all important towns." The Commission noted that, in order that this might be accomplished, town and country planning legislation should be enacted in all states and the necessary machinery for its implementation should be set up.

Work of Sir Patrick Geddes

Sir Patrick Geddes was an innovative thinker in the fields of urban planning and education. He was responsible for introducing the concept of "region" to architectural planning. In India Geddes extended his ideas about regional surveying, cooperation between man and the environment, synthesis of knowledge, historical traditions, involvement of the people in their own betterment and the rediscovery of past traditions of city building. Among the many problems in India were the extreme poverty and obscenely overcrowded slums plaguing India's rapidily growing cities. In addressing these problems, Geddes wanted to revive indigenous customs and use them for modern purpose.

Geddes influenced the urban planning movement in many different ways. His work on regional surveying influenced Lewis Mumford and numerous others. Mumford, however, did not totally accept Geddes' ideas on social reconstruction. Yet, the method of considering social implications in city planning has carried over to the sustainable city projects of today. His understanding of the connection between the individual and the environment, as described in his last major work, Life Outlines of General Biology, constitutes the core of modern planning. In the last years of his life, Geddes settled in southern France, building a school at Montpellier. He tried to teach his views of life and the sciences.

While his son Arthur helped Geddes with his school in Montpellier, the Outlook Tower in Edinburgh received less attention and eventually had to close. Still, Geddes was recognized for his lifelong efforts by being knighted in 1931.

Key Features Of Urban Planning In India

Urban Planning in India includes the following:

- Town planning
- Regulation of land use for residential and commercial purposes
- Construction of buildings
- Planning for economic development
- Planning for social development
- Construction of roads
- Constructions of bridges
- Water supply for domestic use, industrial and commercial purposes
- Public health care management
- Sewerage, sanitation and solid waste management
- Proper fire services
- Urban forestation and maintenance
- Protection of environment through sustainable development
- Promotion of ecological balance and maintenance
- Safeguarding the interests of weaker parts of society

- Offering proper infrastructural help to the handicapped and mentally retarded population of the society
- Organized slum improvement
- Phased removal or alleviation of urban poverty
- Increased provision of basic urban facilities like public urinals, subways, footpaths, parks, gardens, and playgrounds
- Increased public amenities including street lighting, parking lots, bus-stop and public conveyances
- Continual promotion of cultural, educational and aesthetic aspects of the environment
- Increased number of burials, burial grounds, cremation grounds and electric crematoria
- Proper regulation of slaughter houses and tanneries
- Absolute prevention of/ zero tolerance of cruelty to animals
- Proper maintenance of population statistics, including registration of births and deaths records.

CASE STUDIES

Delhi

History

Delhi remains one of the oldest surviving cities in the world today. In fact, it is an amalgam of eight cities, each built in a different era on a different site – each era leaving its mark, and adding character to it – and each ruler leaving a personal layer of architectural identity. It has evolved into a culturally secular city – absorbing different religions, diverse cultures, both foreign and indigenous, and yet functioning as one organic entity.

Mir Taqi Mir, a poet from Delhi, wrote:

"The streets of Delhi are not mere streets;
They are like the album of a painter"

The first city of Delhi was Indraprastha founded by the Pandavas at the time of Mahabharata. Much later, the Tomar Rajputs, who ruled over Delhi, founded Dhillika; Alauddin Khilji built Siri; Tughlaqs added Tughlaqabad, Jahanpanah and Firozabad.

Humayun constructed his capital city Din Panah. His grandson Shahjahan built Shahjahanabad and almost a century and a half later Lutyen designed New Delhi – the Imperial capital of the British Raj. New Delhi was inaugurated in 1931. Today Delhi spills into the adjoining states of Haryana and Uttar Pradesh – still thriving in different eras of its rich history – and in step also with the rest of the world.

The Making of Modern Delhi

Delhi assumed its modern form when in 1912 the imperial capital of British India was shifted from Calcutta to Delhi.

Since then it has undergone 3 distinct phases of City Planningi:

1. The building of New Delhi by a team of British town- planners and architects led by Lutyens
2. The setting up of the Delhi Improvement Trust and the efforts at renovation of Old Delhi and then in the post-independence period.
3. The setting up of the Delhi Development Authority and its combined task of developing new areas and improving old ones 1950 onwards.

Phase 1

In 1912 the government decided to build a new capital city at Delhi separate from the existing city of Delhi. The Delhi Town Planning Committee consisted of the architect Edwin L Lutyens, captain G S Swinton and John A Brodie.

The new city was planned as a garden city with conscious symbolisation of British imperial power in India. Vast stretches of land were to separate the New city from the old city. Lutyens also planned the residential area for the government officials and the 'rajas' etc assisting the British Raj. But in this whole process almost no attention was paid to the problems of Old Delhi which suffered a lot in the times to come. Due to the creation of New Delhi, Old Delhi experienced a 28% surge in population from 1916-1926 resulting in the spilling over of the population from inside the walled city to the Paharganj area, whose restructuring was later abandoned by Lutyens due to resource constraints.

Also, no provision of housing was premeditated for the large no. of skilled and unskilled workers which immigrated in for the construction work of New Delhi. This negligence of the planners towards Old Delhi resulted in its transformation to a large slum area through deterioration and dilapidation.

Phase 2

In 1936, the declining public health of the Old Delhi led to the appointment of AP Hume, an officer on special duty, to suggest measures for relieving congestion in Delhi. In his Report on Relief of Congestion in Delhi Hume wrote "the city contains numerous welldefined slum areas of the meanest type and abounds in insanitary lanes and dwellings of constituting a menace to the public health of the whole urban area of Delhi." The report suggested the setting up of an Improvement Trust, a social body equipped with statutory authority for planning and executing a programme for decongestion of the city along with administration of public lands.

This led to the setting up of the Delhi Improvement Trust in March 1937. The stated purpose, however, was primarily administrative and only secondarily to deal with public health. However the slum clearance schemes prepared by the DIT could not get under way for the first three years because it had not provided for re-housing of the inmates of the slum to be cleared!

The government refused to sanction the schemes. On this ground and it was only then that re-housing of the displaced was planned. When it was eventually executed, fewer than 300 families were all could be re-housed over almost 13 years.

Phase 3

Post-independence Delhi was immediately overwhelmed by a deluge of refugee immigrants from west Pakistan as a result of partition. Many colonies were setup in the south and west like Kailash Colony, Kalkaji, Malaviya Nagar, Moti Nagar and Kirti Nagar to provide for this huge Punjabi population influx.

In the 1950s, it was realised that if the development of Delhi was to be a controlled and channelized process, then it was necessary to provide a Planning Body which could have a broad perspective and take decisions after conducting proper surveys of the area. There was political will behind it to develop the modern capital city of independent India. In December 1957 the Delhi Development Authority was constituted through an act of parliament. It evolved a draft plan in June 1960 and submitted it to the public for objections and suggestions. With due changes the final master plan was ready in November 1961 and in 1962 it was made law.

The plan was basically a land-management plan. It took into consideration the increase in Delhi's employment potential in government, trade and industry. On that basis it projected an increase in population up to 50 lakhs by 1981 and set 'urbanisable limits" which were to be enclosed by a 1 km wide 'green belt' to restrict further urbanisation and prevent surrounding urban areas from merging with Delhi. The plan basically marked out commercial areas, residential areas, industrial and educational areas, etc. Urban renewal rather than mere slum clearance was set as the approach to planning for redevelopment of the existing city.

Schemes for slum clearance were executed and 27 resettlement colonies were laid out relocating 1.2 lakh squatter households from squatter clusters near the heart of the city to its periphery. The squatter resettlement colonies were developed with metalled roads, public parks, water supply, public lavatories, street lighting, drains, shops, schools, dispensaries and community centres. Small-scale industrial units were located close to these colonies to ensure employ-ment in the neighbourhood. This was done to ensure it was a 'resettlement' and not just 're-housing'. The lands in the heart of the city from which the squatters were evicted and slums demolished were developed into parks and picnic spots especially around historic monuments, commercial centres, and some for residential areas.

Flaws in the Planning

But this rehabilitation plan itself was not successful as no significant attention was paid to the needs and requirements of the colonies and hence gradually the rehabilitation colonies themselves turned into planned slums and cholera epidemic occurred in them in 1988. The lowering of standard for housing plot size, for the quality and quantity of basic amenities such as latrines, drainage and water supply was the chief reason behind this problem. If citizens have to fight for the basic needs of life like a decent water supply and a clean latrine, it is nothing but an illusion to expect them to be happy by open spaces, roads and non-functional community centres.

Thus the residents of the resettlement colonies live crowded into small accommodation, with a absence of basic, everyday requirements such as a safe water supply, facilities for defecation and bathing, an adequate drainage system to remove rain water, etc, in the midst of wide roads and lanes, parks converted into reservoirs for the rain water, nonfunctional or under-utilised facilities such as the community centre. Distinctly separated from the better-off residential areas into large environmentally degraded expanses, these colonies are 'slums' if 'lack of sanitation' and 'an environment detrimental to health' are some of the basic characteristics of slums. The plans adopted were all based on dominant city planning practices of that time, that is, on models developed in the west, probably suited to their conditions. These models had to be imitated seemingly to give the citizens of this country, the best, to become developed. But in this approach the city planners forgot to take into account the fact that the conditions social, economic and political as well as the infrastructural base of Indian cities had a stark difference from the west.

The outcome of this planned development can be seen as a few obvious trends- Public health was one of the major goals of town planning. Over the years, however, public health was replaced by real estate as the major issue. The state, which began town planning partly as a means of discharging its responsibility towards the health of the citizens, became the monopolist real estate agent of Delhi. The DDA master plan was basically a 'land use plan' marking out commercial, industrial and residential areas and deciding upon the density per acre in residential areas. The DDA under- took large-scale acquisition of land in order to control future development of Delhi, and to make its own task of development economical.

Thus, it acquired almost sole monopoly on land available for development in Delhi. The acquisition, development and disposal of land became the major preoccupation of the DDA and considerations of social development, public health, progressive planning for the poor got left further behind. Slum clearance was 'necessary' in order to 'make better use' of the commercially valuable land available after clearance and not to rehabilitate the evicted.

Criticism by Sir Patrick Geddes

To take in view the ideas of Sir Patrick Geddes, we have a look at his chief guiding principles can be interpreted from the large number of reports and plans he had drawn up.

These include:

- To start from a given situation and let the plan evolve itself.
- To make best use of resources existing within the setting.
- To understand social, economic and cultural conditions through direct contact and to plan accordingly. The residents' physical, social and psychological needs to be taken into account.
- To take the residents along by use of cultural symbols which will be supported by the positive beneficial results they will themselves perceive because of the appropriate planning and solid action taken.
- To conserve and promote the good in local tradition, without any emotionalism about 'tradition'.
- To take a humanistic approach considering people's life as a whole and not just, say sanitation.
- Special attention to be given to the poor but basic principles to be applied to all.

Geddes came to India in 1915 and produced many town planning studies. He expressed his unambiguous disagreement with Lutyens' plan for New Delhi. For example, Geddes' method of decongestion was a 'conservative' survey. Intensive, on-the- spot surveying led to working out the minimum number of the most dilapidated houses to be pulled down in a manner such that open spaces were created within the congested areas allowing ventilation for each surrounding house. The fewer families displaced can then be resettled in to a developed area with a basic standard of housing and environmental hygiene. The new open spaces would be used for tree planting, as community squares, as a little green patch for kitchen-gardening, etc.

The DDA master plan incorporated a lot of his ideas-detailed surveys to know the existing situation and project into the future, a comprehensive plan, an attempt at categorising areas meant for conservation, rehabilitation or clearance, the 'mohalla' concept for residential areas. By this time, the civic survey and preparation of master plans had become accepted ingredients in the 'science' of town planning though without really acknowledging Geddes. Many components of the DDA plans show that the stream of thought was of Geddes. Prototype plans prepared for redevelopment of different types of slums, the concept of village clusters within the city, the experimentation with local tube- wells and piped water system in resettlement colonies all reflect the Geddesian approach at work. However, what one finds in implementation is that those parts of this approach which applied to the poor were either not implemented.

Present Day Scenario and Future Planning

However, even to the present date there are multiple problems that still exist in Delhi and the NCR region. The New Delhi area is still the only region that is a bit devoid of problems and congestion that the rest of the Delhi faces.

The biggest problem that modern day Delhi faces is the Transport Problem. The Plan of Lutyens to make the central New Delhi area a non-residential area and separating it completely from the residential zone itself has led to long daily commuting hours for the large workforce. And apart from the Government offices, there are many private corporate firms which have their offices in that area, so the no. of commuters multiplies manifold. The Bus service run by Delhi Transport Corporation has always been inadequate to bear such great no. of commuters and if all the citizens were to use private vehicles for commuting, there would not be an inch of space left on the 6-lane roads of Delhi.

Even though the construction of the Ring Road and the Outer Ring road has helped to divert the heavy long distance traffic away from the central area, still the no. of commuters is a gigantic figure. The city of Delhi with a population of round 12 million should have had a Mass Rapid Transit System network of at least 100 km by this time. The Delhi Metro project scheduled to have been completed fully by 2021 is aimed to cover whole of Delhi and provide for the commuting needs of the people. Apart from this, a mono-rail transport system is also expected to kick off.

The primary goal of DDA and planning authorities presently is to deflect the rising population of Delhi outwards to the NCR region chiefly Noida, Gurgaon and Ghaziabad. The development of these areas has been through the Sectoral approach which comprises development of the urban region in sets of small self sufficient units providing all basic civic amenities to its residents. This has been more or less a successful effort but still due to political pressures some villages and rural land could not be acquired which have been surrounded by city from all sides and now serve as a slum region and a source of crime. Also, no logical pattern has been followed in naming numbering these sectors, which is a pain for visitors in the city in locating an address.

Lucknow

The distinctive culture of Lucknow represents an important phase of transition in the definition of modern identities that coincided with the decline of the Mughal empire and the increasing role of the East India Company in Indian affairs. Lucknow's architecture, its town planning and monuments, mirrors the refashioning of identities through the fusion of different cultures and styles.

Lucknow traces its origin to the Suryavanshi dynasty of Ayodhya in ancient times, and derives its name from Lakshman, brother of Lord Rama the hero of the Indian epic, Ramayana. The city came into eminence only during the 18th century. In 1732, Muhammad Shah, one of the later kings of the once powerful Mughal dynasty, appointed Mohammad Amir Saadat Khan, a Persian adventurer of noble lineage, to the viceroyalty of the area known as Avadh, of which Lucknow was a part.

Saadat Khan was the founder of the famous dynasty known as the Nawab Wazirs-a dynasty that changed the face of this hitherto little-known place. Under his successors, Lucknow flowered as never before and all but became the cultural nerve centre of northern India. The rapid growth of Lucknow dates from 1755 when the fourth Nawab, Asaf-ud-Daula transferred the capital of Avadh from Faizabad to Lucknow and set about gifting to the city some of its most splendid architectural marvels, a tradition that was sustained by these successors.

Lucknow Metropolis, The State Capital of Uttar Pradesh has emerged as one of the most important cities of India in terms of modern technology, level of investment, institutional development and a progressive outlook. The projected population of Lucknow Urban agglomeration is 71.66 Lac which is covered by an area of 369.01 Sq.Km. The present metropolitan area of Lucknow is envisaged to be 3091.40 Sq.Km.

The city is situated at the junction of three national highways *viz.* NH 24 connects Delhi, NH. 25 connects Bhopal via Jhansi, NH. 28 connects Patna and four State highways *viz.* SH 25 connects Hardoi, SH 36 connects Raibareli, SH 56 connects Sultanpur and SH 40 connects Mohaan. Lucknow is well connected by rail and air route from different parts of India.

Moreover, as the spirit of vandalism is not yet extinct, the edifices, which have historical association or otherwise any architectural pretension, are gradually transformed into debris and ruins; while none yet takes the trouble to prepare a pictorial record of what Lucknow was,—so as to snatch whatever he can from the inevitable oblivion that follows. It is a matter of deep regret to see how the city is throwing off its skin; and its arts and manufactures, its old picture squeness, and its peculiar civilization, for which Lucknow was famous, are dying an unnatural death. The citizens look on, shed tears like women; and there their business is ended. They do nothing more; for deterioration, the daughter of idleness, is taking place in their physical and mental formations, as in all things else.

Among the extant Lucknow buildings we find two broad categories of buildings:

1. Religious buildings like: Imambaras, Mosques and other Islamic Shrines
2. Secular structures like: Enclosed Gardens, Baradaris, Palace Complexes.

The following are distinct features of Lucknow buildings:

- Use of Fish as as a decorative motif especially on Gates
- The use of Chattar as in the Chattar Manzil
- The Bardari
- Darwaza like Roomi Darwaza
- Enclosed Baghs like Sikandar Bagh
- Vaulted Halls like in the Asafi Imambara
- The labyrinth Bhool Bhulaiyan
- Taikhanas

Spatial Patterns

The Master Plan 2021, which is the source of the information, estimates that Lucknow covered an area of 16,270 hectares in 2004-05. Compared to 1987 when the area was estimated at 9170 hectares, there has been a 77.4% increase in the total area in 2004-05. Trends in land uses has been interesting, especially the fact that residential use has grown dramatically in comparison to all other uses, although there has also been notable growth in commercial, industrial and public service land use. While population densities in core areas, which include the major part of Cis-Gomti specially the old habitations, are around 600 persons/hectare or more the densities in peripheral Trans-Gomti area; vary from 400 to 600 persons/hectares. The total Municipal area as per 2001 census is 143 sq.km. With the radial growth of the city, the Cantonment has gradually been engulfed and is today more centrally located. A Ring Road system has been developed to connect the new development around the Old City and the Cantonment and the Trans-Gomti areas.

The Lucknow Development Authority has planned to develop the intervening open spaces to take advantage of the Ring Road. New housing colonies are already in the south-eastern and eastern parts of the City. It is interesting to note that the Master Plan 2021 does not take into account the development that is taking place on account of the entry of private developers. Like most cities, Lucknow is witnessing a real estate boom with a large number of private developers coming in – this additional development will necessarily require infrastructure that needs to be taken into account when planning investments in the future.

Table. Existing Land Use — Lucknow City Area (in Hectares)

1987		2004-05			Growth Percentage
Land Use	**Area**	%		**Area**	%
Residential	4,485.98	48.92	8,945.00	54.98	99.40
Commercial	223.77	2.44	360.00	2.21	60.88
Offices	474.69	5.18	560.00	3.44	17.97
Industrial	596.22	6.50	990.00	6.08	66.05
Parks/Playgrounds	346.48	3.78	435.00	2.67	25.55
Public Services	902.02	9.84	1,410.00	8.67	56.32
Traffic	952.00	10.38	1,240.00	7.62	30.25
River/water bodies	193.66	2.11	310.00	1.91	60.07
Open Land	996.14	10.86	2,020.00	12.42	102.78
Total	9,170.96	100.00	16,270.00	100	77.43

Reconstruction of Lucknow after Mutiny

There had been an earlier destruction of Lucknow after the mutiny and

Geddes worked towards the 'real' reconstruction of Lucknow; not of merely buildings; however venerable and beautiful, but of 'social life'. Architecture and architects played an important role in the renewal of social life. The suggested reconstruction of Victoria Street, for example, was more than the provision of shaded walkways and new shops and offices; it was a reclamation by citizens of a primarily military space for civic and public uses, while accepting -in accordance with Geddes' theory of evolutionary city growth - the scar the street had left in Lucknow's urban fabric.

Architecture, Geddes explained, was crucial to the success of the civic reclaiming of the street. Traditionally it had organized 'the visible arts, with their many detailed crafts and industries and all their accessories in turn, thus covering well-nigh the whole field of industry'. This organizing function centred on family, household or the city. The service architecture offered these entities was the creation of long-lasting, beautiful goods which constituted real wealth. But once architecture was 'taken away from the city and cathedral building after the Renaissance to fortify power, to adorn its magnificence and exalt its pretensions', it began to fail society and itself by changing from a life-enhancing and supporting art to an ally of destructive forces.

This situation was about to change once more as in recent years and decades architecture became reconnected again with the city, though no longer on its own but under the guidance of town planning, which meant in co-operation with the other arts and subjects such as economics or politics. Geddes and Slater recognized a coalition of forces of architecture, arts, crafts, education, civic service and city development which all worked together to achieve the reconstruction of cities. Architects were the driving force in this coalition for they could visualize reconstruction proposals in the form of plans and perspectives, something Geddes, who fiercely believed in the power of visualization to activate energies. Even more important was that architects could create what distinguished a mere town from a city:... in every urban community what makes an aggregation of buildings something more than a mere aggregation is the presence of an appeal to the sense of beauty, the feeling of a common life, and the prompting of noble aspirations. To fulfil these three criteria by designing adequate architecture was not a waste of money - especially unrealistic in times of war - but belonged to the 'economies of the higher elements of life'.

Accordingly, Geddes demanded an increase in the employment of architects by organizing city surveys and public-building commissions rather than a cutting back due to the constraints of a war-time.

Key Issues of Planning in Lucknow

- While there is a real estate boom on the one hand, however, there has been a growth in slum conditions on the other. There is consensus that there are large numbers of poor people in the city –

more than 60 to 70% population live below the poverty line. The city continues to attract new migrants, many of who end up in informal settlements that would generally be regarded as slums. These areas are spread across the city, so that any action to deal with the related challenges has to be on a citywide scale. It is not a physical pattern that clearly separates better-off areas from others.

- In the absence of adequate measures taken to protect the environment, urban development and expansion has resulted in steady deterioration of the City's environment resulting in adverse impacts on water, air, land-ecology, and public health and has even caused serious damage to heritage properties.
- Increasing population growth of the city coupled with increasing commercial and industrial activity has resulted in rising water pollution both in the River Gomti as well as of the ground water sources. The River Gomti water is fit for drinking after treatment at Dandnamau Ghat, but when it enters Lucknow city at Gaughat, 27 drains carrying domestic sewage discharge directly into it thus deteriorating the water quality. It is estimated that these drains discharge around 32 million litres of sewerage and household wastes each day into the River Gomti. The release of industrial effluents along the course of the river further aggravates the problem and the water is rendered highly unfit for drinking. Although the Jal Sansthan treats the river water before supplying to the City, consumers do not consider this to be safe. Being able to address the pollution of the River Gomti is an area of great concern for the residents of the City.

Spatial and Environmental Issues

- Significant numbers of poor people live in the city, settled in slums without access to basic services. These slums are distributed fairly uniformly across the City, and dealing with the challenges they face cannot be done in isolation from a wider city development strategy. The integration of these areas within the larger fabric of the city in a manner that ensures basic services without encouraging further illegal occupation of land and encroachments is a major challenge. Finding ways to provide security of tenure to the urban poor and/or providing alternate land for relocation are key issues therefore.
- The City is growing rapidly in all directions but with a higher rate of growth along Faizabad Road in the Trans-Gomti area. The new development areas have inadequate infrastructure.

Heritage Issues

- The well-known monuments are relatively better maintained

although the attention seems skewed in favour of the monument with lesser attention to its surroundings. Most of the heritage sites need maintenance and designated parking places and space for food stalls. These places also require public toilets.

- There is need therefore to widen the definition of 'heritage' from just monuments to entire precincts and strategise at city level in order that visitors are treated to a holistic 'heritage experience'

Inner City Renewal Challenges

The inner city area was one of the first to be provided infrastructure in the form of water supply and sewerage systems, drainage, street lighting etc. The pressure of population in this zone has increased significantly both as a result of natural increase as well as its attraction of low rents and large numbers of migrant families. There are few remnants of the once effective infrastructure with the majority of the area facing problems of water supply, inadequate sewage disposal, practically non-existent solid waste management, encroachment of drains etc. Interventions are necessary not only from the point of improving the quality of life of residents but also from the perspective of restoring its past heritage.

The old settlements like Chowk, Kashmisi Mohalla, Nakhas, Aminabad, Saadatganj, Asharafabad, Nawabganj, Rakabganj, Ganeshganj, Chaupatia, Raja Bazar, Daliganj, and Balaganj, etc form the 'inner city'. Daliganj and Balaganj fall on the Trans -Gomti side while the others are on the Cis Gomti side. These localities are centuries old, having been established in the Nawabi period. Today they are densely populated with grossly inadequate infrastructure and some of the old buildings in a dilapidated condition. This locality is home to a number of handicraft 'factories' for Zardosi and Chikan work, alongside people from varying socio-economic groups, ranging from wealthy established families to poor people with vulnerable livelihoods.

Key Issues: Inner City

- Grossly inadequate infrastructure for water supply and sewerage
- Poor solid waste management
- Encroachment of drains and blockages leading to water logging
- Urban decay.

Gomti River Pollution Issue

There are a large number of katcha slum bastees and low income mohallas located along the main nullahs in the core area of the city where the problems of poor solid waste management, drainage and sanitation are closely interrelated and particularly severe. Furthermore, there are up to 607 768 people can be classified as low income groups in the city of Lucknow based on an eightfold classification aggregated from data on caste, occupation, monthly per capita expenditure and capital assets. The urban poor in Lucknow in common with other cities in Asia are marginalised, poorly served by infrastructure and social services in comparison to middle and high income groups and tend to live at severe environmental stress points in the urban fabric. Many of these settlements are unauthorised and therefore unable to access government services. They create major bottlenecks in the successful operation of sewerage and drainage services. It was therefore necessary to adapt the integrated planning approach to the specific requirements of low income areas. Even in urban areas, close to 33 per cent of the state are without toilet facilities, while 50 per cent do not have a sewerage system. The traditional way of ensuring integration is to adopt a completely technocratic top-down approach; however the result of this approach, whilst it may be integrated is rarely appropriate, affordable, sustainable or replicable. The development of local community based plans is a means of moving towards a more appropriate outcome.

Reasons

With increasing urbanisation, there has been an increasing demand for basic amenities like water and sanitation but the service providers have failed to keep pace with the demand. Inadequate sanitation services leading to open defecation on one hand and poor management of sanitation services on the other are the most critical aspects of urban living, which lead to environmental and public health complications.

Child Mortality

There is a huge mortality rate in the children under age of 5 in the urban slums of Lucknow. The families with under five mortality in the 28 randomly selected slums in 1993 were located from the records of the slum health workers and verbal autopsy was conducted to assign a cause of death. There were 71 deaths among 2796 children. The annual under five mortality was 25.4 and the under five mortality rate was 126.7. After the neonatal period, "high fever" that could not be classified into any other disease incorporated in the verbal autopsy instrument, was the most common symptom associated with death, seen in 21.1% cases followed by these diseases: pneumonia in 19.7%, diarrhoea in 18.3% and measles in 11.4%.

"High fever" as the leading symptom associated with death is being reported for the first time from the urban slums of India. There is an urgent need to identify the underlying etiologies of death due to "high fever" and the policy implications are that children with fever must receive immediate and continued medical attention till the symptom persist

Metro Rail to Improve Transportation

People in Lucknow have a lot of problems due to traffic congestions, road jams and shortage of mode of conveyance. A need of Metro Rail was demanded by many similar to Delhi. Now the state government has to think with State Housing and Urban Planning department. Though metro rail is very much needed but it will be difficult because for its implementation a lot of private properties will be demolished and will need large scale of land acquisition. Metro Railway can surely streamline the transport system in the state capital; but lets see how long it takes.

Problems Faced in Bringing Metro Rail in Lucknow

- The topography or terrain of Lucknow is diverse and unpredictable to a considerable extent and would play a key role in the project's implementation.
- There is a limit that the government has put on the minimum population of a city for the metro to be implemented. Lucknow's population lies below that.

Current Lucknow Development Authority (LDA) Schemes

- The Gomti Nagar Scheme by LDA on the Lucknow – Faizabad highway in close proximity of Hazratganj and Vidhan Sabha areas is a highly appreciated housing project by LDA. It consists of sector wise developed residential colonies with adequate commercial spaces, multiplex, office complex and school plots.
- LDA Hardoi Road Scheme located strategically close to the Lucknow Medical College, Sitapur Road Highway, and historical places like 'Bhool Bhulaiya', 'Chota Imambada' and 'Ghantaghar'.
- LDA has also provided development projects of residential colonies on similar lines though the Kanpur Road scheme and Sitapur Road scheme.
- 'Ashrayaheen Yojna' of over 8000 houses in Para, Gomti Nagar, Hardoi Road, Shardanagar and Janakipuram is a housing project under which the land is alloted to people who lost their land in Road broadening or highway construction or other infrastructure development works in the city.
- Auction of undeveloped land to major builders in India like Ansals, Unitech Builders India, Eldeco Constructions etc.
- Beautification of Begum Hazratmahal Park, Subhash Park, Parivartan Chownk, and Laxman Park.
- Kudiyaghat Picnic Spot at Hussainabad Chownk on the banks of River Gomti.
- Gomti Nagar Extension being developed by LDA.
- One Time Settlement Scheme for the defaulters in the previous housing allotment schemes.

Chandigarh

The History

August 15, 1947, the day of independence of India was also the day of division of a nation into India and Pakistan, this was also the day of division of State of Punjab being divided into two states.West Punjab went in Pakistan with retaining Lahore as its capital and East Punjab remained in India. It became a state without a capital. Shimla which used to be the summer capital of India and had the required infrastructure was selected as the temporary capital of Punjab.

The Government of Punjab selected brilliant young engineer Mr. P.L. Verma to undertake the tasks of search for a permanent Capital City for the State of Punjab. At that time the Punjabis were very nostalgic about Lahore. Till the last moment they hoped that Lahore would remain with India. The loss was felt acutely and people were eager for a city similar to Lahore. So Verma and his team of engineers savoured the concept of a larger independent town, when most of the bureaucrats and politicians favoured the concept of a small settlement attached to one of the existing towns.

It was in a speech on January 16, 1948 delivered by Jawaharlal Nehru where he mentioned the need to develop new cities to absorb the flow of refugees from the other part of the subcontinent, as the existing towns and cities would have limited scope to do so. Consequently, Chandigarh was decided to be built After investigating a no. of sites, the team of engineers and bureaucrats headed by Mr. P.L. Verma, selected the existing site of Chandigarh which met almost all the requirements for a new city. Pandit Nehru immediately took the final decision and on his visit to the project site on April 2, 1952, said," *The site chosen is free from the existing encumbrances of old towns and old traditions. Let it be the first expression of our creative genius flowing on our newly earned freedom-Let it be a new town symbolic of the freedom of India unfettered by the traditions of the past and expression of the nation's faith in the future.—The new capital of Punjab will be christened as Chandigarh-a name symbolic of the valiant spirit of the Punjabis.* "

When Chandigarh was contemplated, the focus of urban planning in India was unclear. In the 1950s and '60s, the idea of a modern city was vital, especially to a new independent country. Therefore, it was to serve as a model in city planning for India and even the world. With just 300 architects in the country at the time of independence, this was to be achieved by using the best expertise in the west. It was necessary to look abroad for a man to carry out the Chandigarh scheme. The search led to the USA and Albert Mayer who later withdrew because of the death of his partner. With the withdrawal of Mayer, Mr. P L. Verma and P N Thapar formed a committee to search able architects and town planners who would lead the project upto completion. Charles-Edouard Jeanneret popularly known as Le Corbusier agreed to take on this project along with *Piere Jeanneret, Maxwell Fry and Jane Drew.* Le Corbusier was assigned to look at the master plan prepared by Mayer and make modifications, or make new master plan. Later he would design the capitol complex buildings and work on the architectural control of various areas.

He prepared the plan in a matter of weeks and gave it to Govt. justifying that it was cheaper and space efficient. It was on this basis that his master plan was accepted but he did incorporate some features of the Mayer plan. The two plans remained practically the same with the shifting of certain functions. He retained most of Mayer's organizational features but did away with its adaptation to the landscape, its allowances for unplanned growth, and its use of native Indian building types.

Plans and Principles

The new capital required a secure and central location, easily accessible from all parts of the state. The site had to accommodate an initial population of 100 000. It had to be away from existing towns, with an adequate supply of water, easy drainage and a suitable climate. There was also to be a minimum dislocation to existing landowners and proximity to appropriate building materials for large-scale construction.

Chandigarh was seen as a low-density and low-rise city, with a regular traffic system, so reducing cost of roads and infrastructure. his city was to be free of the familiar overcrowding, pavement dwellings and squatters' shanties of many Indian towns.

Making of the City

As the first example of a town consciously built where two cultures, the Indic and the Western, entered redefined relationships under the relatively freer powers of postcolonialism, cross-breeding political, town-planning and architectural ideas and elements, Chandigarh offers us a case-study of Indic-Western hybridity; that is, "the blending of two diverse traditions into something heterogeneous. Le Corbusier replaced the native Indian town plan with a rectangular grid based on the metaphor of a human body but totally divorced from ideas about complex, vibrant Indian cities. He placed the Capitol Complex at the top resembling the head, the intellectual base, reflecting his conviction that government should rule a city as the head rules the body.

The industrial and educational belts on either side of the city symbolized the limbs. The city center with commercial buildings, shopping, and offices represented the heart. The city was further starkly separated into inward-looking sectors of 2600 by 4000 feet dimensions, each considered to be a self-sufficient neighbourhood. A hierarchy of roads separated pedestrian and vehicular traffic into seven different road types, from V1 for the fast-moving inter-city traffic to V7 for pedestrians within the sectors.

The most positive aspect of the sectors is that they provide a safety area for children, they can play, walk to school, and to shopping areas, usually without crossing a street. All this was based on his designs for the "Radiant City" — the ideal city of an omnipotent Western machine-age civilization promising a decongested city center, filled with sun, space, and greenery.

The speed with which Le Corbusier came up with the master plan is not surprising considering that he had made similar but previously unrealized suggestions starting with the planning of Athens in 1930. The architecture of Le Corbusier at Chandigarh will be remembered primarily for his capitol complex, which is composed of three monumental buildings: the Secretariat, the Assembly, and the High Court. Here Le Corbusier uses much of the technology and ideas that he had developed for the sunny Mediterranean climate and his Marseilles apartment block, particularly its utilisation of rough concrete. This vision was completely at odds with the conditions in India, where 70 per cent of the economy was still agricultural and where people were deeply rooted in their traditions and beliefs and had little understanding of Le Corbusier's "modern man" and industrial-age aspirations.

The Civic Life

However questionable the planning and architecture forced on the city, it did succeed in providing clean hygienic environments, ample green open space, and the basic amenities of civic life — schools, hospitals, and parks. Such amenities are lacking in many Indian cities even today.

But as a city, Chandigarh lacks the vitality, noise, and charisma of most Indian towns and cities, where the streets and bazaars are dynamic places of public gathering, filled with mystique, colour, and allure.

The Problems

Whatever the failings or triumphs of Chandigarh as a symbol of a transformed culture, its existence as an actual city where people live and work has been complicated by two sets of external problems,

1. The explosive growth of the city over the past forty years
2. Political problems of the region.

Explosion of Population

While the original plan called for "an administrative center accommodating half a million people and expandable to one million" the population today stands at just under seven million, and this does not include the numerous, unplanned satellite cities which have sprung up around Chandigarh.

Political Intervention

The matters got worse when the communal tensions of 1966 led to the creation of two states, Punjab and Haryana each of which demanded Chandigarh as its capital. To resolve this predicament, Chandigarh was made into a "union territory", except that it was to serve as the joint capital of Punjab and Haryana, and the two chambers of Le Corbusier's bicameral Assembly building each became the legislature for a different state!

This has also fuelled the growth of the Chandigarh region as the two states have encouraged the development of adjacent satellite cities and industrial sectors as a way of increasing their competing claims to the capital. These new cities are completely unplanned, with no urban infrastructure, so that they depend on Chandigarh for medical services, education and other social services, even as they have sprung up in what were to be greenbelt in the original plan.

Isolation and Alienation of the Capitol Complex

The limits or failings of Chandigarh stem not only from its explosive, unplanned growth, but also from the design decision that separated the capitol complex from the city. This act rendered the monumental dimension of Le Corbusier's vision remote and distant from the citizens of Chandigarh. The sad irony of Le Corbusier's monument of the Open Hand—a symbol of "peace and reconciliation" —is rendered even more distant and remote by the difficulties one encounters in trying to visit Le Corbusier's buildings, for the Secretariat and the Legislative Assembly, following the assassination of the chief minister of Punjab by Sikh militants in 1995, are now guarded by the army, leaving only the Courts open to the public.

The Zonal Approach

At the level of daily life, the critics argue that such "sacred" planning concepts as zoning and single-use neighbourhoods produce buildings and living spaces which are profoundly alienating, particularly because of the absence of street life. Some of these criticisms can be found in Ravi Kalia's ambivalent characterization of Chandigarh, as safe and yet boring, unIndian and yet an inspiration for Indian architects.

Lack of Landmarks

The sectors, which make up the residential part, are marked by a sameness that leaves a visitor lost, without landmarks. Each sector is self-contained, providing essential services within walking distance of every dwelling.

The Missing Indianness and Culture

Chandigarh was meant to be something beyond a new state capital. But it lacks a culture. It lacks the excitement of Indian streets. It lacks bustling, colorful bazaars. It lacks the noise and din of Lahore. It lacks the intimacy of Delhi. It is a stay-at-home city. It is not Indian. It is the anti-city.

The Present Condition

Now, Chandigarh is a hub of economic activity, with large numbers of vehicles and huge rush-hour congestion. Moreover, much of the housing and some public buildings from the first phase are now unsuitable, and small units accommodating as many as three generations in a family. The city has to evolve, change and adapt to the twenty-first century.

Inferences

Although Le Corbusier took courageous risks at all levels of design, neither the city, nor the buildings have been a practical success. He did not master the climate in terms of hot breezes, the monsoon and uninsulated concrete. Similarly, at city scale, the isolation of the routes and avenues, together with zoning regulations, do not encourage intense urban activity to take place. The city's own rigid character, lacking urbanity, is an image of a vast series of metropolitan hamlets. In his book The City of Tomorrow, Le Corbusier shows a vacant rectangle with the following words within it: 'Left blank for a work expressing modern feeling'. With his great concern for area design, there was the hope that Le Corbusier himself could have fulfilled the ambitions of such an urban space admirably within the Capitol of Chandigarh. Yet, like most of his exciting concepts that have influenced generations of architects, Chandigarh is important for what it could have been, rather than what it is today. Chandigarh may well be one of India's greatest achievements in urban town planning. But despite Nehru's enthusiasm, and the evident success of the experiment, the Indian political establishment seems to have learned nothing from it.

Chandigarh ought to have become the harbinger for more planned cities. What came instead was unplanned urban sprawl, dispiriting shanties, and creaking infrastructure, punctuated now by gated enclaves built for the rich by a land-grabbing mafia of private developers. That Chandigarh did not inspire a hundred planned cities points to a colossal failure of the Indian imagination.

URBAN LIVES

THE GROWTH OF CITIES

Accelerating urbanization is powerfully affecting the transformation of Indian society. Slightly more than 26 per cent of the country's population is urban, and in 1991 more than half of urban dwellers lived in 299 urban agglomerates or cities of more than 100,000 people. By 1991 India had twenty-four cities with populations of at least 1 million. By that year, among cities of the world, Bombay, in Maharashtra, ranked seventh in the world at 12.6 million, and Calcutta, in West Bengal, ranked eighth at almost 11 million. In the 1990s, India's larger cities have been growing at twice the rate of smaller towns and villages. Between the 1960s and 1991, the population of the Union Territory of Delhi quadrupled, to 8.4 million, and Madras, in Tamil Nadu, grew to 5.4 million. Bangalore, in Karnataka; Hyderabad, in Andhra Pradesh; and many other cities are expanding rapidly. About half of these increases are the result of rural-urban migration, as villagers seek better lives for themselves in the cities.

Most Indian cities are very densely populated. New Delhi, for example, had 6,352 people per square kilometer in 1991. Congestion, noise, traffic jams, air pollution, and major shortages of key necessities characterize urban life. Every major city of India faces the same proliferating problems of grossly inadequate housing, transportation, sewerage, electric power, water supplies, schools, and hospitals. Slums and jumbles of pavement dwellers' lean-tos constantly multiply.

An increasing number of trucks, buses, cars, three-wheel autorickshaws, motorcy-cles, and motorscooters, all spewing uncontrolled fumes, surge in sometimes haphazard patterns over city streets jammed with jaywalking pedestrians, cattle, and goats. Accident rates are high and it is a daily occurrence for a city dweller to witness a crash or the running down of a pedestrian. In 1984 the citizens of Bhopal suffered the nightmare of India's largest industrial accident, when poisonous gas leaking from a Union Carbide plant killed and injured thousands of city dwellers. Less spectacularly, on a daily basis, uncontrolled pollutants from factories all over India damage the urban environments in which millions live.

URBAN INEQUITIES

Major socioeconomic differences are much on display in cities. The fine homes—often a walled compound with a garden, servants' quarters, and garage—and gleaming automobiles of the super wealthy stand in stark contrast to the burlap-covered huts of the barefoot poor. Shops filled with elegant silk saris and air-conditioned restaurants cater to the privileged, while ragged dust-covered children with outstretched hands wait outside in hopes of receiving a few coins.

The wealthy and the middle class employ servants and workers of various kinds, but *jajmani* -like ties are essentially lacking, and the rich and the poor live much more separate lives than in villages. At the same time, casual interaction and physical contact among people of all castes is constant, on public streets and in buses, trains, and movie theaters. As would-be urbanites stream into the cities, they often seek out people from their village, caste, or region who have gone before them and receive enough hospitality to tide them over until they can settle in themselves. They find accommodation wherever they can, even if only on a quiet corner of a sidewalk, or inside a concrete sewer pipe waiting to be laid. Some are fortunate enough to find shelter in decrepit tenements or in open areas where they can throw up flimsy structures of mud, tin sheeting, or burlap. In such slum settlements, a single outhouse may be shared by literally thousands of people, or, more usually, there are no sanitary facilities at all. Ditches are awash in raw sewage, and byways are strewn with the refuse of people and animals with nowhere else to go. Despite the exterior appearance of chaos, slum life is highly structured, with many economic, religious, caste, and political interests expressed in daily activity. Living conditions are extremely difficult, and slum dwellers fear the constant threat of having their homes bulldozed in municipal "slum clearance" efforts; nonetheless, slum life is animated by a strong sense of joie de vivre.

In many parts of Indian cities, scavenging pigs, often owned by Sweepers, along with stray dogs, help to recycle fecal material. Piles of less noxious vegetal and paper garbage are sorted through by the poorest people, who seek usable or salable bits of things. Cattle and goats, owned by entrepreneurial folk, graze on these piles, turning otherwise useless garbage into valuable milk, dung and meat. These domestic animals roam even in neighbourhoods of fine homes, outside the compound walls that protect the privileged and their gardener-tended rose bushes from needy animals and people.

Finding employment in the urban setting can be extremely challenging, and, whenever possible, networks of relatives and friends are used to help seek jobs. Millions of Indians are unemployed or underemployed. Ingenuity and tenacity are the hallmarks of urban workers, who carry out a remarkable multitude of tasks and sell an incredible variety of foods, trinkets, and services, all under difficult conditions. Many of the urban poor are migrant laborers carrying headloads of bricks and earth up rickety bamboo scaffolding at construction sites, while their small children play about at the edge of excavations or huddle on mounds of gravel in the blazing sun. Nursing mothers must take time out periodically to suckle their babies at the edge of construction sites; such "recesses" are considered reason to pay a woman less for a day's work than a man earns. Moreover, women are seen as physically weaker by some employers and thus not deserving of equal wages with men.

These construction projects are financed by governments and by business enterprises, which are run by cadres of well-educated, healthy, well-dressed men and, increasingly, women, who occupy positions of power and make decisions affecting many people. India's major cities have long been headquarters for the country's highest socioeconomic groups, people with transnational and international connections whose choices are taking India into new realms of economic development and social change. Among these well-placed people, intercaste marriages raise few eyebrows, as long as marital unions link people of similar upper- or upper-middle-class backgrounds. Such marriages, sometimes even across religious lines, help knit India's most powerful people together. Increasingly conspicuous in India's cities are the growing ranks of the middle class. In carefully laundered clothes, they emerge from modest and semiprosperous homes to ride buses and motorscooters to their jobs in offices, hospitals, courts, and commercial establishments. Their well-tended children are educated in properly organized schools. Family groups go out together to places of worship, social events, snack shops, and to bazaars bustling with consumers eager to buy the necessities of a comfortable life.

Members of the middle class cluster around small stock-market outlets in cities all over the country. Even in Calcutta, notorious for slums and street dwellers, the dominant image is of office workers in pressed white garments riding crowded buses—or Calcutta's world-class subway line—to their jobs as office workers and professionals. For nearly everyone within the highly challenging urban environment, ties to family and kin remain crucial to prosperity. Even in the harshest urban conditions, families show remarkable resilience. Neighbourhoods, too, take on importance, and neighbours from various backgrounds develop cooperative ties with one another. Neighbourhood solidarity is expressed at such annual Hindu festivals as Ganesh's Birthday in Bombay and Durga Puja in Calcutta, when neighbourhood associations create elaborate images of the deities and take them out in grand processions.

CITIES AS CENTERS

Cosmopolitan cities are the great hubs of commerce and government upon which the nation's functioning depends. Bombay, India's largest city and port, is India's economic powerhouse and locus of the nation's atomic research. The National Capital Territory of Delhi, where a series of seven cities was built over centuries, is the site of the capital—New Delhi—and political nerve center of the world's largest democracy.

Calcutta and Madras fill major roles in the country's economic life, as do high-tech Bangalore and Ahmadabad, famous for textiles. Great markets in foods, manufactured goods, and a host of key commodities are centered in urban trading and distribution points. Most eminent institutions of higher learning, cradles of intellectual development and scientific investigation, are situated in cities. The visual arts, music, classical dancing, poetry, and literature all flourish in the urban setting. Critical political and social commentary appears in urban newspapers and periodicals. Creative new trends in architecture and design are conceptualized and brought to reality in cities.

Cities are the source of television broadcasts and those great favourites of the Indian public, movies. Bombay, sometimes called "Bollywood," and Madras are major centers of film production, bringing depictions of urban lifestyles before the eyes of small-town dwellers and villagers all over the nation. With the continuing national proliferation of television sets, videocassette recorders, and movie videocassettes, the influence of such productions should not be underestimated. Social revolutions, too, receive the support of urban visionaries. Among the more important social developments in contemporary India is the growing women's movement, largely led by educated urban women. Seeking to restructure society and gender relations, activists, scholars, and workers in the women's movement have come together in numerous loosely allied and highly diverse organizations focusing on issues of rights and equality, empowerment, and justice for women. Some of these groups exist in rural areas, but most are city based.

The escalating issues of dowry-related murder and suicide are most pressing in New Delhi, where groups such as Saheli provide essential support to troubled women. The pathbreaking feminist publication *Manushi* is published in New Delhi and distributed throughout the country. The overwhelming economic needs of self-employed poor female workers in Ahmadabad inspired Ela Bhatt and her coworkers in the Self-Employed Women's Association, which has been highly successful in helping poor women improve their own lives. Urban women have initiated protests challenging female feticide, child marriage, child prostitution, domestic violence, polygyny, sati, sexual harassment, police rape of female plaintiffs, and other gender-related injustices. Their efforts have brought new ways of thinking out of elite, educated circles into the broader public arena of India's multilevel society.

In 1994, two attractive urban Indian women won the most prominent international beauty contests, the Miss Universe and the Miss World competitions. Thousands of young Indian women idolized the glamorous beauties and many newspapers gushed about the victories, but women's groups and feminist commentators decried this adulation. They pointed out that the deprivations and injustices experienced by a high proportion of Indian women were being given short shrift.

While the beauty contest winners were being paraded about in crowns and white chariots before admiring throngs, almost ignored by the public and the media were the torture-slaying of a village woman accused of theft by a soothsayer and the historic qualification of six women as the Indian air force's first female pilots. In 1995, the All India Democratic Women's Association and other groups protested in New Delhi against the Miss India contest.

URBAN VIOLENCE

VIOLENCE HAS REACHED record levels in many cities in Africa, Asia and Latin America, and has become a critical threat to the security of urban dwellers and to productivity and development. But as we try to comprehend the complex, multi-layered nature of urban violence, the phenomenon itself is not static. Along with newer preoccupations such as globalization, post-9/11 fears and insecurities, international migration and "failing" states, not to mention long-term difficulties of exclusion, poverty and inequality, the face of urban violence itself is also rapidly changing.

DEFINITIONS AND CATEGORIES

VIOLENCE IS USUALLY defined as the use of physical force, which causes hurt to others. Broader definitions include psychological hurt and material deprivation. Most definitions recognize that violence involves the exercise of power to legitimize the use of force for specific gains. Definitions of violence often overlap with those of conflict and crime, although there are important distinctions. Conflict-based power struggles do not necessarily inflict physical or mental harm on others, while violence by its very nature does. Crime, similarly, does not have to entail violence.

The insecurity generated by violence is expressed in fear, which has been defined as "the institutional, cultural and psychological repercussion of violence", and identified as an outcome of destabilization, exclusion and uncertainty. Although perceptions of insecurity cannot be reflected in statistical evidence, they fundamentally affect well-being.

The ability of the poor to access resources for survival is closely linked to violence, relating not only to the spatial, economic and social constraints imposed by endemic violence but also to the failure of the state to provide protection. Although there are no hard boundaries between different types of urban violence, policy makers and practitioners need to categorize the phenomenon in order to design interventions to prevent or reduce it. Four categories – political, institutional, economic and social violence – pointing to some of the more common perpetrators and manifestations of each category.

Much social violence is gender-based, linked to gendered power relations and constructions of masculinities, and includes intimate-partner violence and child abuse inside the home as well as sexual abuse in the public arena. Social violence also includes ethnic violence, or territorial or identitybased violence linked to gangs. Economic violence, motivated by material gain, is associated with street crime, including mugging, robbery and violence linked to drugs and kidnapping.

Closely related is institutional violence, perpetrated by state institutions, especially the police and judiciary, but also by officials in sector ministries such as health and education, as well as groups operating outside the state, such as social cleansing vigilante groups. Political violence, driven by the will to win or hold political power, includes guerrilla or paramilitary conflict or political assassination. Although closely linked to conflict and war, political violence is also committed during peacetime. Since any categorization is, by definition, too static to represent a dynamic and holistic phenomenon, the four-fold typology is conceived as an interrelated continuum with close linkages between different types of violence.

Table. Categories, Types and Manifestations of Violence in Urban Areas

Category of Violence	Types of Violence by Perpetrators and/or Victims	Manifestations
Political	• State and non-state violence	• Guerrilla conflict • Paramilitary conflict • Political assassinations • Armed conflict between political parties
Institutional	• Violence of state and other "informal" institutions • Including the private sector	• Extra-judicial killings by police • Physical or psychological abuse by health and education workers • State or community vigilante-directed social cleansing of gangs and street children • Lynching of suspected criminals by community members
Economic	• Organized crime • Business interests • Delinquents • Robbers	• Intimidation and violence as means of resolving economic disputes • Street theft, robbery and crime • Kidnapping • Armed robbery • Drug-trafficking • Car theft and other contraband activities • Small-arms dealing • Assaults including killing and rape in the course of economic crimes • Trafficking in prostitutes • Conflict over scarce resources
Economic/ social	• Gangs • Street children (boys and girls)	• Territorial or identity-based "turf" violence; robbery, theft

	• Ethnic violence	• Petty theft • Communal riots
Social	• Intimate partner violence inside the home • Sexual violence (including rape) in the public arena • Child abuse: boys and girls • Inter-generational conflict between parent and children • Gratuitous/routine daily violence • Incivility in areas such	• Physical or psychological male–female abuse • Physical and sexual abuse, particularly prevalent in the case of stepfathers but also uncles • Physical and psychological abuse as traffic, road rage, bar fights and street confrontations • Arguments that get out of control

Violence may not always be just a physical act but also "structural", as explained by Galtung, who extended the notion of violence beyond overt brutality to include the exploitation, exclusion, inequality and injustice implicit in social structures.

THE TRENDS AND MEASUREMENT OF URBAN VIOLENCE

Although accelerating rates of violence and crime are not only urban problems, they are particularly problematic in many urban areas. The sheer scale of violence in many poor areas or slums means that it has become "routinized" or "normalized" into daily life, provoking references to "failed cities" and "cities of chaos". Fear and insecurity pervade people's lives, with serious implications for trust and well-being among communities and individuals.

What Taussig calls "terror as usual" can exhibit itself through street crime, a growing gang culture and high levels of violence in the private realm. The range of types of urban violence and crime is both complex and context-specific. In an urban Jamaican community, for instance, local residents listed 19 types of violence; the average number identified in nine Guatemalan poor urban communities was 41, while in Colombia the comparable average was 25. Despite the high prevalence of rural violence in the past, violence is commonly most severe in large urban areas.

City-level differences in homicide levels can be striking. In Latin America in 2000, rates ranged from 6.4 per 100,000 per year in Buenos Aires to 248 per 100,000 in Medellín. Violence is not manifested in the same way in different cities, even within the same nation. For example, in Brazil, between 1979 and 1998, the homicide rate in Metropolitan Rio de Janeiro rose by 35 per cent, but in Metropolitan São Paulo it increased by 103 per cent. Differences in rural–urban violence levels are less marked in post-conflict countries, where rural violence is often still more extreme than in urban areas. In El Salvador, 76 per cent of homicides occur in rural areas, as against only 24 per cent in urban areas. Within cities, variations in violence levels are related to neighbourhood income levels, gender and age.

More prosperous areas suffer from violent crime, usually property-related, but severe violence is generally concentrated in lower-income areas, particularly in the marginal periphery. However, increases in vehicle robbery – with the growing risk of being killed in the process – have heightened insecurity among the wealthier population. Young men are most likely to be both the victims and the perpetrators of violence. Even in countries with relatively low levels of violence, not only is male juvenile violence rising, but its intensity is increasing.

The measurement of violence is limited by a number of constraints. Mortality statistics, often used as proxies for violence, are notoriously unreliable. The most commonly used indicator of violent crime, the homicide rate, disregards non-fatal violence, and generally includes both intentional *and* unintentional violence National and regional differences in data collection methods, recall periods and cultural definitions of crime and violence also limit the validity of cross-country comparisons. The measurement of such intangible but significant factors as fear is also problematic. A useful contribution to measurement is the incorporation of questions on violence into broader household surveys – a low-cost way to procure data that is probably more accurate than police statistics. Growing recognition that quantitative methodologies fail to capture people's daily experience has resulted in increased use of complementary qualitative sociological and anthropological methodologies, including the use of solicited personal diaries. Other participatory appraisal techniques have also proved invaluable in giving voice to people's perceptions of violence.

CAUSES, COSTS AND CONSEQUENCES OF VIOLENCE

It is important to distinguish between *structural* causes of violence and *trigger risk* factors. Trigger risk factors for gender-based violence, for instance, frequently include drug and alcohol use. Understanding *structural factors* requires a holistic approach, one of the best-known of which is the "ecological model", which maps the way in which factors at different levels combine to contribute to violence. Another holistic framework locates the situation-specific nature of people's experience of violence within a broader structural context, identifying underlying factors in terms of structure, identity and agency. Since issues of power and powerlessness are fundamental to understanding violence, this allows for the analysis of the wider political and socioeconomic power structure within which individual realities are manifest, and recognizes that experiences of violence depend on such elements as gender, age, ethnicity and race.

Finally, identity is closely related to "human agency", or the recognition that individuals are social actors who face alternative ways of formulating their objectives, however restricted their resources. Socially constructed levels of tolerance to violence can vary considerably, and are vital to any policy to reduce violence. For instance, the social acceptance of domestic violence and of substance abuse within communities can not only contribute to violence but also stand in the way of effective prevention.

In urban contexts, a particularly important debate concerns the extent to which crime and violence are causally rooted in poverty or inequality. Poverty has long been considered the predominant determinant of violence, but more recently this relationship has been challenged as too simplistic. Interpretations based on statistical modelling have demon-strated that inequality is more influential than poverty, with income inequalities being generally more marked in urban than rural areas.

Some analysts argue that increased levels of violence are also closely tied to processes of globalization and structural adjustment as well as political democratization. At the same time, the daily living conditions of the urban poor heighten the potential for conflict, crime or violence. The new theme of the "politicization of crime" is a growing concern in contexts where state institutions are challenged or superseded by non-state forms of social governance. The "urbanization of warfare" is becoming a common phenomenon in regional conflict zones or in those that have recently emerged from war. The changing nature of warfare also benefits those most involved in organized crime – with "open-war economies" serving to integrate the urban with global criminal economies.

The spatial causes of violence are particularly important in cities and their peripheries, which often contain unsafe spaces where rape, robbery and violent crime take place. Urban space is increasingly being reorganized in response to high levels of crime and violence and to the lack of confidence in the state's capacity to provide effective security. The rich retreat to "fortified enclaves", or make use of sophisticated transport networks and privatized security systems that effectively isolate them from the poor, who are seen as the perpetrators of violence.

Closely related to the causal factors underlying violence are the costs and consequences of violent action. Most relevant research is based on the categorization of direct and indirect costs. Probably the greatest advances have been made with measurements of direct economic costs, such as the associated losses due to deaths and disabilities, and "transferrals" resulting from property crimes, calculated as percentages of GNP or GDP. Such measurements are useful for understanding the impact of crime on both individuals and society, and for allowing for a comparison with the costs of other social ills, with important policy implications in terms of cost-benefit assessments.

However, constraints include, in many contexts, lack of access to information on violence-related expenditure assessments of the police, the judiciary, the penal system and even the armed forces. At the same time, many components of indirect costs, both for individuals and society as a whole, are intangible, and no reliable quantitative data exist.

From the extensive "livelihood" debate, a consensus has emerged with regard to the identification of five types of capital assets: physical, financial, human, social and natural; the multiple outcomes of violence can also be analysed in terms of their direct and indirect effects on each of these. Violence erodes financial capital through its drain on criminal justice services and the health care system, decreased investment and institutional costs. Human capital costs also have financial implications. The consequences for social capital include insecurity, fear and a deteriorating quality of life, with ramifications in terms of trust and restrictions on community life.

VIOLENCE REDUCTION INTERVENTIONS THAT FOCUS ON THE URBAN POOR

Urban crime and violence prevention and reduction is now a growth industry. Table identifies some policy approaches and their associated urban-focused interventions. These include such sector-specific approaches as criminal justice to control and treat economic violence, and the public health approach aimed at prevention. Newer approaches such as conflict transformation and human rights reflect increasing concern with political and institutional violence. Recent recognition of the importance of more integrated, holistic approaches has encouraged cross-sectoral approaches such as citizen security, CPTED and urban renewal. Still in the process of development are local-level community-based approaches to rebuild trust and social capital.

Table. Policy Approaches to Violence and Associated Urban-Focused Interventions

Policy Approach	Objective	Types of Violence	Innovative Urban-Focused Interventions
Criminal justice	Violence *deterrence* and *control* through higher arrest, conviction rates and more severe punishment	• Crime • Robbery • Corruption	Judicial reform
		• Crime • Robbery	Police reform
		• Delinquency	Accessible justice systems
		• Robbery • Family violence	Mobile courts
		• Family violence	Community policing All-women police stations
Public health	Violence *prevention* through the	• Youth violence	Youth policies/social protection Education

	reduction of individual risk factors		reform Entrepreneurship
		• Youth violence	Vocational skills training Cultural and recreational activities Promotion of behavioural change
Conflict trans-formation human rights	Non-violent *resolution* of conflict through negotiation and legal *enforcement* of human rights by states and other social actors	• Political violence • Institutional violence • HR abuses • Arbitrary detention	Traditional systems of justice Government human rights / advocates or ombudsman Civil society advocacy NGOs
CPTED/ urban renewal	*Reduction* in violence opportunities through focusing on the *settings* of crime rather than on the perpetrators	• Economic violence • Social violence	Municipal-level programmes
Citizen/ public/ community security	Set of cross-sector measures to *prevent* or *reduce* violence	• Economic violence • Social violence	National-level programmes Municipal-level programmes
Social capital	*"Rebuilding"* social capital, trust and cohesion in informal and formal social institutions Communication	• Youth gangs/ *maras* • Domestic/family violence	Community-based solutions Crisis services for victims Ongoing support and prevention campaigns School programmes Programmes for perpetrators

Such policies are essentially ideal types. In reality, policy makers have shifted towards more integrated approaches that acknowledge not only the multiple forms of violence but also the identity and agency of different social actors. To date, there has been little rigorous evaluation of violencereduction interventions; this leads to an expectation that a diversity of interventions will together achieve the desired result. It is widely recognized that there are no magic bullets or one-off solutions to violence reduction. Some approaches work better than others and are more appropriate in some settings than in others.

There are some common themes, however:

- The almost universal distrust and lack of confidence in the state's capacity to control or prevent crime and violence, and the associated structural problems within existing police and judiciary systems.
- The rapid expansion of non-state forms of social governance. This can support social cohesion and the mitigation of conflict, but it can also generate perverse rather than productive forms of social capital, such as revenge violence, vigilante crime and other extra-judicial forms of justice.
- The privatization of security, with state authorities either contracting or condoning private security firms to conduct public policing – solutions that focus more on the rich than on the poor.

There is growing consensus about the importance of consulting local communities in designing appropriate solutions, whether in drawing on young people's perceptions about solutions for gang violence, facilitating face-to-face communication with excluded communities, or promoting, in a range of ways, productive partnerships between the police and local communities.

Finally, there is the issue of fear. In cities across the world, relentless "routinized" daily violence dominates the lives of local populations. Fear of such violence isolates the poor in their homes and the rich in their segregated spaces. This isolation, in turn, perpetuates a fear of the "other" and contributes to the social, economic and political fragmentation of cities. To date, few violence-related strategies have confronted or addressed the issue of fear or its associated relationship to power and powerlessness. Ultimately, this may provide a critically important mechanism for redressing the impact of violence on the daily lives of the poor and excluded in cities throughout the world.

2

Nature and Scope of Industrial Sociology

SOCIOLOGY

The science dealing with the origin, evolution and development of human society and its organization, institution and functions, is known as Sociology. Coming together to live in a group is the compulsion of man, not his choice as there are stronger animals than man. Food gatherer to food producer, the long journey of evolution of man made him develop the group living ways and thus society is formed.

Thus, the study dealing with requirements of men living in group led to development of Sociology. That is why man is popularly known as '*social animal.*' Behaviour of man ought to be different when living in group as individual behaviour should not disturb others. Then need of norms, rules and laws was felt.

INDUSTRY

It is an economic activity concerned with the processing of raw materials and manufacture of goods in factories. Industry also means hard work. That is why it is well said by AMYOB "To shine your personality enters into industry." The need of industrial sociology, its development and put it on solid foundation is felt by man on the path of progress of mankind. After India got freedom, Jawaharlal Nehru, the first Prime Minister of independent India, gave name to industries, *Temples of Modern India*. From the dawn of civilization man has been making rules of behaviour so that human activities may be bound into the formation of society.

Manmade laws differ from those which are natural and universal, for instance, the rule that human beings must grow and mature. Industrial Sociology deals more with soft skills of man. It plays vital role in building nation as it helps in increasing the production and thus helps in Gross Domestic Product (GDP) rising. More so with quality as competition can be faced. Today, there is noticeable increase of interest in quality, on the part of both industry and society. There are several reasons for the greater interest in quality-higher demands for quality from customers, greater competition, demands for better profitability and legislation on product liability. Good results can not be achieved through work on a single department in the enterprise. It is necessary for all those functions which come into contact with the product during its development, manufacture and use, to cooperate in this work.

This means that quality must be considered and controlled by all these functions—market research, product development, manufacturing engineering, purchasing, production, inspection, marketing and after-sales service. It is also necessary to coordinate the work of these functions on quality that the enterprise should have a wide approach to quality. Our lives are dependent in many ways on industrial products; shelter, nutrition, communications, healthcare, work, recreation and national security.

One basic aspect of products of this type, goods or services, is that they must be fit to use. Failure in use may lead to injury, discomfort, death or economic loss. Since all these functions are created by men in manufacture of any product, those involved form a group and thus society is formed. The periphery of this society is also affected or for that matter they may come from general public and thus role of corporate comes into play. This is popularly known as Corporate Social Responsibility (CSR).

INDUSTRIAL SOCIOLOGY

DEFINITION

Industrial Sociology, a term came into use in the middle of twentieth century owing to the famous experiments conducted by George Elton Mayo and his associates during late twenties and early thirties at Hawthrone Works in Chicago.

It is the application of sociological approach to the reality and problems of industry. The importance attached to the subject can be gauged to the fact that India has committed to the industrial development as a necessary means to solve its economic and social problems. Here, we have to understand key terms: *'industry'* and *'sociology.'*

Industry

Industry may be understood as, *'the application of complex and sophisticated methods* for the *production* of *economic goods and services'*. These complex methods, implying use of machinery, have been devised to improve quality and quantity of production. To shine, enter into industry. From food gatherer to food producer, man has always been industrial, *i.e.*, hard-working. Coming together and start living in a group, man always tried to develop. He has always used tools to get food and satisfy his needs. To get his daily breads, pre-literate man used digging stick, *hoe* or *bow* and *arrow*. Anthropology and Histroy show that man has always been not only user of tools but also maker of tools, *i.e., homo faber*. Adjustment, one of the characteristics of man, makes man move from *means* to *ends*, to achieve his objectives. That is why man is also called *homo sapiens* (intelligent man) and so *homo industrialis* (industrial man). From French *industrie* or Latin *industria,* here group of diligent and hard-working men came together and formed a unit to carry economic activity concerned with the processing of raw materials and manufacture of goods in factories.

Sociology

The Science, dealing with the behaviour of man living in group, which developed over a period of time, is known as Sociology or Science of society. Society itself consists in the web of social relationships with the combinations and complexities arising from them, as clique, groups, associations, institutions, systems, etc. The root or beginning of society is the social relationship which essentially develops on mutual awareness, followed by reciprocal interrelations and interactions. Thus, we may say that strangers do not make society. Like, two students come to college from different areas, different backgrounds and never seen each other in past. Though physically present in college, they have not found occasion to start talking.

But when they come close to each other on introduction, the social relationship begins to emerge and may even become more complex when they begin to deal with each other or talk business. Generally, sociology is restricted to the field of study of social institutions or social systems as the family or state, the village or factory etc. The objectives are undoubtedly legitimate, but there does not seem to be any cogent reason to exclude other social realities, such as group or social relationship itself. Any reality, especially a complex reality like industry, can be studied from various points of view, such as technological, physical, psychological etc. But we must give emphasis to the sociological aspect or social element that manifests itself in industry.

PSYCHOLOGY, SOCIOLOGY AND ECONOMICS

Human behaviour is now given importance. It is the concern of everyone. Parents are unhappy about the behaviour of their children, teachers find students disinterested in study, employers find lack of commitment from their employees. '*Why people behave as they do*', is subject of study, full of mystery. Here study of Psychology plays great role paving the way for Sociology and Economics. Mutual awareness or reciprocity is what characterises social reality and distinguishes it from other sciences. Psychology has much affinity with sociology. When Kumar quarrels with his tool, we call it psychological phenomenon in which only one man is involved. But when Kumar is fired by supervisor Vishnu, a sociological reality has emerged. Whereas, Industrial Psychology deals mostly with individual and personal behaviour and problems, as selection of personnel, definition of basic personal factors in job satisfaction, internal work motivation, accident proneness, etc., Industrial Sociology stresses, on the contrary, the social or interactional factors as industrial and human relations, formal and informal organisation, team work, communication, etc. Though communication or motivation is common to both disciplines of Industrial Psychology and Industrial Sociology, approaches and characteristic viewpoints of these are clearly distinct.

Economics is mainly concerned with the traditional activities of production, distribution and consumption, giving due significance to the problems of finance, exchange, etc. Profits, finance, monopoly, taxation, viability etc., are the question raised by economists without any emphasis given to human, social or psychological aspects. But now ideas have greatly changed in this respect and today not only are these sciences becoming more specialised and objective but their fields of collaboration and mutual support are also expanding rapidly. Organisational Sociology is the latest branch of Sociology which is closely related to Industrial Sociology.

TASK OF INDUSTRIAL SOCIOLOGY

From the discussion we have here, we may say that Industrial Sociology is an applied discipline. Not merely concerned with general sociological concepts, but it is related to concepts which specially refer to industry. Thus task of industrial sociology is to select and study its social elements even when they are combined or interacting with other realties. Industrial Sociology is concerned with industry as social system. Factors like technical, economic, political affect structure and working of the system. In view of these factors playing great role, study of industrial sociology assumes much importance. Economist talks of prices and wage rates, Psychologist speaks of vocational guidance and tests, Physiologist thinks in terms of fatigue and nutrition. Lawyers are imported by collective bargainer, *i.e.,* trade union leaders into the discussion and then things get messed up. But none considers the group (industry) and its functions in society as a constituent unit of integrity.

Yet the group has an impulse to self-preservation as, or stronger than that of an individual and many industrial strikes are actually symptomatic of the attempt of group to hold together. Economist, psychologist, physiologist, ...all ignore the fact that complex group association is the distinguishing character of human beings.

PERSONNEL ADMINISTRATION AND SOCIAL WELFARE

Industrial Sociology has considerably widened its scope but its method and approach remain essentially same. The social sciences especially psychology, economies and sociology provide tools to correct deficiencies and improve society and the practical social sciences, among which social welfare is prominent, apply them. Personnel Management or Personnel Administration, of which industrial social welfare is a part, is mainly the application of social sciences to the human problems of industry. That is the reason personnel manager of any industry is supposed to have adequate knowledge of sociology, psychology, economics etc., as they affect industry. If personnel man is trained psychologist or sociologist, he will definitely be more successful in his job.

SOCIAL RELATIONS

In modern times, we have discovered to realise that industry itself, which originally was considered to be only economic or technical organisation, is eminently a social organisation, or institution devoted to the production and marketing of goods and services. Thus the importance of social sciences in general and sociology in particular is understood.

Sociology, therefore, is concerned with social relations in industry and their influence on industrial phenomena like productivity, morale, attitude, functional authority etc. and thereby affecting quantity and quality of goods and services. These social relations in industry may be internal or external. Internal relations are those existing within industry itself concerning management, operations or both, whereas external relations are between industry and outside bodies as government, community, educational institution etc. The internal relations, which are more important in industry to take mission forward, are further divided into formal, informal and mixed categories.

Formal relations immediately arise from performance of one's approved duties to the organisation, may be *managerial* or *operational* depending upon whether these are proper to the management or workmen or operations. Formal relations may also be *statutory* or sanctioned by law or custom or those implied in collective bargaining, grievance procedure, industrial councils, adjudication etc. Popularly known as *Industrial Relations*, they literally go more extensively.

Informal relations spontaneously arise everywhere in industry. Though hardly ever officially regulated, they are ordinarily sustained by common rules of ethics and customs. Informal relations may exist among individuals as when two or more workmen criticise or grumble against their supervisor, agree to play cards, interaction between different groups or individuals such as trade union groups.

Like unions and associations of all banks came together to form United Banks Federation or union of workmen from same village, or aggrieved workmen who temporarily unite to protect their own interest and have their complaints heard. Once, Prime Minister Rozgaar Yojana borrowers, who defaulted, formed union in A.P. When matter is taken up with grievance committee, their informal relations become formal relations. The informal relations in nuclear groups and clique, though informal, are more or less defined and stable. They may be seen at all levels of industry, office workers, managers etc. and are known as informal organisations of the industry. Mixed relations, also described by social scientists as *socio-technical* relationship, play great roles in the industry. Arising out of discharge of one's duties which may be of managerial or technical nature, mixed relations are also called *socio-functional*.

While instructing a trainee on the job, trainer cracks joke or drops some pleasantries, commenting like lazy-bones, sociofunctional relations are developed. No industry can exist and thrive without taking external relations into consideration. Growing in importance, external relations are given due weightage and so Public Relations Officers (PROs) are appointed.

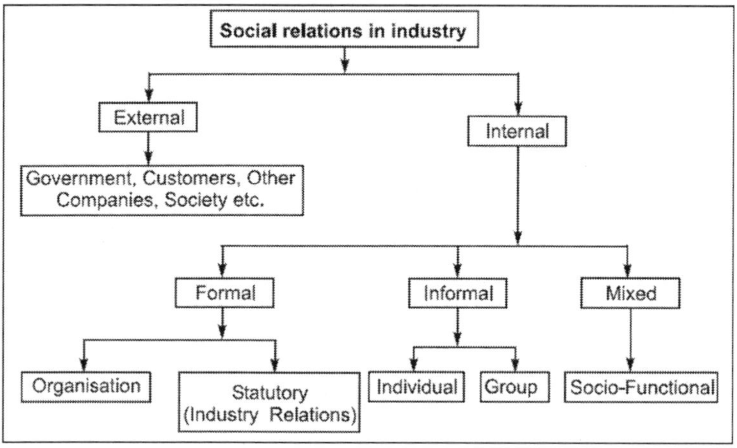

QUICK REVIEW

Preliminary concepts of Industrial Sociology deal with application of sociological approach to the problems of industry in order to achieve objects. Here key words are Industry and Society. Industry, part of society, is the application of complex and varied methods for the production of economic goods and services, that is application of tools for economic production. As man is endowed with intelligence, he has always been an industrial being, *homo industrialis*. As manifest in society, sociological approach to industry consists in the study of social relationships, groups, institutions, behaviour of man in group of men, in isolation affecting the outcome. Industrial Psychology differs from Industry Sociology as former is individual-oriented but latter is group oriented.

However, combination of both sciences results in Social Psychology of Industry or Industrial Psycho- Sociology depending upon emphasis given to psychological or sociological behaviour of men. Economics is an important connector in all social sciences in industry as all activities are carried out by men together or alone. Industrial Sociology is a specialised subject and is distinct from disciplines as industrial or social welfare or personnel management which are concerned with practical problems of industry. Industrial Sociology has paved the way for the development of these disciplines and now help one another, that is, from theory to practice or practice to theory, *i.e.,* empirical in order to achieve the objects, that is the quest of man. Various types of social relations in industry, as charted earlier, particularly formal and informal relations play great roles in development of industry. Both soft touch and hard touch are needed in the administration of industry and many times on the spot decision based on established norms of industry are needed.

SIGNIFICANCE OF INDUSTRIAL SOCIOLOGY

Industrial Sociology has acquired significance in progressive society where industrial revolution played great role which was necessitated to cater the growing demands of ever increasing population. Following benefits increase the significance of Industrial Sociology.

USE OF SCIENTIFIC METHODS

Industrial Sociology acquires great significance in view of scientific methods adopted to study. To understand it by establishing cause-effect relationship, scientific knowledge helps. All round progress of mankind depends upon moving up the ladder of Maslow's hierarchy of needs, *i.e.,* food.

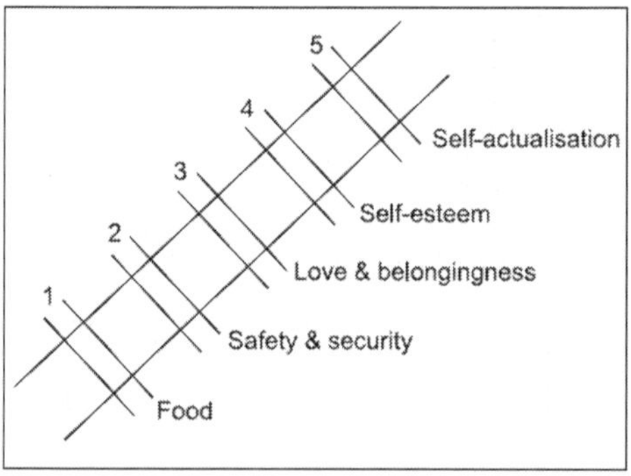

Fig. Maslow's Hierarchy of Needs

With the onset of industrial revolution, development of industries took the centre stage. Industrial development in any nation became a key factor in deciding the progress of that nation. As science helped in industrial development, the systematic knowledge acquired using scientific methods human behaviour became very handy. Thus industrial sociology as a subject of study gained currency. Various institutions dealing with industrial society, its social control, social dynamics, social change, problems and their remedies came up and thereby widened the scope of industrial sociology. It would not be exaggeration to say that without knowledge of industrial sociology industrial progress could not have been achieved. The importance of industrial sociology made the premise of setting up Tata Institute of Social Sciences in Mumbai.

UNDERSTANDING THE SOCIAL ASPECT OF INDUSTRY

The orderly movement of things based on certain rules takes any work to logical conclusion. That is the importance of science and that is why it is called specialised knowledge. To gauge the development of any nation, the position of its industries plays a great role. The contribution of industries to the well-being of citizens of its country and humanity at large has become now predominant in the index of development of any nation. That is why Corporate Social Responsibility (CSR) has become a buzzword in developing country like India.

Industrial Sociology has added new dimension to the knowledge of humanity. The workmen, who do work, execute the design, that is taken from drawing board to floor, are vital link between theory and practice. So called labour class, workmen are to be trained, taught and toughened so that they become finest craftsmen. The social strata, importance of roles and problems of workmen are to be addressed in such a way that there ever remains cordial industrial relations and industrial peace should bring development in industries.

SOLUTIONS FROM INDUSTRIAL SOCIETY TO THE PROBLEMS OF INDUSTRY

Based on knowledge and experience people are employed in industries leading to formation of various layers taking care of different job roles and responsibilities. Industrial Revolution gave birth to industries which were organised to achieve its objectives. Job roles decided expertise, division of labour and degree of responsibility and thus created vertical and horizontal set up in the organisation. Occupation hazards are associated with industries which require matching counter balance in the form of money, perks, glamour and other welfare measures. As workmen, supervisors, executives, policymakers are associated with any industry, a stratum is formed which gives feeling of differentiation, status-consciousness, inferiority-superiority complex etc.

INDUSTRIAL RELATIONS

Industrial relations play vital role in development of industries in any country. The management policies, its objective, long-term and short-term goals decide its working environment. In-short, we can say the mission and vision of any company in theory and practice speak about the company. The relationship between workman and management has to be harmonious for industrial rest and once that is there, industrial progress is bound to happen.

Production has to multiply. The production coupled with quality is the need for growth of any industry. Industrial Sociology helps in achievement of this objective. Important factors playing great roles in good industrial relations are rates of wages, working conditions, welfare measures, recruitment policy, job-security etc.

Welfare measures are widely covered under the heading of food, cloth and house. Industrial Sociology is gaining importance due to its role played in taking care of all these discussed matters. Mutual trust, sense of belonging, feeling of ownership, team spirit are knitting social industrial fabric which ultimately result into higher quality production and give sustenance and thus growth is achieved. Initial steps of ladder of hierarchy of needs of Maslow *viz.* food, safety and security are very important to be given top-most priority to make workmen take their duty seriously.

DIVISION OF LABOUR

Every one cannot do everything. In India, caste system worked well earlier. In fact, people were easily adopting family profession. However, with good progress in education people started coming out of family business. The sharpening of mind, learning skills of other's profession and zeal and zest make people go for the occupation which make them happy. Thus caste system, which earlier caused impediment in economic progress, is losing its effect.

Not by design but by default, industrial progress caused mingling particularly in industrial society. Thus caste-system is being eliminated and division of labour is made based on certain other factors *viz.* innate ability, training, choice etc. Now scientific division of labour in industry demands good knowledge as per profession. Here, role of industrial sociology comes to play.

ECONOMIC PLANNING

After India gained freedom, the progress of nation was to be carried out on solid foundations and thus it adopted Five-Year Plan growth approach. Called temples of modern India by first Prime Minister of India Jawaharlal Nehru, industrial growth was aimed in five-year plan to solve many problems arisen mainly out of population.

Illiteracy, low level of wages, corruption, lack of trained people and professional approach are some of the problems which require intervention of industrial sociologists.

INDUSTRIAL AUTOMATION

Industrial revolution came with onset of mechanisation. The increased requirements of people necessitated invention of steam engine to mechanise processes such as cloth weaving in England. More automation means less manual work and in turn less employment. It gave more profits to industrialists and so more automation was opposed by workmen's unions. Here role of industrial sociologist brings solution to the dispute.

INDUSTRIAL MANAGEMENT

Industrial management requires scientific approach to take care of turnover, sustenance of activity, quality and other variable factors. Human approach is given in industrial management where all elements of production are most efficiently employed without any exploitation.

INTEGRATION OF FAMILY

The unit of any society is family which requires special attention. Any disturbance caused due to any social evil such as alcoholism, insufficient housing, bad recreation, uncontrolled media, print as well as electronic would disorganise industrial society in particular. Disintegration of family is bound to happen. Industrial Sociology gives insight leading to solutions of many problems arisen out of progress in industries.

3

Rise and Development of Industry

EARLY INDUSTRIALISM

EARLY INDUSTRIALIZATION

Starting in the early 19th Century the United States underwent an industrial revolution. The work that many people did changed as they moved from farms and small workshops into larger factories. They tended to buy things in stores, rather than make them at home or trade with their neighbours. They used machines, and purchased the products of machines, more than they ever had.

Fig. Left: Spinning Wheel, Possibly for Flax.
Right: Mechanized Spinner from the Progress of Cotton, 1835-40.

The small-scale centers of textile production lasted well into the 19th century. But the manufacture of textiles began to change dramatically, starting as early as the 1790's, as these traditional sources were first joined, and then replaced, by a new material, a new kind of agriculture, and a new kind of factory. The material processed changed, from linen and wool to cotton; the way that cotton was grown and prepared changed, with the invention of the cotton gin and the reinvention of the plantation; new machines, invented to process the cotton, found a new setting in larger and more complex factories. Together, these changes added up to an industrial revolution. This textile revolution did not happen everywhere in the United States at the same time, and its effects were quite different in different areas. Perhaps the largest change came in the South, where the new demand for cotton was supplied by plantations based on slave labor and mechanized processing of the cotton by the cotton gin. The Northeastern United States changed dramatically as home spinning and weaving, and small-scale carding and fulling mills gave way to large integrated mills where a new kind of worker used new machines to produce cotton cloth on a scale previously unimagined. Smaller mills remained, and would remain for the rest of the century, but for the most part, only in areas of low population far from the commercial markets of the Northeast. This account of the American Industrial Revolution is different from the usual one found in textbooks. Many textbooks claim, for example, that the Industrial Revolution did not occur until the end of the 19th century, with the coming of massive steel mills and the end of small-scale production. And they omit the mechanization and reorganization of Southern plantations, on the grounds that agricultural production is not part of the history of industry. While this traditional story is not wrong, it leaves out an important part of the story.

It also leaves out many people who participated in and whose lives were changed by industrialization. To focus on factories, which have traditionally employed native white and immigrant workers, and from which African Americans were kept by racial prejudice, leaves out a large group whose story is a key element of American history. Slaves produced the cotton that made possible Northern factories, a piece of history often slighted in favour of stories about those factories. In this curriculum we have widened our point of view to include Southern cotton production as part of textile history. So slavery, and later sharecropping, becomes an important part of the story of Northern textile mills; African Americans become part of the history of technology; and technology becomes part of African American history. Such an inclusionary view should help students of colour imagine themselves as people who, like their ancestors, use and control technology.

The South

It is right to start the story of the industrialization of the textile industry in the South, because that is where the story of cotton starts. Southern plantations underwent an industrial revolution of a sort: one of the key new technologies of the textile revolution, the cotton gin, made possible a new, much larger scale of production, and that increased scale demanded new organization and management. Before the American Revolution, tobacco, rice, and indigo were the major crops produced for market in the South. Cotton was not produced for market because it was so hard to remove the sticky seeds from inside each cotton ball; it could not be done fast enough to make cotton profitable. Since the first millenium B.C., people around the world used roller gins to speed the cleaning of cotton. The saw gin, patented in 1793, made processing cotton even easier, faster, and cheaper.

Based on an ancient technology, the introduction of the saw gin at the end of the 18th century changed the nature of American cotton cultivation. Developed just as the world-wide demand for raw cotton was skyrocketing because of the expansion of textile mills in Britain and the United States, the machine removed the principal bottleneck to cotton production. Even the early machines allowed one person to clean the seeds from fifty pounds of green-seed cotton in one day. Soon cotton became the most important market crop in the South. Production went from 3,000 bales in 1790 to 1 million bales in 1835.

With the opportunity to make a good profit from cotton came dramatic changes in Southern agriculture: increased size of plantations, and to work them, increased numbers of slaves. African slaves had been used in Southern agriculture almost from the beginning of European settlement. Tobacco planters had used slaves since the 17th century; slaves were critical to the rice cultivation that developed in the 18th century. Plantations, large farms using slave labor to grow a single crop, were created to make a profit for the owners before technology made cotton a cash crop and before slavery was the only labor system. But plantations were adapted to produce cotton in the 19th century and by then many of them employed only slaves. Planters became wealthy by exploiting the labor of Africans in America, men and women who could not choose another way of life. The growth of cotton as a cash crop in the 19th century meant the growth of slavery throughout the South. Slavery, which had been in decline, became an integral part of the new agriculture. It might seem odd that a new labor-saving machine like the cotton gin meant an increase in the size of the labor force. But the lower price meant an enormous increase in cotton production, and even with the cotton gin, cotton production still required an enormous amount of labor. Cotton demanded large plantations; it made money only when plantation owners could put more workers in the field.

From an investor's point of view, slaves were a capital investment, comparable to the machinery a northern factory owner might purchase. The cotton gin was one of those inventions that brought about an enormous change in the way people lived and worked, and even in their politics, and so it is appropriate that much of the southern part of this Unit is focused on the gin. The exercise on "Inventing the Cotton Gin" raises issues about the nature of invention. The exercise on fixing a gin raises questions about technological skills. Both of these include a discussion of race and technology.

The North

The invention of the cotton gin was only one of the technological innovations that propelled the growth of cotton as a cash crop. The other important new technology was new machines for the manufacture of cloth, which lowered the price and increased the speed of production. These technological developments were crucial in the growth of cotton as a commodity crop, as was a commercial and market revolution that created a growing demand for cotton. The new technology and new demand meant changes in northern industry every bit as extensive as those in the South.

Textile manufacturing in the 18th century occurred mostly in homes. Farm women worked hard to turn raw wool into finished cloth, first picking and breaking it, then spinning, and then weaving. For some farm women this work was a full-time winter job, for some a job done between other chores. Towards the end of the century, small water-powered carding and fulling mills became increasingly common. Thus, some of this work was industrialized. Women might take the wool to the local carding mill for cleaning and carding, then take it home for spinning. They might do the weaving themselves, or perhaps take the yarn to a professional weaver. Finally, they would take the cloth to a mill to be fulled and finished. This division of labor brought some of industrial work into the home, but, for the most part, women worked alone, in control of the details of their own time and pace. They used machinery, but very simple machinery. Hand powered, individually controlled, and highly dependent on the skill of the user, home textile production made use of mechanisms that were more tools than machines

In the late 18th century, a new kind of textile mill, invented in England, began to be found in the United States. The first was the Pawtucket, Rhode Island, mill of Almy, Brown and Slater. It was the first mill in the United States set up on an English pattern, as well as the first to use water-powered spinning machines. The men, women, and children who worked at the mill produced yarn, which was sent out to hand weavers for production into cloth. Samuel Slater, trained in England as a mill manager, brought the knowledge of technology with him. He also called on local experts: millwrights to place and build the waterwheel and mill, and iron and wood workers to build the machines. Almy and Brown were merchants; they provided the capital, and took responsibility for the purchasing of materials and the sale of product.

Mills like that of Almy, Brown, and Slater were soon found throughout Southern New England, especially after the 1809 Embargo on shipping with England led to an enormous increase in American textile production. These mills changed the lives of their thousands of workers, who had to learn a new time discipline, and of their workers' families. But they also changed the lives of those who bought the cloth the workers produced—cloth became cheaper, and part of a system of commercial exchange, impacting the lives of those who lived nearby. The dams required to provide water power to the mills flooded farmers' fields and stopped fish from their annual migration. Industry did not coexist easily with traditional ways of life.

A different sort of textile industry developed in the cities, which had always been centers of manufacturing. Philadelphia, which became the largest producer of textiles, pioneered a style of production quite different from that found in New England. Philadelphia's textile industry was quite diverse. There were a few large mills that used water or steam power to drive machinery, but, for the most part, Philadelphia's textiles were produced in small shops or home-based operations. The workers who produced them, many of them British immigrants, tended to be highly skilled workers, able to undertake a variety of jobs.

The management too was highly skilled, not only knowledgeable about the machines and processes under its control, but skilled in rapid shifts of resources, product, and market. The products tended to be of high quality. The machines reflected what historian Philip Scranton has called "productive flexibility," their complexity and ease of adjustment allowing a broad range of output.

A third style of textile mill was found in Lowell, Massachusetts. The city had been founded in 1822; by 1840, it had 26 cotton mills, employing some 7,000 workers. Almost all of these mills produced the same basic product—a low-grade cotton cloth. The mills, all of them enormous, were powered by water wheels, and all were basically identical, both inside and out. The workers, almost all of them young unmarried women who would work there for only a few years, possessed only the specialized skills they were taught for the machines they ran.

The machines were largely devoid of adjustable features. Mechanical ingenuity went into increasing automatic operations and speed, not improving the machines' quality or variability of output. Managers were more knowledgeable about the control of workers than the details of machinery or of markets; other specialists dealt with those departments of the business. It is worthwhile to look more deeply into the story of Lowell, for it was, at its start, a unique industrial city—a city that raises key questions about the nature of American industrialization. Designed as an explicitly American style of industry, the mills at Lowell were unique in their utopian aims, their workforce, their managerial style, and their machines. Not that the Lowell mills had no predecessors—these mills had a heritage that stretched back to the English mills of Arkwright and Robert Owen, to the many industrial experiments that were part of the American attempts to win economic independence from England, and to the small textile mills of New England—but the Lowell mills compounded these all, and at a scale so much larger as to be something new in industrial history.

In developing this experimental city, the developers of Lowell broke new ground. They had to solve a new set of problems, and they solved them in a different way than anyone else. The problem was simple: how to make money in manufacturing in a nation unused to manufacturing. That is, in a country without skilled machine makers, without skilled workers—for that matter, without many workers available at all—without a great deal of capital or a tradition of manufacturing—indeed, with a strong philosophical bent against manufacturing, and against managerial prerogative. Many of the beliefs, ideas, skills, and machines that modern industrialists take for granted, or assume they can purchase, were missing in Lowell. So too were most of the economic assets. The solutions found by the owners and managers of Lowell—solutions managerial, technological, social, cultural, and political in nature—took a large step towards the modern industrial style. Lowell was to become one of the places where American manufacturing and managerial traditions were born. By 1840, more than 50,000 people worked in the cotton textile industry in New England.

Perhaps the most important tradition to which the founders of Lowell helped contribute was that of managerial expertise, separate from engineering or technological or financial expertise. Managers at Lowell were hired for their skills as managers, not their technical abilities or their financial prowess. The textile mills of Lowell drew on traditions of authority that existed elsewhere—in schools, prisons, on ships—and reshaped them to the needs of industry. Managers at Lowell brought a new rationality of production, a new precision of understanding of processes, and also a new way of looking at the men, women, machines, and materials of industry.

It is the beginning of the abstraction from reality into information that is essential to modern economic life, the origin of a new belief in the efficacy of numbers as a means of control. The workforce at Lowell, and the way it was managed, was also something new. The young women who left their family's farms expected to stay there only a few years. Millgirls were expected to abide by a list of "General Regulations" that outlined the new world of bureaucracy They were about to enter. The rules were part moral exhortation, part guide to duties and the duties of the managers under whom they would work, and part legal contract stating obligations as an employee. They were required, the Regulations stated, to "attend assiduously" to duties, to "aspire to the utmost efficiency" in work, and "to evince... a laudable regard for virtue temperance." They would be expected to attend public worship, to observe the Sabbath, and not to drink or gamble. At work, they would "conform to regulations."

The social, cultural, and technological innovations of the New England corporations were important elements in the industrialization of the United States. Not so much because these mills set the style for other industries; the Lowell mills, with their millgirls and "moral" boardinghouses, were not widely copied outside of northern New England. They also did not last long; by 1860 the so-called "golden age" of Lowell was over, and the utopian dreams of its founders had disappeared as Lowell became simply another textile city. But, as the first large-scale industrial experiments, the mills at Lowell brought with them much that would be found in later factories—not only large-scale production, but also some profound opposition to industrial capitalism. The opposition was in part theoretical and in part practical. The theoretical aspects were based on philosophical beliefs about the nature of American democracy.

America would only stay a republic, Thomas Jefferson and others of his period believed, as long as it stayed agricultural. "God forbid," wrote Zachariah Allen, an American mill owner, "that there may arise a counterpart of Manchester in the New World." Thomas Mann put the same sentiments in even stronger terms. A sometime mill worker and teacher, he made up in feeling what he lacked in poetic ability in his

Portrait of a Factory Village:
For liberty our fathers fought
Which with their blood, they dearly bought,
The Factory system sets at naught.
A slave at morn, a slave at eve,
It doth my inmost feelings grieve;
The blood runs chilly from my heart,
To see fair Liberty depart;
And leave the wretches in their chains,
To feed a vampyre from their veins.
Great Britain's curse is now our own;
Enough to damn a King and Throne.

Another mill worker was less poetic and more straightforward. Jabez Hollingworth, an English immigrant who had worked in several American mills, combined in one sentence the two comparisons that came to a textile mill operative's mind when management was oppressive: "Management breeds lords and Aristocrats, poor men and slaves." Some of the Lowell millgirls felt the same way. The rhetoric of their early strikes showed the influence of radical democratic ideas: The millgirls called themselves "daughters of freemen" and feared that the "oppressing hand of avarice would enslave us."

The mention of slavery brings us back to the beginning of this thesis. Clearly, the use of the word "slavery" by radical Northern workers is more rhetorical than real; industrial work, as hard and unpleasant as it might have been, was not slavery. Workers were not property like slaves were. They were, in principle anyway, always free to leave. But there are some comparisons that are useful. Both factory workers and slaves were treated, to some extent, as cogs in a larger machine. Northern factory owners as well as Southern plantation owners used similar imagery in describing their operations as machines. Andrew Ure, a British scientist, wrote in his *Philosophy of Manufactures*: "The main difficulty in training human beings to renounce their desultory habits of work, and to identify themselves with the unvarying regularity of the complex automaton." A plantation owner echoed Ure when he wrote a few years later: "A plantation might be considered as a piece of machinery, to operate successfully, all of its parts should be uniform and exact, and the impelling force regular and steady." Both systems of labor demanded a strict adherence to the rules set down by those in charge.

New systems of rules, along with the new machines and new products, are the legacy of the Industrial Revolution of the early 19th century, for the second Industrial Revolution of the later part of the century, and, to a large degree, for today. We have come to accept the necessity of technology, products, and hierarchy. The exercises in this unit suggest that they came about not out of necessity, but as the product of specific historical circumstances.

In her 1931 history of the early New England textile industry, historian Caroline Ware asked: "Could political democracy encompass industrial autocracy, could it harbor a working class and a moneyed power and survive?... These problems which New England faced before 1860 have confronted other American communities as one by one they have experienced the process of industrialization. Their solution still lies in the future."

TYPES OF PRODUCTION SYSTEMS

Three types of production system can be identified certain features of which influence the actions of production managers:

1. Small batch and unit production
2. Large batch and mass production
3. Continuous process production

Woodward compared the affect of these on the span of control of the first line supervisor and levels in the management hierarchy. She drew conclusions on how different approaches to operational systems design affect management control over work done. The importance of information is paramount.

A few points to note are:

- Products can be divided into those a customer regards as single items or multi-component assemblies. Few companies produce single item products n.b. packaging is a product in itself. Subcontractors may produce single components for someone else to assemble.
- Most production in engineering, electronics, furniture etc is concerned with assemblies of manufactured internally or 'bought in' components. "Make or buy" decisions are important and considerable cost information is required.

Production system are often split between the part that produces components and the part that assembles them and certain basic organisation structures can be identified in a production plant:

- Functional production facilities grouped by function *e.g.* All furniture drilling machines together, all sanding and finishing machines together. Orders are routed through the functional departments where each operation is performed. The benefits of 'collective expertise' are obtained but the operators are 'task specialists'. This can result in motivational and attitudinal problems. Functional organisation is flexible but needs much close control and information on the progress of 'batches' between shops.

- Line materials flows through the manufacturing facilities are uni-directional and any product flowing along the line usually requires all the facilities on the line. With computer control of materials movements far more flexibility vis a vis exactly what components go into each product as it passes down the line can be built in. This is a feature of the modern computer controlled car assembly line where so long as the car is a micra different versions will sit side by side on the line. This type of approach needs a well trained, flexible workforce with supervisors and workers on the shop-floor possessing up-to-the-minute information. When the product type is changed-complex resetting is necessary.
- Continuous process is a special form of line organisation that is-plant dominated. The operation of the system is defined almost completely when the plant is designed constant control of the process is needed for efficient control operations *e.g.* To adjust temperatures.
- Group organisation is similar to line except that a group or cell of facilities processes a range of items with similar facility requirements. All items produced by the group won't need all the facilities. Different facilities within the group will be working on different items. again material flows should be uni-directional as possible and immediate information on work flows and priorities is needed by the supervisors and workers.

These modes of production have substantial implications in terms of ability to control stocks, supplier-customer relationships and the sophistication of purchasing systems.

COMPARING PHYSICAL ORGANISATIONS

Manual assembly of products for stock in high volumes is usually line organisation because of use of semi-skilled staff, size of work-in-progress inventories, training time and the efficiency of the work design. However unit assembly by small group or individual is more likely to be MTO or jobbing work. Component manufacture is usually batch or functionally organised because of the need for machine stations and the inflexibility of machine cycle times. Low utilisation of facilities is a problem. The flexibility of functional organisation has a cost of high work-in-progress inventories to stabilise uneven workflow. Line organisations have efficient throughput rates with low inventories. The use of computers to minimise the inefficiencies of each is therefore obvious.

EXAMPLE: FUNCTIONAL ORGANISATION

An order requires 10 operations with a total batch work content time of 20 hours only. However work in progress queues may involve 2 days waiting at each work centre. Thus an order would take 3 weeks to have only 20 hours work done on it.

- Throughput Efficiency = 20 hours → 3 weeks
- Thus a typical functional organisation will have a T.E. of 10-20% rarely higher.

PROBLEMS IN MTO AND MFS

Control-ables:

- Capacity
- Finished stock levels
- Customer delivery times.

The OPS Mgr needs data on these to manipulate efficiency to the best.

Examples:

- Poor quality control at Jaguar Cars in the 70's led to considerable employee alienation. The company's high quality standards now and emphasis on employee excellence are reaping dividends.
- A restaurant chain decides to re-design its franchise outlets so that only a limited range menu is offered. Any change in eating habits or in the cost structure of the menu will render the design partial

THE MANORIAL OR FEUDAL SYSTEM

LANDLORD AND PEASANT: 9TH-15TH CENTURY AD

Life on a manor is the medieval version of a relationship which occurs, between landlord and peasant, in any society where a leisured class depends directly on agriculture carried out by others. Such landlords may be patricians living in their Roman villas or feudal knights ensconced in castles and fortified manor houses. Records suggest that the work of between fifteen and thirty peasant families is required to support one knight's family. The relationship between the knight and his peasants is the manorial system. The knight has force on his side. Even in normal circumstances he may be able to terrify his peasants into subjection. In unruly times-characteristic of much of the Middle Ages-his armour becomes even more significant. The peasants need his protection from marauding enemies. They are less likely than usual to assert themselves. On the other hand a cooperative labour force is more productive than a resentful one, so the lord of the manor may be inclined to use his natural advantages with moderation. And occasionally, when labour is in short supply-as after the Black Death in the 14th century-the peasants themselves acquire a measure of economic strength.

The resulting balance of power varies greatly in different places and times. There is an important distinction between free peasants and serfs. Serfs are the descendants either of slaves who have been given a measure of freedom, or of free peasants who have accepted legal restrictions in return for the lord's protection. Serfs are slaves only in the one crucial sense of being tied to their lord's land. That distinction comes to seem a quibble where serfdom continues into modern times outlasting the abolition of true slavery. The system of labour and of rent which develops on a medieval manor is also immensely variable. It is further complicated by the fact that part of any manor is farmed by the lord on his own account, using peasant labour, and part is cultivated by the peasants for their subsistence-paying the lord some form of rent, whether in natural produce, days and weeks of their own labour, or money. Gradually, as in any long-established social system, the lords devise more and more dues to supplement their revenue. These may be direct taxes or fees for the functions of the manorial court.

THE MANORIAL COURT: 9TH-15TH CENTURY AD

The court is the judicial basis of the manorial system. In the decentralized and unruly regions of medieval Europe, some measure of control is achieved by giving lords legal powers over the peasants on their manors. A large estate will consist of many manors, acquired not only by feudal grant but also by marriage, purchase and even outright seizure. The lord or his representatives move from one manor to another, holding court and consuming the produce gathered since their last visit. The court dispenses justice for crimes committed on the manor, hears civil disputes between tenants, and collects rents, fines and fees.

Fees are claimed by the lord of the manor on a wide range of events in the life of the community. They may be required for the issue of a legal document, for the buying and selling of property and even-most notoriously-for permission to marry. These rights over the community last long after the economic basis of the manor has crumbled. They are the final residue of feudalism, and the most resented. Beaumarchais' radical comedy *The Marriage of Figaro* hinges on the question of whether the count will give permission for the wedding-or will attempt to revive a less authentic seigneurial right to the bride's virginity.

This supposed right, known as the *jus primae noctis* (right of the first night) or *droit du seigneur* (right of the lord), gives an intriguing glimpse of the nature of the manorial system at the time when feudalism is declining into decay and corruption. There is no evidence that any lord ever claimed this outrageous prerogative, but there are several cases of people in the late Middle Ages paying money to avoid the exercise of the *jus primae noctis*. It is an unusually imaginative example of the feudal system of rights and privileges, with their inherent potential for abuse.

FARMING THE MANOR: 9TH-18TH CENTURY AD

The Frankish empire under Charlemagne is the source of feudalism and the manorial system. It also introduces a related revolution in agriculture. Rotation of crops to conserve the soil has been a standard part of agricultural practice since the Neolithic Revolution. The classic method is the simple two-field system. Of every two fields, one is planted each year. The other is allowed to lie fallow, grazed by the cattle and fertilized by their manure. The Franks introduce a major improvement, extending the rotation to three fields. One field is now planted in the autumn with winter wheat or rye. One field is planted in the spring with oats, barley or vegetables such as peas and beans. The third field is left fallow.

The new arrangement requires summer rain for the crop planted in the spring, so it is suitable only in the cooler regions of Europe. It seems to have been introduced, perhaps in the late 8th century, between the Loire and the Rhine.

The advantages are considerable. The most obvious is an increase of one third in the crop. The work of preparing and harvesting the fields is more efficiently spread out through the year. The ripening of crops in two seasons rather than one reduces the risk of famine from freak weather. And there is a benefit, in terms of health and variety, in the addition of vegetables to a previously all-grain diet.

STRIP-FARMING AND ENCLOSURE: 9TH-20TH CENTURY AD

The fields of a medieval manor are open spaces divided, almost imperceptibly, into long narrow strips. Only the fields being grazed by cattle are fenced. The others are open and are identifiable as separate fields only by the crops which they bear. The unusual detail is that the single crop in each field is separately farmed-in individual strips-by peasant families of the local village.

Some of the strips may also belong to the local lord, farmed for him by the peasants under their feudal obligations. But more often the lord's land is in a self-contained demesne around the manor. Strip-farming is central to the life of a medieval rural community. It involves an intrinsic element of fairness, for each peasant's strips are widely spread over the entire manor; every family will have the benefit of good land in some areas, while accepting a poor yield elsewhere.

The strips also enforce an element of practical village democracy. The system only works if everyone sows the same crop on their strip of each open field. What to sow and when to harvest it are communal decisions. The field cannot be fenced, or the cattle let into it, until each peasant has reaped his own harvest. Ploughing too is a communal affair. The heavy wheeled plough needed for northern soils is expensive, as are horses to pull it. So a team of horses and plough works successive strips of an open field for different peasants. The long narrow shape of the strips reflects the difficulty of turning the team at each end. In addition to the open fields, each village or manor has common land where peasants have a right to graze cattle, collect wood, cut turf and perhaps catch fish. From about the 13th century there are pressures on this agricultural system for two different reasons. One is the wish to rationalize the use of the land by changing each peasant's rights from scattered strips to a unified plot surrounding a family cottage. There is considerable resistance to this, because it eliminates the old safeguard by which good and poor land was evenly shared out.

The other motive is the greed of lords of the manor, who regularly attempt to enclose the common land and incorporate it in their own demesne. Enclosure of common land causes particular unrest, not only for the loss of an ancient right but because the poorest peasants rely on these pastures and woods for subsistence.

The issue becomes a crisis at different times in different parts of Europe, in some places even in the 20th century. But the trend is everywhere the same-transforming the open fields of the Middle Ages into the fenced, hedged or walled fields of the individual farms which are characteristic of today's landscape.

LANDLORD, TENANT AND LABOURER: FROM THE 13TH CENTURY AD

The gradual move towards enclosure brings with it a change in the employment system in European agriculture. The feudal relationship of lord and peasant gives way to a system of landlord, tenant and labourer which is entirely based on money. The tenant pays money to the landlord for the use of his land; the landlord pays money to the labourer for his work. In broad terms the free peasants, who have owned a share of the land in the open-field system, become the tenants.

The serfs become the labourers. The new system probably begins during the prosperous 13th century. With the growth in national and international trade, the subsistence farming of the feudal manor is unable to meet the demands of the market. England is one of the first regions to make the change, owing to its prosperous trade with Flanders in wool. In the 14th century a different pressure continues the process; shortage of labour after the Black Death leads to an increased use of wages to pay for work done in the fields. The change gradually introduces the system of land tenure and labour which has prevailed in most of Europe ever since.

THE GUILD SYSTEM

GUILD

A guild is an association of craftsmen in a particular trade. The earliest types of guild were formed as confraternities of workers. They were organized in a manner something between a trade union, a cartel, and a secret society. They often depended on grants of letters patent by a monarch or other authority to enforce the flow of trade to their self-employed members, and to retain ownership of tools and the supply of materials. A lasting legacy of traditional guilds are the guildhalls constructed and used as meeting places. An important result of the guild framework was the emergence of universities at Bologna, Paris, and Oxford around the year 1200; they originated as guilds of students as at Bologna, or of masters as at Paris.

The economic consequences of guilds have led to heated debates among European historians. Ogilvie argues that their long apprenticeships were unnecessary to acquire skills, and their conservatism reduced the rate of innovation and made the society poorer. She says their main goal was rent seeking, that is, to shift money to the membership at the expense of the entire economy. Epstein and Prak's book rejects Ogilvie's conclusions. Specifically, Epstein argues that guilds were cost-sharing rather than rent-seeking institutions. They located and matched masters and likely apprentices through monitored learning. Whereas the acquisition of craft skills required experience-based learning, he argues that this process necessitated many years in apprenticeship.

Early Guildlike Associations

In pre-industrial cities, craftsmen tended to form associations based on their trades, confraternities of textile workers, masons, carpenters, carvers, glass workers, each of whom controlled secrets of traditionally imparted technology, the "arts" or "mysteries" of their crafts. Usually the founders were free independent master craftsmen.

During the Gupta period in India, craftmen's associations, which may have had archaic antecedents, were known as *shreni*. Greek organizations in Ptolemaic Egypt were called *koinon*, starting from their 3rd century BC origins of Roman *collegia*, spread with the extension of the Empire. The Chinese *hanghui* probably existed already during the Han Dynasty:, but certainly they were present in the Sui Dynasty. Roman craftsman's organizations continued to develop in Italy of the Middle Ages under the name *ars*. In Germany they are first mentioned in the 10th century.

The German name is *Zunft* for guilds of craftsman and *Gilde* for guilds of merchants. *Métiers* in France and *craft gilds* in England emerged in the 12th century. Craft organizations stemmed from the 10th century in Iran, and were seen to spread also in Arabia and Turkish regions under the name *futuwwah* or *fütüvvet*. 900 of the carvers of Benin are said to have founded their own organization.

In the neighbouring tribes of Yoruba and Nupe the organizations were given the names *egbe* and *efakó*. Specifically, within the medieval Oyo Empire of present day southwestern Nigeria and Benin, separate guilds developed for professional dancers, mask carvers, and musicians associated with *egungun* ancestral masquerade performances often regarded as the predecessor to the traveling Alarinjo theatre.

European History

The connecting sense is of a tribute or payment to join a protective or trade society. But some see the root in its alternative sense of "sacrifice," as if in worship, and see the word as meaning a combination for religious purposes, either Christian or pagan. The Anglo-Saxon guilds had a strong religious component; they were burial societies that paid for masses for the souls of deceased members as well as paying fines in cases of justified crime. The continental custom of guilds of merchants arrived after the Norman Conquest, with incorporated societies of merchants in each town or city holding exclusive rights of doing business there. In many cases they became the governing body of a town. Trade guilds arose in the 14th century as craftsmen united to protect their common interest.

The early egalitarian communities called "guilds" were denounced by Catholic clergy for their "conjurations"—the binding oaths sworn among artisans to support one another in adversity and back one another in feuds or in business ventures. The occasion for the drunken banquets at which these oaths were made was December 25, the pagan feast of Jul: Bishop Hincmar, in 858, sought vainly to Christianize them.

In the Early Middle Ages, most of the Roman craft organizations, originally formed as religious confraternities, had disappeared, with the apparent exceptions of stonecutters and perhaps glassmakers. Gregory of Tours tells a miraculous tale of a builder whose art and techniques suddenly left him, but were restored by an apparition of the Virgin Mary in a dream. Michel Rouche remarks that the story speaks for the importance of practically transmitted journeymanship.

In France, guilds were called *corps de métiers*. Viktor Ivanovich Rutenburg, "Within the guild itself there was very little division of labour, which tended to operate rather between the guilds. Thus, according to Étienne Boileau's Book of Handicrafts, by the mid-13th century there were no less than 100 guilds in Paris, a figure which by the 14th century had risen to 350." The most striking example of an elaborate classification according to craft is found in the metal-workers: the farriers, knife-makers, locksmiths, chain-forgers, nail-makers, often formed separate and distinct corporations; the armourers were divided into helmet-makers, escutcheon-makers, harness-makers, harness-polishers, etc.

In England, specifically in the City of London Corporation, more than 100 guilds, referred to as livery companies have been in existence for over a thousand years. They continue to exist and several still play a role today. Membership in a livery company is expected for individuals participating in the governance of *The City*, as the Lord Mayor and the Remembrancer. A recent guild is the Worshipful Company of Tax Advisers. The guild system reached a mature state in Germany circa 1300 and held on in the German cities into the 19th century, with some special privileges for certain occupations remaining today. In the 15th century, Hamburg had 100 guilds, Cologne 80, and Lübeck 70. The latest guilds to develop in Western Europe were the *gremios* of Spain: *e.g.*, Barcelona, Valencia and Toledo. Not all city economies were controlled by guilds; some cities were "free". Where guilds were in control, they shaped labour, production and trade; they had strong controls over instructional capital, and the modern concepts of a lifetime progression of apprentice to craftsman, journeyman, and eventually to widely-recognized master and grandmaster began to emerge. In order to become a Master, a Journeyman would have to go on a 3 year voyage called Journeyman years. This was also known as the Waltz and is the origin of the Australian song Waltzing Matilda. The practice of the Journeyman years still exists in Germany.

As production became more specialized, trade guilds were divided and subdivided, eliciting the squabbles over jurisdiction that produced the paperwork by which economic historians trace their development: there were 101 trades in Paris by 1260, and earlier in the century the metalworking guilds of Nuremberg were already divided among dozens of independent trades, in the boom economy of the 13th century.

In Ghent as in Florence the woolen textile industry developed as a congeries of specialized guilds. The appearance of the European guilds was tied to the emergent money economy, and to urbanization. Before this time it was not possible to run a money-driven organization, as commodity money was the normal way of doing business. The guild was at the center of European handicraft organization into the 16th century. In France, a resurgence of the guilds in the second half of the 17th century is symptomatic of the monarchy's concerns to impose unity, control production and reap the benefits of transparent structure in the shape of more efficient taxation.

The guilds were identified with organizations enjoying certain privileges, usually issued by the king or state and overseen by local town business authorities. These were the predecessors of the modern patent and trademark system. The guilds also maintained funds in order to support infirm or elderly members, as well as widows and orphans of guild members, funeral benefits, and a 'tramping' allowance for those needing to travel to find work. As the guild system of the City of London declined during the 17th century, the Livery Companies transformed into mutual assistance fraternities along such lines.

European guilds imposed long standardized periods of apprenticeship, and made it difficult for those lacking the capital to set up for themselves or without the approval of their peers to gain access to materials or knowledge, or to sell into certain markets, an area that equally dominated the guilds' concerns. These are defining characteristics of mercantilism in economics, which dominated most European thinking about political economy until the rise of classical economics. The guild system survived the emergence of early capitalists, which began to divide guild members into "haves" and dependent "have-nots". The civil struggles that characterize the 14th century towns and cities were struggles in part between the greater guilds and the lesser artisanal guilds, which depended on piecework. "In Florence, they were openly distinguished: the *Arti maggiori* and the *Arti minori*—already there was a *popolo grasso* and a *popolo magro*".

Fiercer struggles were those between essentially conservative guilds and the merchant class, which increasingly came to control the means of production and the capital that could be ventured in expansive schemes, often under the rules of guilds of their own. German social historians trace the *Zunftrevolution,* the urban revolution of guildmembers against a controlling urban patriciate, sometimes reading into them, however, perceived foretastes of the class struggles of the 19th century.

In the countryside, where guild rules did not operate, there was freedom for the entrepreneur with capital to organize cottage industry, a network of cottagers who spun and wove in their own premises on his account, provided with their raw materials, perhaps even their looms, by the capitalist who reaped the profits. Such a dispersed system could not so easily be controlled where there was a vigorous local market for the raw materials: wool was easily available in sheep-rearing regions, whereas silk was not.

Organization

The structures of the craftsmen's associations tended everywhere in similar directions: a governing body, assisting functionaries and the members' assembly. The governing body consisted of the leader and deputies. In Ptolemeic Egypt the presidents were known as *presbyter,* in Roman Egypt as *proestotes, egoymenos* or *archonelates,* in Byzantine Egypt *epistates,* in the Roman Empire as *decurio,* in Florence of the Middle Ages as *consul, officialis* or *rector,* in France as *consul, recteur, baile* or *surposé,* in Germany *Zunftmeister* or *Kerzenmeister,* in England *alderman, graceman* or *master,* in Iran as *rish safid* or *pishavaran,* in India as *adhyaksha, mukhya, pamukkha* or *jettaka,* in Tibet as *dbu chen mo,* in China as *hangshou, hangtou* or *hanglao,* in the West African Yoruba region as *bale* or *baba egbe* and in the Nupe region as *dakodza, muku* or *ndakó,* depending on the type of craft.

The guild was made up by experienced and confirmed experts in their field of handicraft. They were called master craftsmen. Before a new employee could rise to the level of mastery, he had to go through a schooling period during which he was first called an apprentice. After this period he could rise to the level of journeyman. Apprentices would typically not learn more than the most basic techniques until they were trusted by their peers to keep the guild's or company's secrets. Like *journey,* the distance that could be travelled in a day, the title 'journeyman' derives from the French words for 'day' from which came the middle English word *journei.* Journeymen were able to work for other masters, unlike apprentices, and generally paid by the day and were thus day labourers. After being employed by a master for several years, and after producing a qualifying piece of work, the apprentice was granted the rank of journeyman and was given documents which certified him as a journeyman and entitled him to travel to other towns and countries to learn the art from other masters. These journeys could span large parts of Europe and were an unofficial way of communicating new methods and techniques, though by no means all journeymen made such travels-they were most common in Germany and Italy, and in other countries journeymen from small cities would often visit the capital.

After this journey and several years of experience, a journeyman could be received as master craftsman, though in some guilds this step could be made straight from apprentice. This would typically require the approval of all masters of a guild, a donation of money and other goods, and the production of a so-called masterpiece, which would illustrate the abilities of the aspiring master craftsman; this was often retained by the guild.

The medieval guild was established by charters or letters patent or similar authority by the city or the ruler and normally held a monopoly on trade in its craft within the city in which it operated: handicraft workers were forbidden by law to run any business if they were not members of a guild, and only masters were allowed to be members of a guild. Before these privileges were legislated, these groups of handicraft workers were simply called 'handicraft associations'. The town authorities might be represented in the guild meetings and thus had a means of controlling the handicraft activities. This was important since towns very often depended on a good reputation for export of a narrow range of products, on which not only the guild's, but the town's, reputation depended.

Controls on the association of physical locations to well-known exported products, *e.g.* wine from the Champagne and Bordeaux regions of France, tin-glazed earthenwares from certain cities in Holland, lace from Chantilly, etc., helped to establish a town's place in global commerce—this led to modern trademarks.

In many German and Italian cities, the more powerful guilds often had considerable political influence, and sometimes attempted to control the city authorities. In the 14th century, this led to numerous bloody uprisings, during which the guilds dissolved town councils and detained patricians in an attempt to increase their influence. In the early 14th century, some guilds in the cities of North-East Germany introduced statutes, under which persons of Wendish, *i.e.* Slavic, origin were forbidden from joining the guild. Wilhelm Raabe, *"down into the eighteenth century no German guild accepted a Wend."*

Fall of the Guilds

As Ogilvie argues, the guilds negatively affected quality, skills, and innovation. They were control mechanism —or what economists now call "rent-seeking" and imposed deadweight losses on the economy. Ogilvie says they generated no demonstrable positive externalities and notes that industry began to flourish only after the guilds faded away. Guilds persisted over the centuries because they redistributed resources to politically powerful merchants.

On the other hand, Ogilvie agrees, guilds created "social capital" of shared norms, common information, mutual sanctions, and collective political action. This social capital benefited guild members, even as they hurt outsiders. The guild system became a target of much criticism towards the end of the 18th century and the beginning of the 19th century. They were believed to oppose free trade and hinder technological innovation, technology transfer and business development.

According to several accounts of this time, guilds became increasingly involved in simple territorial struggles against each other and against free practitioners of their arts. Two of the most outspoken critics of the guild system were Jean-Jacques Rousseau and Adam Smith, and all over Europe a tendency to oppose government control over trades in favour of laissez-faire free market systems was growing rapidly and making its way into the political and legal system. The Le Chapelier Law of 1791 abolished the guilds in France, which it called *corporations*, according to Fernand Braudel.

Smith wrotes in the Wealth of Nations:

- It is to prevent this reduction of price, and consequently of wages and profit, by restraining that free competition which would most certainly occasion it, that all corporations, and the greater part of corporation laws, have been established. and when any particular class of artificers or traders thought proper to act as a corporation without a charter, such adulterine guilds, as they were called, were not always disfranchised upon that account, but obliged to fine annually to the king for permission to exercise their usurped privileges.

Karl Marx in his *Communist Manifesto* also criticized the guild system for its rigid gradation of social rank and the relation of oppressor/oppressed entailed by this system. From this time comes the low regard in which some people hold the guilds to this day. In part due to their own inability to control unruly corporate behaviour, the tide turned against the guilds.

Because of industrialization and modernization of the trade and industry, and the rise of powerful nation-states that could directly issue patent and copyright protections—often revealing the trade secrets—the guilds' power faded. After the French Revolution they fell in most European nations through the 19th century, as the guild system was disbanded and replaced by free trade laws. By that time, many former handicraft workers had been forced to seek employment in the emerging manufacturing industries, using not closely guarded techniques but standardized methods controlled by corporations.

Influence of Guilds

Guilds are sometimes said to be the precursors of modern trade unions, and also, paradoxically, of some aspects of the modern corporation. Guilds, however, were groups of self-employed skilled craftsmen with ownership and control over the materials and tools they needed to produce their goods. Guilds were, in other words, small business associations and thus had very little in common with trade unions. Guilds were more like cartels than they were like trade unions. However, the journeymen organizations, which were at the time illegal, may have been influential.

The exclusive privilege of a guild to produce certain goods or provide certain services was similar in spirit and character with the original patent systems that surfaced in England in 1624. These systems played a role in ending the guilds' dominance, as trade secret methods were superseded by modern firms directly revealing their techniques, and counting on the state to enforce their legal monopoly.

Some guild traditions still remain in a few handicrafts, in Europe especially among shoemakers and barbers. Some of the ritual traditions of the guilds were conserved in order organizations such as the Freemasons, alleging deriving from the Masons Guild. These are, however, not very important economically except as reminders of the responsibilities of some trades towards the public. Modern antitrust law could be said to derive in some ways from the original statutes by which the guilds were abolished in Europe.

Modern Guilds

Modern guilds exist in different forms around the world. In many European countries guilds have had a revival as local organizations for craftsmen, primarily in traditional skills. They may function as forums for developing competence and are often the local units of a national employer's organization.

In the United States guilds exist in several fields. The Screen Actors Guild, Writers Guild of America, East and the Writers Guild of America, West are capable of exercising very strong control in Hollywood because a very strong and rigid system of intellectual property rights exists. These guilds exclude other actors and writers who do not abide by the strict rules for competing within the film and television industry in America. The Newspaper Guild is a labor union for journalists and other newspaper workers, with over 30,000 members in North America.

Real estate brokerage is an example of a modern American guild. Signs of guild behaviour in real estate brokerage include: standard pricing, strong affiliation among all practitioners, self-regulation, strong cultural identity, little price variation with quality differences, and traditional methods in use by all practitioners. In September 2005, the U.S. Department of Justice filed an antitrust lawsuit against the National Association of Realtors challenging NAR practices that, DOJ asserts, prevent competition from practitioners who use different methods. The DOJ and the Federal Trade Commission in 2005 advocated against state laws, supported by NAR, that disadvantage new kinds of brokers. *U.S. v. National Assoc. of Realtors*, Civil Action No. 05C-5140.

The practice of law in the United States is also an example of modern guilds at work. Every state maintains its own bar association, supervised by that state's highest court. The court decides the criteria for entering and staying in the legal profession. In most states, every attorney must be a member of that state's bar association in order to practice law. State laws forbid any person from engaging in the unauthorized practice of law and practicing attorneys are subject to rules of professional conduct that are enforced by the state's high court. Medical associations that might be compared to guilds are the American Medical Association, and the American Dental Association.

Scholars from the history of ideas have noticed that consultants play a part similar to that of the journeymen of the guild systems: they often travel a lot, work at many different companies and spread new practices and knowledge between companies and corporations. Many professional organizations similarly resemble the guild structure. Professions such as architecture, engineering, geology, and land surveying require varying lengths of apprenticeships before one can be granted a 'professional' certification. These certifications hold great legal weight and are required in most states as a prerequisite to doing business there. Thomas W. Malone of the Massachusetts Institute of Technology champions a modern variant of the guild structure for modern "e-lancers", professionals who do mostly telework for multiple employers. Insurance including any professional liability, intellectual capital protections, an ethical code perhaps enforced by peer pressure and software, and other benefits of a strong association of producers of knowledge, benefit from economies of scale, and may prevent cut-throat competition that leads to inferior services undercutting prices. And, as with historical guilds, resist foreign competition. The free software community has from time to time explored a guild-like structure to unite against competition from Microsoft, *e.g.* Advogato assigns journeyer and master ranks to those committing to work only or mostly on free software.

In the City of London, the ancient guilds survive as Livery Companies, most of which play a ceremonial role. Guilds also survive in the UK in Preston, Lancashire as the Preston Guild Merchant where among other celebrations descendants of Burgesses are still admitted into membership. In 1878 the London Livery companies established the City and Guilds of London Institute the forerunner of the engineering school at Imperial College London. The aim of the City and Guilds of London Institute was the Advancement of Technical Education. Today City and Guilds is an examining and accreditation body for vocational, managerial and engineering qualifications from entry level craft and trade skills up to post doctoral achievement. In Australia, there exists the Guild of Commercial Filmmakers, a collection of commercial, short film and feature filmmakers. In some online computer games, players can form groups called player guilds, wherein people can socialize and organize various in-game activities.

THE GREAT WEAKNESS OF THE GUILD SYSTEM

I shouldn't really be answering this question but I think it is important for you to be aware of the weakness in the system. Just don't go talking about it in earshot of any of the masters. They won't take kindly to any talk against the guild system. Although the guild system has many obvious advantages such as providing a large measure of social and economic security for its members and supplying the means for guild members to co-operate for social, economic, and political activities, it has a great weakness. This weakness is its inability to adjust itself to technological progress. A guild member can not use a new method of manufacture until it has been accepted by the guild and provided for in the regulations. In practice, this acceptance of new methods is next to impossible. This means that any innovators are forced to work outside the jurisdiction and protection of the guilds.

An example is the wool industry. During the twelfth century the regular method of fulling cloth was to put it in water and stamp on it or beat it with paddles. It occurred to someone late in the century that water power could perform this task more effectively. Fulling mills began to sprout up but the guilds refused to have anything to do with them. Therefore, the fulling mills were built outside the towns away from the jurisdiction of the guilds.

By building their mills on land of a powerful Nobel, the millers insured that the guilds dare not refuse to accept the product of their mills. As a result, much of the wool industry of late medieval England grew up in the countryside to avoid the guilds. This scenario continues to repeat itself during the Renaissance period as other technological improvements are developed.

THE DOMESTIC OR PUTTING-OUT SYSTEM

The putting-out system was a system of domestic manufacturing that was prevalent in rural areas of western Europe during the seventeenth and eighteenth centuries. It evolved out of an early form of independent commodity production, constituting a transitional phase to what German social theorist Karl Marx called the "formal" subordination of labor to capital. The subordination of labor to capital refers to a situation in which the direct producers are separated from the means of production, depending on capitalists to provide them with the necessary tools, machinery, and raw materials to produce commodities. Such producers also receive a wage from the capitalists and have no control over the disposition of the products of their labor. Wage-earners who still retain considerable control over their own labor process, however, are subject merely to "formal subordination" rather than to the "real subordination" to capital that characterizes the fully developed factory system of industrial capitalism. Domestic workers involved in the putting-out system typically owned their own tools but depended upon merchant capitalists to provide them with the raw materials to fashion products that were deemed the property of the merchants. Semi finished products would be passed on by the merchant to another workplace for further processing, while finished products would be taken directly to market. The typical commodity product of the putting-out system was cloth, although other commodities were also produced under this system.

A salient feature of the putting-out system was the high degree of control that the direct producers retained over their own labor processes. Working at home and at their own pace, domestic producers were well positioned to balance work-time and leisure-time in accordance with the pre-capitalist preference for leisure. The system also allowed adult family members to develop a domestic division of labor in which their children could contribute productive labor under direct parental supervision. These circumstances were conducive to the rise and consolidation of the nuclear family as a dominant family form—a form that was also encouraged by the earlier system of independent commodity production.

With time, it became clear to the merchant "putter-outs" that their domestic employees required a greater degree of supervision to maximize their productivity and discourage "embezzlement" of raw materials or even finished products. Stephen Marglin argued in his 1974 article "What Do the Bosses Do? The Origins and Functions of Hierarchy in Capitalist Production," that it was these social considerations rather than any technological imperative that accounted for the rise of the factory system. By removing wage-earners from their own domestic environments and assembling them in a common workplace, merchant capitalists were in a better position to control the hours and pace of work and, through vigilant surveillance, to prevent embezzlement. By doing this, of course, many merchant capitalists transformed themselves into industrial capitalists, inaugurating the long transition to a "specifically capitalist" as opposed to an artisanal mode of commodity production.

Dan Clawson argued in his 1980 publication Bureaucracy and the Labor Process that Marglin's "social control argument" for the disappearance of the early putting-out system and the rise of the factory has many strengths but is one-sided in its dismissal of the important role played by new technologies in facilitating the subordination of labor to capital. Clawson "It is much more fruitful, and obviously the only Marxist approach, to understand the process as one of class struggle: Capitalists tried to impose social control in the form of factories, while workers struggled to resist. In this struggle, technological innovations were crucial capitalist weapons to help change the balance of power". Furthermore, noted Clawson, by assembling workers in large factories and workshops, capital could significantly improve their productivity by imposing ever-more detailed divisions of labor and taking advantage of machinery requiring a central power source.

The putting-out system all but disappeared in western Europe by the nineteenth century. However, by the late twentieth century it experienced a revival, stimulated by the advent of new computer and information technologies. Thanks to computer technology, the Internet, and new systems of inventory control, it has become increasingly possible for capital to employ stay-at-home workers without sacrificing productivity, control over hours, or effective cost accounting. The products of this new putting-out system are varied, but its most typical product is information.

FACTORY SYSTEM

The factory system was a method of manufacturing first adopted in England at the beginning of the Industrial Revolution in the 1750s and later spread abroad. Fundamentally, each worker created a separate part of the total assembly of a product, thus increasing the efficiency of factories. Workers, paid by wage, and machines were brought together in a central factory. All the processes of production would be carried out under one roof, and would continue as long as it was practical. Arguably the first was John Lombe's water-powered silk mill at Derby, operational by 1721.

However, the rise of the factory came somewhat later when cotton spinning was mechanised. Much manufacturing in the 18th century was carried out in homes, especially the weaving of cloth and spinning of thread and yarn, often with just a single loom or spinning wheel. As these devices were mechanised, they replaced the cottagers, who were forced to work in a central factory. Other products such as nails had long been produced in factory workshops, increasingly diversified using the division of labour to increase the efficiency of the system.

INDUSTRIAL REVOLUTION

The factory system was largely responsible for the rise of the modern city, as large numbers of workers migrated into the cities in search of employment in the factories. Nowhere was this better illustrated than the mills and associated industries of Manchester, nicknamed "Cottonopolis", and arguably the world's first industrial city. For much of the 19th century, production was done in small mills, which were typically water-powered and built to serve local needs. Later each factory would have its own steam engine and a chimney to give an efficient draft through its boiler.

The transition to industrialisation was not without difficulty. For example, a group of English workers known as Luddites formed to protest against industrialisation and sometimes sabotaged factories. They continued a tradition already established where new machines threatened existing jobs.

Numerous inventors in the textile industry such as John Kay and Samuel Crompton for example, suffered harassment when developing their machines or devices. In other industries the transition to factory production was not so divisive. Some industrialists themselves tried to improve factory and living conditions for their workers.

One of the earliest such reformers was Robert Owen, known for his pioneering efforts in improving conditions for workers at the New Lanark mills, and often regarded as one of the key thinkers of the early socialist movement. By 1746, an integrated brass mill was working at Warmley near Bristol. Raw material went in at one end, was smelted into brass and was turned into pans, pins, wire, and other goods. Housing was provided for workers on site. Josiah Wedgwood in Staffordshire and Matthew Boulton at his Soho Manufactory were other prominent early industrialists, who employed the factory system.

ARKWRIGHT

Richard Arkwright is the person credited with being the brains behind the growth of factories. After he patented his water frame in 1769, he established Cromford Mill, in Derbyshire, England. The factory system was a new way of organizing labour made necessary by the development of machines which were too large to house in a worker's cottage. Working hours were as long as they had been for the farmer, that is, from dawn to dusk, six days per week. It reduced the worker to an unskilled commodity who could be easily replaced.

CONTROVERSY

Debate arose concerning the morality of the system, as workers complained about unfair working conditions prior to the passage of labour laws. One of the problems concerned women's labour, which in many cases women were paid almost a quarter of what men made. Child labour was also a major part of the system, and was vehemently argued by those who deemed it immoral. Robert Owen created his utopian socialist factories at New Lanark which provided better working conditions. It was common to work 12 hours a day, six days a week in most factories.

CAUSES AND CONSEQUENCES OF INDUSTRIALIZATION

Industrialisation is the process of social and economic change that transforms a human group from an agrarian society into an industrial one. It is a part of a wider modernisation process, where social change and economic development are closely related with technological innovation, particularly with the development of large-scale energy and metallurgy production. It is the extensive organisation of an economy for the purpose of manufacturing.

Industrialisation also introduces a form of philosophical change where people obtain a different attitude towards their perception of nature, and a sociological process of ubiquitous rationalisation. There is considerable literature on the factors facilitating industrial modernisation and enterprise development. Key positive factors identified by researchers have ranged from favourable political-legal environments for industry and commerce, through abundant natural resources of various kinds, to plentiful supplies of relatively low-cost, skilled and adaptable labour.

As industrial workers incomes rise, markets for consumer goods and services of all kinds tend to expand and provide a further stimulus to industrial investment and economic growth. The first country to industrialise was the United Kingdom during the Industrial Revolution commencing in the eighteenth century. By the end of the 20th century, East Asia had become one of the most recently industrialised regions of the world.

DESCRIPTION

The original sector classification of Jean Fourastié, an economy consists of a "Primary sector" of commodity production, a "secondary sector" of manufacturing and processing and a "Tertiary Sector" of service industries. The industrialisation process is historically based on the expansion of the secondary sector in an economy dominated by primary activities. The first transformation to an industrial economy from an agricultural one is called the Industrial Revolution and took place from the mid 18th to early 19th century in certain areas in Western Europe and North America, starting in Great Britain Derby, followed by Germany, f.i. Bergisches Land and France. This now is called the first industrial revolution.

The Second Industrial Revolution describes the later changes that came about in the mid 19th century after the invention of steam engine, internal combustion engine, electricity and the construction of canals, railways and electric power lines. The invention of the assembly line gave this phase a boost. The lack of an industrial sector in a country can be a handicap in improving the country's economy and power, so governments encourage or enforce industrialisation. On the other hand, the presence of industry in a country does not mean in general that it will bring wealth and prosperity to the people of that country.

And third, the presence of an industry in one country can make it more difficult for other countries to develop the same type of industry. This can be seen in the computer- software-, and internet industries. Started from the U.S.A. around the 1990's these industries seemed to spread over the world. But after a period of monopolisation less than a decade long, the globally leading companies are concentrated in the U.S.A. Their economic power and capacity to dominate the media work against the developing of the same types of industry in other states.

HISTORY OF INDUSTRIALIZATION

Most pre-industrial economies had standards of living not much above subsistence, among that the majority of the population were focused on producing their means of survival. For example, in medieval Europe, 80% of the labour force was employed in subsistence agriculture.

Some pre-industrial economies, such as classical Athens, had trade and commerce as significant factors, so native Greeks could enjoy wealth far beyond a sustenance standard of living through the use of slavery. Famines were frequent in most pre-industrial societies, although some, such as the Netherlands and England of the seventeenth and eighteenth centuries, the Italian city states of the fifteenth century, the medieval Islamic Caliphate, and the ancient Greek and Roman civilisations were able to escape the famine cycle through increasing trade and commercialisation of the agricultural sector. It is estimated that during the seventeenth century Netherlands imported nearly 70% of its grain supply and in the fifth century BC Athens imported three quarters of its total food supply.

Industrialisation through innovation in manufacturing processes first started with the Industrial Revolution in the north-west and Midlands of England in the eighteenth century. It spread to Europe and North America in the nineteenth

Industrial Revolution in Western Europe

In the eighteenth and nineteenth centuries, the United Kingdom experienced a massive increase in agricultural productivity known as the British Agricultural Revolution, which enabled an unprecedented population growth, freeing a significant percentage of the workforce from farming, and helping to drive the Industrial Revolution.

Due to the limited amount of arable land and the overwhelming efficiency of mechanised farming, the increased population could not be dedicated to agriculture. New agricultural techniques allowed a single peasant to feed more workers than previously; however, these techniques also increased the demand for machines and other hardwares, which had traditionally been provided by the urban artisans. Artisans, collectively called bourgeoisie, employed rural exodus workers to increase their output and meet the country's needs. The growth of their business coupled with the lack of experience of the new workers pushed a rationalisation and standardisation of the duties the in workshops, thus leading to a division of labour, that is, a primitive form of Fordism. The process of creating a good was divided into simple tasks, each one of them being gradually mechanised in order to boost productivity and thus increase income.

The accumulation of capital allowed investments in the conception and application of new technologies, enabling the industrialisation process to continue to evolve. The industrialisation process formed a class of industrial workers who had more money to spend than their agricultural cousins. They spent this on items such as tobacco and sugar, creating new mass markets that stimulated more investment as merchants sought to exploit them. The mechanisation of production spread to the countries surrounding England in western and northern Europe and to British settler colonies, helping to make those areas the wealthiest, and shaping what is now known as the Western world.

Some economic historians argue that the possession of so-called 'exploitation colonies' eased the accumulation of capital to the countries that possessed them, speeding up their development. The consequence was that the subject country integrated a bigger economic system in a subaltern position, emulating the countryside, which demands manufactured goods and offers raw materials, while the colonial power stressed its urban posture, providing goods and importing food. A classical example of this mechanism is said to be the triangular trade, which involved England, southern United States and western Africa.

Critics argue that this polarity still affects the world, and has deeply retarded industrialisation of what is now known as the Third World. Some have stressed the importance of natural or financial resources that Britain received from its many overseas colonies or that profits from the British slave trade between Africa and the Caribbean helped fuel industrial investment.

Early Industrialisation in other Countries

After the Convention of Kanagawa issued by Commodore Matthew C. Perry forced Japan to open the ports of Shimoda and Hakodate to American trade, the Japanese government realised that drastic reforms were necessary to stave off Western influence. The Tokugawa shogunate abolished the feudal system. The government instituted military reforms to modernise the Japanese army and also constructed the base for industrialisation. In the 1870s, the Meiji government vigorously promoted technological and industrial development that eventually changed Japan to a powerful modern country.

In a similar way, Russia suffered during the Allied intervention in the Russian Civil War. The Soviet Union's centrally controlled economy decided to invest a big part of its resources to enhance its industrial production and infrastructures to assure its survival, thus becoming a world superpower. During the Cold war, the other European socialist countries, organised under the Comecon framework, followed the same developing scheme, albeit with a less emphasis on heavy industry.

Southern European countries such as Spain or Italy saw a moderate industrialisation during the 1950s-1970s, caused by a healthy integration of the European economy, though their level of development, as well as those of eastern countries, does not match the western standards.

The Third World

A similar state-led developing programme was pursued in virtually all the Third World countries during the Cold War, including the socialist ones, but especially in Sub-Saharan Africa after the decolonisation period. The primary scope of those projects was to achieve self-sufficiency through the local production of previously imported goods, the mechanisation of agriculture and the spread of education and health care.

However, all those experiences failed bitterly due to a lack of realism: most countries did not have a pre-industrial bourgeoisie able to carry on a capitalistic development or even a stable and peaceful state. Those aborted experiences left huge debts towards western countries and fuelled public corruption.

Petrol-producing Countries

Oil-rich countries saw similar failures in their economic choices. An EIA report stated that OPEC member nations were projected to earn a net amount of $1.251 trillion in 2008 from their oil exports. Because oil is both important and expensive, regions that had big reserves of oil had huge liquidity incomes. However, this was rarely followed by economic development.

Experience shows that local elites were unable to re-invest the petrodollars obtained through oil export, and currency is wasted in luxury goods. This is particularly evident in the Persian Gulf states, where the per capita income is comparable to those of western nations, but where no industrialisation has started. Apart from two little countries, Arab states have not diversified their economies, and no replacement for the upcoming end of oil reserves is envisaged.

Industrialisation in Asia

Apart from Japan, where industrialisation began in the late 19th century, a different pattern of industrialisation followed in East Asia. One of the fastest rates of industrialisation occurred in the late 20th century across four countries known as the Asian tigers thanks to the existence of stable governments and well structured societies, strategic locations, heavy foreign investments, a low cost skilled and motivated workforce, a competitive exchange rate, and low custom duties. In the case of South Korea, the largest of the four Asian tigers, a very fast paced industrialisation took place as it quickly moved away from the manufacturing of value added goods in the 1950s and 60s into the more advanced steel, shipbuilding and automobile industry in the 1970s and 80s, focusing on the high-tech and service industry in the 1990s and 2000s. As a result, South Korea became a major economic power.

This starting model was afterwards successfully copied in other larger Eastern and Southern Asian countries, including communist ones. The success of this phenomenon led to a huge wave of offshoring–*i.e.*, Western factories or Tertiary Sector corporations choosing to move their activities to countries where the workforce was less expensive and less collectively organised. China and India, while roughly following this development pattern, made adaptations in line with their own histories and cultures, their major size and importance in the world, and the geo-political ambitions of their governments. Currently, China's government is actively investing in expanding its own infrastructures and securing the required energy and raw materials supply channels, is supporting its exports by financing the United States balance payment deficit through the purchase of US treasury bonds, and is strengthening its military in order to endorse a major geopolitical role. Meanwhile, India's government is investing in economic sectors such as bioengineering, nuclear technology, pharmaceutics, informatics, and technologically-oriented higher education, exceeding its needs, with the goal of creating several specialisation poles able to conquer foreign markets. Both China and India, particularly the Chinese, have also started to make significant investments in other developing countries, making them significant players in today's world economy.

Newly Industrialised Countries

In recent decades, a few countries in Latin America, Asia, and Africa, such as Turkey, South Africa, Malaysia, Philippines, Mexico, Costa Rica, and El Salvador have experienced substantial industrial growth, fueled by exporting to countries that have bigger economies: the United States, China, India and the EU. They are sometimes called newly industrialized countries. Despite this trend being artificially influenced by the oil price increases since 2003, the phenomenon is not entirely new nor totally speculative. Japan and Russia both were successful in the fact that they imitated many other societies giving them flexibility.

Yet they both had very little in common before the 19th century. Japan was isolated from the world with its ongoing traditions and forms of centralized government. Russia featured a more strong centralized government under the emperor. Both would soon to discover that westernization and industrialism were expanding and their own ways would not hold up against the new changing world of industrialization. In the late 19th century the force for them to being industrializing would become even more prevalent for the success of their nation in this new growing societies.

SOCIAL AND ENVIRONMENTAL CONSEQUENCES

Change to Family Structure

The family structure changes with industrialisation. The sociologist Talcott Parsons noted that in pre-industrial societies there is an extended family structure spanning many generations who probably remained in the same location for generations. In industrialised societies the nuclear family, consisting of only of parents and their growing children, predominates. Families and children reaching adulthood are more mobile and tend to relocate to where jobs exist. Extended family bonds become more tenuous.

Environment

Industrialisation had led to its own health problems. Modern stressors include noise, air, water pollution, poor nutrition, dangerous machinery, impersonal work, isolation, poverty, homelessness, and substance abuse. Health problems in industrial nations are as much caused by economic, social, political, and cultural factors as by pathogens. Industrialisation has become a major medical issue world wide. Countries, such as the United States and China are now looking at ways to manage emissions being let off. China, being one of the fastest growing industrialized countries, releases emissions at a much more rapid rate than any other country.

They are burning more fossil fuels and discharge more Carbon emissions. With China's substantial industrialized growth, it is likely that as suggested, see more cars on the road, letting of greater emissions. As more countries begin to develop, the pollution only gets larger, making it harder to improve the air.

On one hand, as the economy rises, so does the amount of fossil fuels being burned daily. On the other hand, there is still the question of whether or not economic development could even happen while protecting the atmosphere. The main problem is that developed countries are competing instead of working together. Even if the countries do work together, there is still not enough participation among other countries to do any drastic change. Countries now need to agree on a low emission standard to cease the competition.

CURRENT SITUATION

China in 2010 became the worlds largest manufacturer, ending the United States run for over a century, the value of China manufacturing output in 2010 was $1.995 Trillion Dollars or 19.8% of the worldwide total, edging out the United States which accounted for 19.4% worth $1.952 Trillion Dollars. Currently the "international development community" endorses development policies like water purification or primary education.

The community does not recognise traditional industrialisation policies as being adequate to the Third World or beneficial in the longer term, with the perception that it could only create inefficient local industries unable to compete in the free-trade dominated political order which it has erected. The relationship between economic growth, employment and poverty reduction is complex. Higher productivity is argued to be leading to lower employment. There are differences across sectors, whereby manufacturing is less able that the tertiary sector to accommodate both increased productivity and employment opportunities; over 40% of the world's employees are "working poor" whose incomes fail to keep themselves and their families above the $2 a day poverty line. There is also a phenomenon of deindustrialisation, such as in the former USSR countries' transition to market economies, and the agriculture sector often is the key sector in absorbing the resultant unemployment.

4

Indian Industrialization

INTRODUCTION

India has become one of the fastest growing economies in the world over the last two decades, arguably aided in this performance by economic reforms. One of the striking aspects of India's recent growth has been the dynamism of the service sector, particularly information technology (IT) and IT enabled services (ITES), while, in contrast, manufacturing has been less robust. The contribution of the service sector was particularly striking in the 1990s, which not only saw rapid growth, but also a high contribution–over 60 per cent–from services. This growth trajectory, which has been termed "services-led" industrialization, or even a "services revolution" seems to stand out from the previous experience of economic development, which followed the traditional path from agriculture to manufacturing, with services becoming important at a later stage.

In India, in contrast, there was a sharp increase in the share of services in GDP, from 37 per cent in 1980 to 49 per cent in 2002, while the share of manufacturing remained about the same, at 16 per cent. Thus questions arise about India's development pattern, including its nature, sustainability and replicability. This document reviews the recent growth experience of India, identifies the major contributing factors to its pattern of development, and examines the prospects for further "services-led" industrialization in India. The analysis will draw on theoretical models as well as case studies of the Indian experience. The structure of the document is as follows. The next part provides a conceptual framework for the examination of the Indian experience. In particular, we discuss the nature of services, their distinction from products, and their categorization.

We argue that the precise nature of the services being considered is important for any analysis of growth impacts, and that one therefore has to go beyond broad national income accounts categories to understand the role of services in industrialization. A brief overview of India's overall growth experience, followed by a more detailed examination of the contribution of the service sector to growth, and the relative performance of manufacturing. The potential for spillovers from IT, ITES and other service sectors such as financial services, to the rest of the economy. We draw on econometric work on productivity growth, as well as input-output analysis of linkages to understand these possible spillovers. It is possible, based on this evidence, to hypothesize that India's manufacturing sector development may have been constrained, at least in part, by weaknesses in key service sectors such as transportation and electricity. In fact, other evidence suggests that telecommunications reforms were also critical for the rapid growth in IT and ITES. We consider the particular role of international trade in services. This deserves special treatment because of its growing importance, and because balance of payments constraints have often been major barriers to stable growth for developing countries.

We discuss the consequences for employment of different growth paths, and the challenges of education and manpower training to support and sustain India's development path. The social and environmental issues associated with "services-led" or alternative development paths. The focus in this part is on regional inequality issues, as well as impacts that do not necessarily manifest themselves in the national income accounts and growth statistics. The Indian experience as analysed in this document to some of the recent discussions of industrial policy, and development policy more generally.

CONCEPTUAL FRAMEWORK

Much of the literature on service-led growth begins with broad national income accounting categories. However, it is important both to disaggregate services to identify important differences within that category, and stepping back from the accounting, to understand the key ways in which services differ from products, which themselves are classified as outputs of the manufacturing sector. A good starting point for analysis is a consideration of the precise nature of services vis-à-vis other kinds of productive activities. The differences will be seen to depend on the nature of market transactions as well as intrinsic characteristics of services vs. products, and both are subject to change as economies and technologies evolve. The classical writers, such as Adam Smith and, earlier, the Physiocrats discussed services from the perspective of a distinction between productive and unproductive labour.

Smith's idea of "unproductive labour" included the servants of wealthy individuals and government employees, as well as the military, the clergy, lawyers, doctors, writers and musicians, all of whom are now included in the service sector. Of course, modern economics, based on utility and demand theory, has jettisoned this view, and services, however defined, are counted as productive activities. Various modern conceptual discussions of the distinct nature of services make similar observations. Hill, for example, emphasizes the non-storability of services, which requires that services must be consumed as they are produced. Griliches defines services as anything that is the result of labour that does not produce a tangible commodity. Lack of tangibility is fundamentally what leads to non-storability, and to non-transferability. However, intangibility must, in the digital age, be carefully interpreted. Thus, software programmes and various forms of digital electronic content have only limited tangibility, but are storable and transferable. The creation of these digital products may often be classified as a service, as also their delivery. The marketing literature pays considerable attention to the nature of services, and in this literature, the dimensions that distinguish services from products are summarized as follows:

- Intangibility,
- Heterogeneity,
- Simultaneity of production and consumption, and
- Perishability.

Several more fundamental economic implications are drawn from these distinguishing characteristics. For example, in this schema, intangibility, perishability and simultaneity all work against maintaining inventories. Heterogeneity and simultaneity makes it more difficult to achieve scale economies. All of these features make display and consumer assessment of characteristics harder to achieve.

Of course, the use of the above four characteristics to distinguish services from products is subject to several caveats. First, the differences are mostly of degree, especially in comparing services to certain kinds of products. Second, and more fundamentally, the distinction between products and services is often based on the contractual nature of the market transaction. At the most fundamental level, every product either provides services directly, or is combined with other products to generate services. Thus, an automobile is purchased as a product, but its value is based on the stream of services that it will provide over time. All such durable goods may be leased or rented, in which case the service is more explicitly contracted for than in the case of a product transaction. The more expensive the product, the less possible or economically desirable it is for an individual to access the services through a purchase.

In fact, contracting for services from specialist providers is often a way to achieve economies of scale in providing services that would not be possible otherwise. The general point is that the boundary between products and services is often a function of market and economic conditions, rather than the intrinsic characteristics of what is being exchanged. Previous analysts of this issue do recognize that the practical application of these conceptual distinctions in classifying services incorporates the contractual nature of the transaction. For example, in the case of utilities, Melvin points out that they are typically classified as services in the national income accounts, although gas, electricity and water are tangible goods. In these cases, the distribution systems are a critical aspect of enabling consumption of these goods, and the contractual relationship is primarily for delivery services using the distribution systems. One exception to this blurring of the boundary between products and services is the case of personal services. To take a simple example, a practitioner of traditional Indian medicine may make a diagnosis based only on an examination of the patient, consisting of visual inspection and pulse reading, without any tools whatsoever. No product is involved in this service provision. Such pure personal services, without the use of any capital or tools, are increasingly rare: a modern doctor's services typically incorporate the use of large quantities of expensive equipment. Other personal services, such as those of lawyers and accountants, also involve the use of physical capital in their delivery. One idea that we develop in this part is the increasingly "industrial" or "manufacturing-like" character of such personal services.

It is also worth noting that knowledge services, which have traditionally been personal services, are becoming more "industrialized" through the use of information technology: we also develop this point further in this part. By these characterizations, we mean the development of standardization, routinization, scalability and replicability for these services. Besides the marketing literature, one area where the conceptual distinction between products and services has been explored in detail is that of international trade, where the categorizations are important for shaping international trade policies and agreements. Locational characteristics are central to discussions of services in international trade. For example, Bhagwati argues that services can be divided into two classes: those that require physical proximity of the user and provider; and those that do not.

Services that require physical proximity can be further divided into three groups:

- Mobile provider and immobile user, *e.g.*, transporting labour to a construction site;
- Mobile user and immobile provider, *e.g.*, a patient going to a hospital;
- Mobile user and mobile provider, *e.g.*, students and professors meeting in a university for lectures.

A variation on the classification is the basis for the World Trade Organization's categorization of services trade, which categorizes different "modes of supply". Digital technology has also reduced the need for contact or physical proximity in many cases–these changes are at the heart of the new tradability of various knowledge-based services.

Bhagwati was an early observer of the trend towards removal of proximity requirements through technological change, *i.e.*, the increased richness and lower cost of long-distance communications. Melvin also explores this trend, characterizing services either as activities that require the double coincidence of time and location, or as activities that overcome constraints of time and location. He describes knowledge or information services as also overcoming a constraint–that of ignorance. Digital communications technology is, of course, behind the new wave of international trade in information or knowledge services. In the international trade context, the skill content of services can be an important distinguishing feature. Some kinds of low-skill services are susceptible to routinization and automation, whereas others are not.

Table. Services Sub-sectors for India

Sector	Activities included
Trade, hotels and restaurant	
Trade (distribution services)	Wholesale and retail trade in commodities both produced at home (including exports) and imported, purchase and selling agents, brokers and auctioneers
Hotels & Restaurants	Services rendered by hotels and other lodging places, restaurants, cafes and other eating and drinking places
Transport, storage and communication	
Railways:	
Transport by other means	Road, water, air transport, services incidental to transport
Storage:	
Communication	Postal, money orders, telegrams, telephones, overseas communication services, miscellaneous
Financing, insurance, real estate and business services	
Banking	Banks, banking department of RBI, post office saving bank, non-bank financial institution, cooperative credit societies, employees provident fund
Insurance	Life, postal life, non-life
Dwellings, real estate	
Business services	
Legal services	
Community, social and personal services	
Public administration, defence	
Personal services	Domestic, laundry, barber, beauty shops, tailoring, others
Community services	Education, research, scientific, medical, health, religious and other community
Other services	Recreation, entertainment, radio, TV broadcast, sanitary services

The former are easier to trade. In some cases, service activities can be unbundled or "splintered" to allow the offshore outsourcing of the lower skill components. One trend that also seems to be emerging, however, is trade in services with higher skill content, such as financial analysis or patent preparation. After one has clarified some of the conceptual characteristics of services, and their distinction from products, it is important to consider how measurement and classification are done in practice: "rather than discussing definitions, it may be more useful to take an operational approach and to examine what are actually called services in the national accounts and related statistical sources".

The Central Statistical Office in India provides a standard breakdown of services into 15 sub-sectors for that country, as shown in Table. Note that this Indian classification does not include utilities, which are often classified as services elsewhere. The salient point is the heterogeneity of the activities that are classified as services, in terms of capital intensity, skill content, need for physical contact, and importance of tangible products as part of the service.

INDIA'S GROWTH EXPERIENCE: OVERVIEW

Since our interest is in the role of services in India's recent growth, it is useful to have some perspective on the nature and extent of that growth. As we noted in the introduction, in the 1980s India's growth sped up from a moderate or slow rate prior to that decade and has since ranked among the highest in the world. There are numerous detailed reviews of India's growth experience in the last couple of decades, and we shall be selective and relatively brief.

These reviews often discuss causal factors, albeit typically without formal econometric modelling, with the importance of economic reforms in the growth acceleration being the subject of some controversy. In other cases, econometric techniques have been used to identify structural breaks in the growth process, but without any causal modelling. In this part, in addition to discussing aggregate growth performance, we also examine studies that focus on the performance of the service sector.

Panagariya provides a very careful appraisal of India's growth experience in the 1980s and 1990s, and of the 'revisionist' view, articulated by DeLong, Rodrik and Rodrik and Subramanian, that economic policy reforms in the 1990s were not key to India's growth performance in that decade. Those authors further argue that India's growth surge is properly understood as beginning in the 1980s, before the 1991 and subsequent economic reforms.

Based on a careful examination of the data, Panagariya reaches three conclusions about India's growth experience in the last 25 years:

- Growth during the 1980s was inconsistent, with the last three years of that decade contributing 7.6 per cent annual growth, without which growth in the 1980s was only marginally better than that of the previous three decades.
- The high growth in the last three years of the 1980s was preceded or accompanied by significant economic reform, including trade and industrial policy liberalization.

- Growth in the 1980s was fuelled by expansionary policies that entailed accumulation of a large external debt and contributed to an economic crisis.

Panagariya's final conclusion from his review of policy changes and growth performance is that it was "the 1991 market reforms and subsequent liberalizing policy changes that helped sustain growth". Ultimately, the positive impact of economic policy reforms seems to have been accepted, even in the revisionist view. For example, while Rodrik and Subramanian– based on their earlier analysis– use a growth accounting methodology to evaluate and project India's growth performance which de-emphasizes economic liberalization policies, they do not dismiss such policies.

They focus on "meta-institutions" such as democracy and the rule of law, as well as conventional economic inputs such as human and physical capital, and productivity growth. In emphasizing these fundamentals, they highlight the infrastructure and human capital built up under the pre-liberalization policy regime. At another level, however, their assumptions about the impacts of policy are not that different from those of Panagariya, since they state that "policy liberalisation will progressively erode the licence-quota-permit raj as a source of corruption and patronage that has had such a corrosive effect on public institutions." In addition to this indirect effect, they also attribute productivity growth directly to reforms that removed the "shackles on the private sector."

The case of IT illustrates the positive impact of the 1990s reforms, with telecommunications reform and liberalization leading the way for that sector. One of the best-known, most successful participants in this industry has documented the positive impact of liberalization, including general steps to ease the conduct of business. While Panagariya shows that average growth rates are very sensitive to how one divides the period under consideration, one might argue that the data itself should be allowed to reveal when a growth acceleration occurred for India, rather than being determined subjectively. Time series methods to test for structural breaks are designed to achieve this. Wallack's study is the most comprehensive along these lines, and examines time series data for 1951-2001.

The tests are applied to aggregate GDP data as well as to sectoral data. The latter, in particular, is of interest for understanding the recent pattern of economic development in India. Since these are pure time series estimations, there are no structural explanatory variables, but one can plausibly compare the identified break dates with what we know independently about policy changes or other macroeconomic events. The results are summarized in Table and provide some plausible connections between growth and economic environment changes. As Wallack herself emphasizes, the results are not as robust as one would like, since other years often have F-statistics close to the maximum values. However, there are two important conclusions. First, there is evidence for a break in the aggregate GDP growth rate in 1980. Second, there is little evidence that this was caused by a break in the growth of any sector–instead, as T.N. Srinivasan has emphasized, much of the growth rate change probably came from a shift in activity from slower-growing to faster-growing sectors. The results of the statistical tests suggest some exceptions to this observation. One is the breaks in financial, real estate and business services in 1974 and 1980.

Table. Structural Breaks in India's Growth Rates

Series	Break year 1	Break year 2
GDP	1980**	
GNP	1987**	
Trade, transport, storage, and communication	1992**	
Finance, insurance, real estate, and business services	1974**	1980**
Agriculture, forestry and logging, fi shing, mining and quarrying	1979	
Manufacturing, construction, electricity, gas and water supply	1964	
Registered manufacturing	1964	
Public administration, defense and other services	1993	

Obs.: ** indicates sup-F statistic signifi cant at 5% level, *** at 1% level.

Wallack suggests these were the result of low interest rates in 1974, and an investment boom beginning in 1980. There is also a break in trade, transport, storage and communication services in 1992: Wallack relates this to telecommunications reform and the growth of IT, but those factors may have come into play somewhat later. Clearly, this empirical approach needs to be explored further to understand the behaviour of the Indian economy. In addition to the time series evidence for structural breaks in some service sectors, there are more general empirical observations on service sector growth in India. For example, the share of services in gross capital formation declined from 57.7 per cent in 1950-51 to 48.8 per cent a decade later, and further to 43.7 per cent in 1970-71.

Thereafter, however, the share has not changed that much, hovering around 40 per cent. One can make conjectures about changes in capital and labour productivity in the service sector but since the composition of the sector has changed substantially over time, and these sub-sectors have different capital intensities, it is difficult to reach any definite conclusion from the data as presented. Hansda also suggests that the terms of trade moved against the service sector in the latter part of the 1990s, with finance, insurance, real estate and business services and trade, transport, storage, and communication together contributing to that decline. Liberalization, competition and technological progress may all have contributed to this development. A disaggregated view of service sector growth in India, using the CSO classification as described in Table gives a stronger indication of growth acceleration than the formal time series analysis. Gordon and Gupta note that 12 of 15 service sub-sectors in India grew faster than GDP over the 50 year period beginning in 1951, but the growth acceleration in the 1990s, which was responsible for India becoming an outlier in the service sector share was the strongest in business services, communication, and banking services, followed by hotels and restaurants and community services. These five sub-sectors together accounted for the entire acceleration in services growth in the 1990s. They assert that growth in other sub-sectors in the 1990s was broadly similar to, or lower than, that in the previous decades. In the context of service sector contributions and linkages in the economy.

Two other aspects of the performance of India's service sector are noteworthy. First, following an international trend, FDI inflows into India have moved increasingly away from manufacturing, and towards services sector, even as they have increased overall. These flows have been heavily concentrated in telecommunications and financial services. Second, the structure of indirect taxation in India, with historically light or zero taxation of services due to the nature of constitutional tax provision, has meant that the recent growth of the service sector has been associated with an overall tax-GDP ratio below the norm for countries at similar income levels. While services crossed 50 per cent as a share of GDP in the 1990s, they contributed only about 10 per cent of total tax revenue. This situation is changing, with moves to change constitutional tax assignments and bring services broadly into the indirect tax base.

In addition to analyses of aggregate and sectoral growth, a recent review of India's pattern of development focuses on skill intensity, and suggests that the nature of the economic policies followed by India from independence onward created a pattern of specialization that was already somewhat distinct from the typical developing country at comparable income levels. This, in turn, shaped the country's development pattern in the post-1980 reform period. In particular, India's manufacturing sector was more diversified, more skill-intensive, and less labour-intensive than average. In fact, it is suggested that the data indicates that India's service sector was smaller than normal up to the early 1980s. Thus, while the last two decades have seen a continuation of unusually skill-intensive growth, the rapid growth since the 1980s in services represents a departure from the past. Kochhar et al. examine the performance of the Indian economy in the 1980s and 1990s, starting from these apparently unusual 1980 preconditions. GDP per worker and total factor productivity both grew more rapidly in these two decades, as compared to the 1970s. Cross-country level regressions for the year 2000 suggest that India's services share of GDP was significantly higher than the norm in that year, but only when a country size variable was included. On the other hand, services employment was always significantly lower than the norm, and by a large magnitude, of 17 percentage points. This result is consistent, then, with the kind of skill-biased development observed in India pre-1980.

Regressions using the change in the share of services also indicated that India was a positive outlier during the period 1981-2000. The 1980s and 1990s also saw an accentuation of the skill bias in India's manufacturing, including whatever is measured of the informal sector. A conjecture is that incomplete labour market reforms and continued skewed education sector spending might be underlying factors behind the observed pattern of growth, in which case it might be altered by policy changes.

On the other hand, hysteresis in development paths might accentuate the observed biases in the future. State-level sectoral growth data seems to support the latter possibility: states such as Tamil Nadu and Maharashtra, according to this analysis, appear to be behaving more like advanced skill-intensive countries in their growth pattern. The concerns raised by Kochhar et al. about India's somewhat skewed pattern of development, and its implications for income and regional inequality particularly in the context of employment, education and training social issues and broader lessons for development policy.

Here, we offer one word of caution on their analysis. Historical patterns of development and cross-country comparisons are an important component of empirical analysis. Nevertheless, these comparisons may miss certain kinds of innovations that are not captured in the data. In particular, the development of modern business process outsourcing represents a rather new form of organizing economic activity, and an opportunity at many skill levels, that may not have been possible in the past. This goes back to our conceptual discussion in the previous part.

To offer an imperfect analogy, Japan in 1950 was not viewed as a likely candidate for building a world class automobile industry. The industry was both capital-intensive and technologically advanced. Nevertheless, Japan not only succeeded, but there were arguably positive spillovers from this effort to other engineering-intensive manufacturing. The imperfections in this analogy include substantial differences in initial conditions and social heterogeneity, but the caveat on extrapolating from the past should be kept in mind.

UNDERSTANDING SERVICE SECTOR GROWTH AND ITS IMPACTS

The discussion in the last part has suggested that India's more rapid growth in the 1980s and, especially, the 1990s has been the result of policy changes as well as initial conditions. The pattern of growth has been skewed towards the service sector, as well as towards skill-intensive activities. As noted in the introduction, India's service sector was responsible for over 60 per cent of its GDP growth in the 1990s, well above the sector's contribution in previous decades. A small number of service sub-sectors seems to have led the overall contribution of services to GDP growth.

In fact, the five fast-growing sub-sectors in the 1990s accounted for effectively all of the more rapid services growth. In this part, we begin with the empirical question of what factors can explain observed service sector and sub-sector growth in India. One possible answer is increased specialization, or splintering which, if it occurs across sectors, would alter the aggregate accounting. More precisely, if services components of manufacturing activity such as accounting, research and development, or logistics are splintered off and outsourced to other firms, they will be accounted for as service sector contributions to GDP, rather than being subsumed in manufacturing value added. Using input-output coefficients constructed by Sastry et al. Gordon and Gupta provide one estimate of this effect, based on changes in those coefficients. The input coefficients of services in agriculture and manufacturing increased enough in the 1980s to add 0.5 percentage points to service sector growth in that decade. Using input-output coefficients constructed from 1998-99 data, we are able to repeat this calculation for the 1990s, obtaining essentially no contribution of splintering in the 1990s, if measured in this manner.

However, this data and methodology does not permit an analysis of the extent to which cross-country splintering, which became more important in the 1990s, *e.g.*, through offshore outsourcing of business services, would explain the observed patterns of service sector growth. In the latter case, there is a real shift in economic activity to India, whereas domestic splintering is more of an accounting change. Even in the latter case, however, when specialization is associated with efficiency improvements, purely domestic splintering may reflect a positive economic change.

Along with increased specialization, another basic reason for an increasing share of services in GDP as an economy grows is a higher than average income elasticity of demand. Thus, the share of services in private final consumption expenditure grew faster in the two decades beginning 1980 than did services as a share of GDP. Aside from a big jump in the share of the sub-category "operation of personal transport equipment" in the 1980s, the shares of different kinds of final consumption services were relatively stable in this period.

Gordon and Gupta estimate that final consumption of services grew at a similar rate to overall services in the 1990s, but slower in the 1980s, which would be consistent with our calculation that splintering through specialization was a less significant contributing factor to services growth in the latter decade. Finally, the accelerated growth in services in the 1990s, along with a decline in their relative prices, is not consistent with a purely demand driven explanation of services growth. A third possible factor in explaining service sector performance in India is the role of policy liberalization. Based on an industry case study, we have noted the importance of liberalization in general, and telecommunications reform in particular, as a factor in the growth of IT and ITES.

Gordon and Gupta make essentially the same point using patterns in the data. In the absence of any good measure of liberalization, they note that the communications sub-sector grew rapidly in the 1990s coincident with deregulation, that the private sector share in the service sector grew in this period, and that FDI was positively correlated with services growth. This period also saw a rapid increase in service sector exports, which may have been aided by domestic liberalization: the international aspects of India's service sector growth. Some further quantification of the contribution of the various factors affecting services growth in the 1990s is provided by Gordon and Gupta through a basic growth accounting exercise. They first estimate a pre-1990 trend growth rate of about 1.5 per cent for service sub-sectors that accelerated in the 1990s. This is assigned to splintering and high income elasticity, as relatively constant factors. The residual is about 1.75 percentage points of service sector growth. Growth due to exports is estimated at about 0.5 percentage point.

The remaining residual, of 1.25 percentage points, is assigned to policy liberalization and technological progress. These estimates are somewhat rough and ready, but can provide a basis for examining more detailed econometric work on the contributions of and to service sector growth. A set of sub-sector specific and pooled time series regressions to estimate the factors determining services growth are consistent with the conclusion of a positive impact of reform on services growth. There also appears to be a positive impact of industrial growth on services growth, as one might expect. A complementary question to that of the impacts of industrial growth on services growth concerns the impact of services on manufacturing production and productivity.

These authors perform a sources-of-growth analysis, in which services are included as an input to manufacturing. They first use panel data for 148 three-digit level industries covering 18 years, 1980-81 to 1997-98, to estimate a production function, and based on this econometric estimation, the sources of growth analysis is carried out. It is estimated that, although service inputs contributed little to the production of the registered manufacturing sector during the 1980s, the contribution of services increased substantially in the 1990s. This, in turn, implies that excluding services inputs overstates the extent of manufacturing TFP growth in the 1990s. In fact, when the authors regress their TFP index on a set of explanatory variables that includes the ratio of services input to employment, a statistically significant positive relationship is found between services input and industrial productivity, though the estimated elasticity is not large. These results suggest that the increasing use of services in manufacturing in the 1990s favourably affected TFP. The results of this analysis also suggest that trade reforms played an important role in increasing the use of services in the manufacturing sector. It is not clear, however, to what extent this increased use reflects splintering, or other changes in the organization of manufacturing. Finally, Bosworth, Collins and Virmani examine the role of services as part of a detailed, up-to-date growth accounting for India. A major result is that TFP growth in the service sector has been very high in recent decades, while the contribution of capital is relatively low. Since half this sector's growth has come in 'traditional' sub-sectors such as trade, transportation, and community and personal services, where great productivity improvements might not be expected, they argue that price increases in services may be underestimated, leading to an overestimate of real growth in this sector.

If correct, this view has serious implications for overall Indian growth measures. However, an alternative explanation may lie in reductions in transaction costs associated with policy reforms. Combined, the empirical results summarized suggest that services have not only played a positive, direct role in India's economic growth in the last decades, but may have also helped spur manufacturing growth. While the latter impact was not visible in aggregate data for the 1990s more recent data suggests stronger manufacturing growth. Furthermore, since the growth of the services sector has been more robust than that of manufacturing, a relatively clear picture emerges of services driving the Indian growth process. There are serious concerns about skill intensity and employment but the central conceptual question from a growth perspective is whether the empirical experience can be related to an underlying theoretical understanding.

The traditional development paradigm of "agriculture to manufacturing to services" not only makes manufacturing central to the transition to modernity, but also necessary for sustained productivity growth, since an increasingly important service sector is viewed as a symptom of a mature economy and slower growth. Therefore, in addition to the empirical studies, we also consider the conceptual role of services, and information technology in particular, in reducing transaction costs and improving productivity in manufacturing. In fact, a recent major empirical study of the United States concludes that services sector productivity increases were responsible for the strong growth in the US in the latter half of the 1990s, with information and communication technologies playing a significant role in this productivity effect. One aspect of this impact is the possibility that technological change, including the use of ICTs in particular, has made some services more routinized, and therefore more like manufacturing. For example, a large-scale call centre is run more like a factory, reaping economies of scale, rather than a traditional services organization, which would have traditionally provided customised or differentiated services at a relatively small scale. While there is some scepticism about the long-run impacts of ICTs, there seems to be a well understood case for focusing on ICTs, providing both services and products, in the growth process. For example, Dasgupta and Singh state that, "IT, however, produces both new products and processes.

Nevertheless, from the Kaldorian perspective, what is important is whether IT, be it product, service or process, and manufacturing are subject to increasing or decreasing returns to scale, to dynamic economies of scale and to spill over effects for the rest of economy." While the macroeconomic data may not answer this question, microeconomic studies of developed countries directly establish the positive impacts of IT use on productivity. Another key aspect of ICTs' development impacts comes through reductions in transaction costs. This term can be interpreted broadly, to include various kinds of costs of communication, transportation, and other aspects of exchange, such as costs of searching for options, negotiating contracts and enforcing agreements.

Singh constructs an illustrative model to show precisely how transaction cost reductions can increase short run efficiency, as well as boost the long run steady state of the economy. The simplest and most basic aspect of transaction costs is that they result in resources' being used up in exchange, and drive a wedge between the supply price and the demand price in a competitive market. If transaction costs are high enough, the relevant market will not exist, in the sense that the quantity exchanged is zero.

If the transaction cost consists purely of resources used up in the process of exchange, then the welfare loss from its existence consists of the usual Harberger deadweight loss triangle, plus the transaction cost rectangle, which can be substantially larger. If the transaction cost is actually a payment to an intermediary, or a tax imposed by the government, then the welfare loss is just the Harberger triangle. Romer, in an influential paper, argues that even if the rectangles represent redistribution, and not a resource cost, there is a welfare cost that goes well beyond the usual Harberger triangles. The basic idea is that if there is a fixed cost of producing a good, transaction costs can reduce operating profits to the extent that some goods are no longer produced, leading to a larger loss of welfare than would otherwise be the case.

From a development perspective, the main implication of domestic transaction costs, *i.e.*, their effect on the equilibrium number of intermediate goods, and hence on output and welfare, must be sought in a dynamic model. Romer hints at this, but the first formal model is that of Singh, building on the analysis of Ciccone and Matsuyama. This uses a dynamic monopolistic competition model, in which an economy that inherits a small range of differentiated intermediate inputs can be trapped into a lower stage of development. In particular, the model may have multiple steady state equilibria, and the starting point of the economy can determine which steady state is approached. Singh shows that if transaction costs determine the initial number of varieties of the intermediate good, then reducing transaction costs can jump start the economy, moving it to a path that leads to a higher steady state.

In addition, transaction costs will affect the long-run equilibrium number of varieties, and hence the level of the steady state. Transaction costs can reduce the long-run steady state level of the economy, and even arrest the process of development. The use of ICTs, by reducing transaction costs, can mitigate both these effects. Note that, although Singh emphasizes ICTs, improved transportation and distribution can also bring down transaction costs. The connection to the empirical work on the growth of the Indian service sector reviewed earlier in this part should be clear: the fast growing services have included some sub-sectors that are critical determinants of major aspects of transaction costs for the Indian economy. From this perspective, one might also view infrastructure constraints in transportation as one manifestation of high transaction costs. In addition to affecting transaction costs, certain kinds of services may impact the rate of innovation, so that their growth is critical in determining development.

The obvious perspective to take in this case is that of the endogenous growth literature, which emphasizes the role of innovation. In this context, the critical aspect of services growth is their knowledge intensity. The comprehensive study of Dahlman and Utz analyses the development of a "knowledge economy" in India. These authors emphasize R&D quite broadly, and range over issues of governance institutions and education, as well as the national system of innovation.

Implicitly their treatment of education partially deals with the concerns about skill intensity expressed by Kochhar, by highlighting the importance of skilled labour in development. Their perspective converges with the transaction cost approach in emphasizing the need to improve the ICT infrastructure, which will in turn speed and enhance the acquisition, creation, dissemination, and use of knowledge. Singh provides a formal analysis of how improving ICTs can enhance growth. His growth model, designed to capture the special role of ICTs in economic growth as an enabler of efficient communication and storage of information, is an extension of the recombinant growth model of Weitzman.

The central idea of this approach is that new ideas are formed through combinations of old ideas. A key property of this formulation is that the increase in the number of ideas is faster than geometric growth. The rate at which potential ideas are converted into new ones depends on a "success rate", which is a function of the current level of resources spent per potential new idea, *i.e.*, the level of R&D. In Weitzman's model, all ideas are the same, and the actual number of new ideas is given by the number of potential new ideas multiplied by the success rate. Singh modifies Weitzman's model to allow the stock of ICT knowledge to independently affect this success rate, so that ICT gives the growth process an extra 'kick,' beyond that which comes from recombinant growth in general.

LINKAGES AND SPILLOVERS

The analysis of the previous part can be extended and complemented by explicitly considering linkages in an input-output framework. The goal is to quantify the extent to which services, manufacturing and agriculture have spillover effects on each other. A single year's input-output data provides this information in a static context, whereas examining changes in coefficients over time can provide some insight into structural changes in the economy. For example, Sastry construct input coefficient matrices for four years: 1968-69, 1979-80, 1989-90 and 1993-94.

Table. Sectoral Production Linkages

	Agriculture	Industry	Services
1968-69			
Agriculture	0.182	0.127	0.017
Industry	0.043	0.333	0.132
Services	0.016	0.135	0.096
1979-80			
Agriculture	0.160	0.130	0.039
Industry	0.068	0.345	0.105
Services	0.020	0.149	0.096
1989-90			
Agriculture	0.160	0.130	0.039
Industry	0.068	0.345	0.105
Services	0.020	0.149	0.096
1993-94			
Agriculture	0.145	0.035	0.034
Industry	0.140	0.365	0.150
Services	0.048	0.213	0.195
1998-99			
Agriculture	0.117	0.081	0.019
Industry	0.075	0.397	0.145
Services	0.050	0.173	0.144

The basic observation is that, over this period, agricultural production became more industry- and services-intensive, whereas industrial production became less agriculture-intensive and more services-intensive.

For the production of services, the main change was greater service intensity. Some of these changes took place more uniformly through this time period, but the greatest changes in the Indian economy's production structure, by this measure, came in the 1980s and 1990s. These observations are, of course, consistent with the analyses presented earlier. The input-output approach is applied at a much more disaggregated level by Hansda.

His goal is to address the larger question of the sustainability of services-led growth for the Indian economy. He uses input-output transactions tables for 1993-94, disaggregated at the level of 115 activities (22 in agriculture, 80 in industry, and 13 in services), as well as at the level of 10 broad sectors. At these disaggregated levels, Hansda's analysis suggests that the Indian economy is quite services-intensive with industry being the most services-intensive sector.

The pattern of average intensity for sectors falling into the three overall categories of agriculture, industry and services. The main conclusion, on the services intensity of industrial activities, is validated by the bold numbers in Table, indicating a large fraction of industrial activities with above-average services intensity.

This conclusion is in line with the Sastry et al. aggregated data for 1993-94, and our calculations for 1998-99. One can also examine the data at an intermediate level of aggregation, as in Table.

Table. Distribution of Activities with above Average Sectoral Intensity

	Agriculture intensive			Industry intensive			Services intensive		
Activity Categories (number)	Direct intensity		Direct & indirect intensity 1993-94	Direct intensity		Direct & indirect intensity 1993-94	Direct intensity		Direct & indirect intensity 1993-94
Agricultural activities (22)	15	14	15	0	0	0	1	1	1
Industrial activities (80)	18	19	22	57	61	55	56	57	59
Service activities (13)	1	1	1	3	3	3	6	7	2
Total activities (115)	34	34	38	60	64	58	63	65	62
Average intensity		7	6	12	29	24	59	15	14

The numbers here are the direct and indirect sectoral intensities, corresponding to the numbers reported by Sastry et al., but at a level of disaggregation that allows a greater understanding of the pattern of linkages of the different services sub-sectors. Note that the columns are further aggregated at the level of the three sectors–agriculture, industry and services. The different aggregation gives intensities somewhat at variance with the Sastry et al. calculations, but the conclusion of the importance of services still emerges clearly. Manufacturing, construction and "electricity, gas and water supply" are all services intensive. On the other hand, among services activities, "transport, storage and communication" are together quite industry intensive, while "personal, social and other services," and "trade, hotels and restaurants" are also somewhat industry intensive.

Table. Sectoral intensity—aggregate Categories

	Agriculture			Industry			Services		
	G (Rank)		G* (Rank)	G (Rank)		G* (Rank)	G (Rank)		G* (Rank)
Sector	93-94	98-99	93-94	93-94	98-99	93-94	93-94	98-99	93-94
Agriculture	0.131 (2)	0.093 (3)	0.172 (3)	0.092 (7)	0.091 (7)	0.211 (8)	0.057 (10)	0.051 (9)	0.122 (8)
Allied activities	0.179 (1)	0.173 (1)	0.220 (1)	0.039 (10)	0.038 (10)	0.127 (9)	0.068 (8)	0.049 (10)	0.121 (9)
Mining and quarrying	0.000 (9)	0.000 (9)	0.028 (9)	0.190 (5)	0.143 (6)	0.358 (5)	0.070 (7)	0.059 (8)	0.152 (7)
Manufacturing	0.091 (3)	0.110 (2)	0.179 (2)	0.420 (2)	0.417 (2)	0.811 (1)	0.185 (2)	0.179 (2)	0.385 (1)
Construction	0.024 (5)	0.021 (5)	0.095 (4)	0.362 (3)	0.340 (3)	0.706 (3)	0.202 (1)	0.171 (4)	0.381 (2)
Electricity, gas and water supply	0.004 (8)	0.003 (8)	0.038 (8)	0.453 (1)	0.440 (1)	0.800 (2)	0.166 (4)	0.176 (3)	0.330 (3)
Transport, storage and communication	0.023 (6)	0.005 (7)	0.074 (5)	0.282 (4)	0.276 (4)	0.560 (4)	0.175 (3)	0.191 (1)	0.317 (4)
Trade, hotels and restaurants	0.034 (4)	0.048 (4)	0.060 (6)	0.091 (8)	0.083 (8)	0.214 (7)	0.160 (5)	0.131 (6)	0.227 (5)
Financing, insurance and real estate	0.000 (10)	0.000 (10)	0.006 (10)	0.044 (9)	0.056 (9)	0.089 (10)	0.061 (9)	0.105 (7)	0.087 (10)
Personal, social and other services	0.016 (7)	0.013 (6)	0.048 (7)	0.152 (6)	0.157 (5)	0.301 (6)	0.090 (6)	0.144 (5)	0.167 (6)
Average Intensity	0.050	0.064	0.092	0.212	0.241	0.418	0.123	0.139	0.229

Definitions: G: Direct sectoral intensity;
G*: Direct and indirect sectoral intensity.

As one might expect, the level of linkages to and from agriculture, as indicated by these intensities, is quite low. Surprisingly, the same is true for "financing, insurance and real estate." The results for 1998-99, for direct intensities only, indicate relatively little change in magnitudes of agriculture and manufacturing intensities, as well as for their rankings, which capture relative intensities. Services intensities seem to have changed somewhat more from 1993-94 to 1998-99.

In particular, "transport, storage and communications," "financing, insurance and real estate," and "personal and social services" all became more services intensive in absolute and relative magnitude. The level of linkages to financial and real estate services remained relatively low, however. Given the expansion of this sub-sector in the 1990s, and policy statements about creating an international financial hub in Mumbai, it would be important to investigate how these linkages have changed since 1998-99. One can also calculate backward and forward linkages more formally, using a procedure due to Rasmussen. Backward linkages refer to stimulus from a sector to its input-providing sectors, while forward linkages capture stimuli in the opposite direction, *i.e.*, downstream in production. Linkage measures are constructed as indices. An index value greater than one indicates a greater than average linkage.

Applying this method to 1998-99 data, we find that 43 out of the total of 115 activities–6 of 22 agricultural activities, 28 of 80 industrial activities and 9 of 13 services activities–had relative backward index values above one. In fact, 8 of the 9 service activities exceeded the threshold by substantial margins. Therefore, we may conclude that services activities had proportionately the largest inducing effect on the rest in terms of backward linkage. The results for the forward linkage indices are qualitatively similar, in terms of the relative importance of services: 19 of 115 activities–5 of 22 agricultural activities, 5 of 80 industrial activities and 9 of 13 services activities–had high forward linkage indices.

Hansda's aggregated results for 1993-94 are quite similar to these disaggregated indicators, finding strong backward linkages for "personal, social and other services" and "transport, storage and communication" in particular. Forward linkages from services are weaker at this level of aggregation, emphasizing the need to consider as disaggregated a view of the economy as possible. Two additional pieces of analysis are possible. Hansda calculates the coefficients of variation for the linkage indices. These coefficients measure the evenness across sub-sectors of a particular sector's purchases or sales. The low proportion of services activities with low backward coefficients of variation suggests that the backward linkages from services tend to be concentrated, *i.e.*, their purchases are from a relatively small segment of the economy. Hansda also finds that the forward linkages from services are more evenly spread.

Second, given conceptual criticisms of the Rasmussen indices of linkages, he constructs an alternative index of vertical integration, based on the work of Heimler. The results are that 14 out of the 115 activities have index values higher than the average, with 7 of those activities in the services sector, 6 in industry and 1 in agriculture. This supports the view that the services sector has the largest multiplier effect on the rest of the economy. One way to interpret the results from the disaggregated input-output analysis is in keeping with the idea that India is a high transaction cost economy.

Transportation, trade and communications in India, all sectors which have high impacts on transaction costs, have all been markedly inefficient, held back by inefficiencies in government and by barriers to private participation. The 1980s and 1990s saw this situation begin to change, and a plausible interpretation of Hansda's results is that, through linkages, this change has stimulated the entire economy to some extent. One must bear in mind that this kind of input-output analysis is static, and there is no growth mechanism postulated. Nevertheless, one can argue that, to the extent that growth is driven by innovation, innovations in the services sector are likely to have positive implications for the growth of the rest of the economy. We can explore this hypothesis more explicitly by selectively perturbing input-output coefficients and tracing out the implications.

The theoretical basis for the following exercise is developed in an important paper by Majumdar and Ossella. They show that in an input-output economy, under some further conditions, the long-run optimal growth factor is given by,

$$g = (\delta\lambda)^{1/\alpha}, \text{ where } \delta$$

is the discount factor for the representative consumer, a is the parameter of the constant elasticity one-period utility function (equivalent to the coefficient of relative risk aversion), and l is the inverse of the largest eigenvalue of the input-output matrix. Efficiency gains in sector *j*, such as would result from any kind of innovation, are modelled as proportional reductions in all the input requirements of that sector, *i.e.*, the elements of column *j* of the input-output matrix.

The maximal eigenvalue decreases in this case, implying an increase in the optimal growth rate of the economy. Since the other two parameters are unchanged, the ranking of growth rates is equivalent to the ranking of the l's across all the individual sector perturbations. Hence, the sectors for which exogenous efficiency improvements would have the greatest growth impacts can be clearly identified.

These sectors are termed "leading sectors" for the economy. Majumdar and Ossella, using data from 1989, consider both 2 and 5 per cent reductions in input requirements, and identify the five leading sectors of the Indian economy for that year in each case as, in order of growth rate impacts:

- Electricity, gas and water supply,
- Iron and steel,
- Paper and paper products,
- Other chemicals, and
- Other manufacturing.

Using α = 0.9, the growth factor for a 5 per cent reduction in input requirements in the electricity, gas and water supply sector, relative to the original growth factor, is 1.0081. To translate this into a growth rate impact, assume that the initial optimal growth rate was 6 per cent–the efficiency gain would change the optimal growth rate to 6.9 per cent.

We carry out the analysis along the lines of Majumdar and Ossella, using input-output data for 1998-99. We have 115 sectors instead of the 60 sectors used in 1989. Nevertheless, major sectoral classifications are quite similar. We only calculate the impacts of 5 per cent efficiency improvements, but consider the 10 leading sectors of the economy. The results are presented in Table.

Table. Leading Sectors

	Relative growth factor	Growth rate (base 6 percent)
Electricity, gas & water supply	1.0108	7.14
Iron, steel and ferro-alloys	1.0049	6.52
Non-ferrous basic metals	1.0037	6.40
Other services	1.0031	6.32
Other transport services	1.0028	6.29
Railway transport services	1.0020	6.21
Coal and lignite	1.0018	6.19
Trade	1.0016	6.17
Miscellaneous manufacturing	1.0016	6.17
Inorganic heavy chemicals	1.0013	6.14

Electricity, gas and water supply remains the most important leading sector, and its growth impact is estimated to be even higher than for the earlier data. Several heavy industry sectors feature in the top 10, paralleling the earlier results. The new feature of our results, however, is the prominence of services. Four services sub-sectors are in the list, and their nature and presence strongly bears out the transaction cost interpretation provided previously in this part. As an alternative to using disaggregated input-output data, it is also possible to undertake a dynamic analysis of sectoral growth and linkages within the Indian economy through reduced-form time series modelling. Sastry et al. add a export sector to agriculture, industry and services, and estimate this four equation specification for annual data from 1981-82 to 1999-2000. Linkages from agriculture and industry to services, and agriculture and services to industry are incorporated by including those sectors' outputs as causal variables. On the other hand, agricultural growth is assumed to be determined independently. Their empirical results for the industrial sector come from a straightforward levels regression, and indicate that a 1 per cent rise in services would stimulate industrial output by 0.40 percentage point. The services sector presents several additional challenges in terms of assumptions required for empirical analysis.

Sastry et al. focus only on construction, "trade, hotel and restaurants" and "transport, storage and communication" as endogenous services, subject to linkages, leaving finance, and "community, social and personal services" as exogenous to the system.

The results for the entire sample period, with the equation estimated in growth rate terms, suggest that a percentage point increase in the growth rate of services would lead to a 0.32 percentage point increase in the growth rate of industry. Given the substantial changes in the input-output coefficients over this period, and tests that reject parameter stability, they re-estimate the equation for the 1990s only. The impact of services growth now increases to 0.49 percentage points, and they argue that this is consistent with the 1993-94 input-output tables. In fact, the match is less good than the authors suggest, since the coefficient for agriculture is much higher in the time series specification than in the input-output table.

Nevertheless, there is broad consistency from this approach concerning the importance of services. The input-output linkage analysis is limited by its focus on what are essentially pecuniary externalities. As noted by Dasgupta and Singh, the Kaldorian hypothesis of the mechanisms of growth through structural change emphasizes technological externalities or spillovers, rather than pecuniary externalities. In this view, technological externalities are what made manufacturing special in the past, and now explain why ICTs are a special driver of growth.

This perspective is also consistent with the analysis of Singh with respect to the special role of ICTs in the innovation process. In this context, Singh also surveys fieldwork and case studies which suggest that there are spillovers from ICTs in rural areas of India. In particular, the introduction of a range of rural ICT-based services not only reduces transaction costs, but also provides spillovers through knowledge acquisition and information access. It has also been argued that there were substantial spillovers from the IT services industry in India to IT enabled services, as well as to knowledge intensive sectors in general. These included specific organizational expertise, customer knowledge, and general reputational effects. In turn, there are linkages and spillovers from ITES to sub-sectors such as construction and transportation, not only through demand stimulus but also by creating a different set of requirements and expectations.

INTERNATIONAL TRADE IN SERVICES

Theoretical considerations and empirical evidence both suggest a positive role for trade liberalization in India's growth since the 1980s. Theories of comparative advantage and inter-industry trade do not necessarily distinguish between agriculture, manufacturing and services as likely export sectors for a developing country, though developing nations are almost invariably those with a relative abundance of unskilled labour. Since much of India's export growth has come in skill-intensive services, the international aspects of India's "services- led" growth bear examination from empirical and theoretical perspectives.

Panagariya summarizes India's experience with external liberalization, starting in the late 1970s. He documents the acceleration in India's growth rate in the 1980s, and ties this improvement to the external liberalization that took place. Several studies formally establish a positive linkage between opening the economy and productivity improvements in manufacturing: this supports the conventional view connecting trade liberalization and development through improvements in manufacturing. Many developing countries have had to struggle with maintaining balance of payments equilibrium. In India's case, balance of payments crises in the 1970s and before tended to shape a policy of keeping the Indian economy substantially closed to international trade and investment. In this respect, one of the most important aspects of services sector growth in India has been its favourable international trade and balance of payments consequences.

Hansda provides some basic documentation of the change in the role of services in India's international trade. For example, India's share in world export of commercial services doubled from 0.6 per cent in 1990 to 1.2 per cent in 2000, while its share in global merchandise exports went up only marginally, from 0.5 per cent to 0.7 per cent, in the same period.

Table. Sectoral employment Elasticities

Sectors	1983 to 1987-88	1983 to 1993-94	1993-94 to 1999-2000
Agriculture	0.87	0.70	0.01
Mining and quarrying	1.25	0.59	–0.41
Manufacturing	0.59	0.38	0.33
Electricity, gas and water supply	0.30	0.63	–0.52
Construction	2.81	0.86	0.82
Trade, hotels and restaurants	0.87	0.68	0.62
Transport, storage and communication	0.47	0.55	0.63
Financing, insurance, real estate and business services	0.49	0.45	0.64
Community, social and personal services	0.52	0.68	–0.25
All	0.68	0.52	0.16

Data going back to the 1950s show that, while India has run a persistent deficit in merchandise trade, there has been a consistent surplus in trade in services. This surplus, only 10 per cent of the merchandise trade deficit in 1990-91, grew to onethird of that deficit by 2001-02. In aggregate, the ratio of services exports to merchandise exports increased from 25 per cent to 45 per cent in that period.

Much of this increase came in the category of miscellaneous services, which include IT services and ITES such as business process outsourcing and call centres. Hansda also notes the higher positive balance in travel services, and suggests this may be related to a more favourable exchange rate, which was also a consequence of liberalization. Travel connected to IT services and ITES may also have contributed to this increase. Numerous authors note the increased ability to deliver services over long distances at a reasonable cost as a result of technological progress in ICTs, which has led to increased worldwide trade in services. Gordon and Gupta estimate that, in India, exports of services grew by an average of 15 per cent a year in the 1990s, compared with 9 per cent annually in the 1980s. Using the Sastry et al. input-output matrix, and making some assumptions about input usage for services exports relative to services overall, they estimate the contribution of exports to annual average services growth to be about 0.2 percentage points in the 1980s, and 0.6 percentage points in the 1990s. In their regression analysis, they find that exports of services were highly significant for explaining overall growth of business services, which includes IT services and ITES–seemingly an unsurprising result. On the other hand, the growth of other kinds of services did not show much sensitivity to exports. We have suggested that, in many respects, the recent services growth in India comes from outsourcing by developed country firms that has characteristics of manufacturing, namely scale and routinization. Even in general, trade in services can be analytically treated as similar to trade in goods.

This includes trade based on comparative advantage as well as that driven by economies of scale and product differentiation. Bhagwati, Panagariya and Srinivasan provide some analytical foundations for understanding outsourcing to countries like India in the context of general trade in services. This offshore outsourcing is properly defined, they note, as "offshore trade in arm's length services," distinct from offshore purchases of manufactured components and FDI. The authors go on to model three kinds of international outsourcing. The result of their analysis in each case is that the welfare impacts of this kind of trade in services are akin to the conventional benefits of trade in goods. These models and some extensions focus on the impacts on the developed country from which the outsourcing comes.

In each case, though, the receiving country should benefit from the new trade, since there is an increased demand for its labour. This kind of theoretical analysis supports the view that new trade in services, such as India is experiencing, provides positive welfare gains. At the same time, these models do not incorporate labour with different skill levels, nor can they quantify the benefits of trade. Putting aside concerns about the magnitude and nature of the growth and employment effects of services trade, one can examine barriers to realizing whatever benefits there are. In addition to IT services and ITES, sub-sectors such as health, education and travel may all have growth and development impacts that are affected by international trade.

One possible focus is on the external and demand constraints on India's international trade in services. External trade barriers can arise from limits on foreign equity participation, licensing provisions, immigration and labour market regulations and discriminatory treatment with respect to taxes, subsidies, and other policies.

Domestic constraints can result from infrastructure inadequacies, poor quality and standards, lack of clear-cut responsibilities between centre and state governments and other policy-related disincentives. To examine the extent of the constraints to trade in India's services sector, Banga classifies services in terms of their external trade barriers, *i.e.*, the extent of liberalization, as well as growth rates and the share in exports of services. The extent of liberalization of services is captured by the FDI cap and restrictions on trade in Mode 4, as classified by the WTO under the General Agreement on Trade in Services. The period considered for the extent of liberalization is from 1997, since many services were liberalized after that, so the average share in exports is estimated for the period 1997-2003. Banga uses this classification to suggest that services that face high trade barriers have mostly grown slowly, while others, which have seen moderate liberalization, such as health and education, have had their growth held back by domestic constraints.

Table. Categorization of Services by Extent of Trade Liberalization and Growth

	Substantially liberalized	**Moderately liberalised**	**Less than moderately liberalized/Restricted**
High growth (10% and above)	Software Services H Telecommunication M	Banking M Insurance M Travel H Health L Education L	
Moderate growth (5-9%)			**Legal L**
Low growth (0-5%)	Road Transport L	Construction L Air Transport M	Professional Services, e.g., Postal, Accountancy L Rail Transport L

The various external and domestic constraints for these sub-sectors include explicit constraints on FDI and other restrictions, but often just a lack of a coherent set of policies and modern regulatory institutions. Banga offers several policy prescriptions. In particular, health and education are identified as service areas with high growth rates and low export shares, suggesting potential for more trade in these services. Currently, India's trade in health services occurs mainly from mode 4 and mode 2. The latter is limited by technological and infrastructure constraints. Continued telecommunication reforms, such as reduced connectivity costs and lower tariffs will expand the scope for crossborder supply of these services. Even with medical tourism to India, where doctors do not go abroad, there can be issues of diverting care from the poor.

Thus, liberalization and investment in this area would ideally be accompanied by a strengthening of the public health care system. Regarding trade in education services, Banga emphasizes the need to develop a more robust system of regulation and accreditation of educational institutions. Srinivasan similarly notes the possibilities and constraints for mode 2 services trade in education. Conventional tourism, which can complement health services in particular, as in medical tourism, is particularly constrained by infrastructural shortcomings. Srinivasan notes that tourism grew by 24 per cent in 2004, making India one of the leading tourist destinations in the world. At the same time, the inadequacy of affordable quality hotel rooms, transport and communications still constrains India's ability to attract and absorb tourists. Even in the case of fast-growing IT and ITES, Srinivasan notes the infrastructure constraints can still hurt growth: "Reliable electric power, efficient and inexpensive telecommunications and access to venture capital are essential infrastructures for the IT sector. Although telecommunications infrastructure has vastly improved, as noted earlier, there are still some unresolved issues relating to the authority of the regulatory agency vis-à-vis the Department of Telecommunications and the state-owned providers. The situation regarding electric power continues to be abysmal". One other important potential growth area is financial services. Banking and insurance have seen high growth with moderate liberalization of the sector. Some of the developments in the financial sector have come from the adoption of information technology, and others from improvements in regulation and legal and institutional frameworks, though much remains to be accomplished in the latter arena.

The problem of financially weak and inefficient public sector banks and insurance companies contrasts with modern equity markets that enjoy high trading volumes and some aggressive and competitive private sector banks such as ICICI Bank. The input-output analyses do not show much evidence of strong linkages to and from the financial sector, but to the extent that the efficiency of capital allocation is increased through financial development, one can make a case for encouraging the financial services sector, as recent government policy pronouncements have suggested.

Since conventional input-output analysis ignores the financial sector, and is static, its enabling role for investment and growth is neglected in that approach. However, several empirical studies for India do support the conclusion that financial sector development would stimulate economic growth.

EMPLOYMENT, EDUCATION AND TRAINING

Studies of the development of the services sector in India typically highlight the lack of job growth that has taken place, even as the sector has, to some extent, driven overall GDP growth. The problem is a bigger one, however, since overall job growth has also been anaemic. For example, organized sector employment in 1991 was 26.73 million. By 1997, this had grown a bit, to 28.25 million. However, in 2003, the numbers had shrunk: 18.58 million public sector employees, 8.42 million private, and 27 million total. Clearly, there are some well-known institutional and legal constraints in the labour market that inhibit job growth.

Aside from these overall constraints, understanding the consequences of India's particular pattern of service sector growth for employment is important. In fact, while some fast-growing segments of IT services have not been subject to restrictive labour laws, they have not altered the overall services employment picture. There are several accounts of the slow growth of employment in services. Hansda points out that, while the share of services in employment increased from 20 per cent in 1970-71 to 23.5 per cent in 1999-2000, this was much less than the growth of the services sector's share of GDP, which was from 32.1 per cent in 1970-71 to 48.5 per cent in 2000-01.

Gordon and Gupta note that, while services rose from 42 per cent to 48 per cent of GDP during the 1990s, the employment share of services actually declined by about one percentage point during the decade. Of course, the flip side of these observations is that labour productivity in services has grown much faster than in the rest of the economy. Hence, one might repose the question of low employment growth in services as one of relatively low productivity growth in the rest of the economy. As suggested, return to this issue later in this part.

The productivity issue may also be examined to some extent through the input-output coefficients of the Indian economy. Lower coefficients imply not only lower linkages, but also simply lower input intensity. Thus the low linkages of financial services may be partly an indicator of high productivity. The caveat in reaching this as a definite conclusion, of course, is that one does not have a technology benchmark for each sector. Furthermore, splintering complicates any attempt to interpret changes in the coefficients over time. More disaggregated data on employment in services is presented in Tables.

Table. Growth of Employment by Sectors

Industry	Employed workers, millions (%)			Annual growth rates, %	
	1983	1993-94	1999-2000	1983-94	1994-2000
Primary	208.99 (69.0)	245.16 (65.5)	239.83 (60.4)	1.60	–0.34
1. Agriculture				1.51	–0.34
2. Mining and quarrying				4.16	–2.85
Secondary	41.66 (13.8)	55.53 (14.8)	66.91 (16.8)	2.91	3.14
3. Manufacturing				2.14	2.05
4. Electricity, gas and water supply				4.50	–0.88
5. Construction				5.32	7.09
Tertiary	52.11 (17.2)	73.76 (19.7)	90.26 (22.7)	3.53	2.42
6. Trade				3.57	5.04
7. Transport, storage and communication				3.24	6.04
8. Financial services				7.18	6.20
9. Community, social and personal services				2.90	0.55
Total employment	302.76 (100)	374.45 (100)	397.00 (100)	2.04	0.98

The difference in the pattern of employment generation as well as overall employment growth in the two periods is striking. Joshi points out that the slowdown in tertiary sector employment growth in the latter period is chiefly due to the sharp decline in the growth of employment in community, social and personal services. Other, more disaggregated data does suggest that a squeeze on public employment in the 1990s may have been behind the slowdown in employment in community, social and personal services, and hence of services employment.

If that was a proper result of controlling wasteful government expenditure, the question that follows is why private sector employment did not compensate more. Possible answers may lie in the quality of the labour force, and the skills it possesses, as well as labour laws. There may also have been cyclical effects at work, since employment growth picked up subsequently. Total employment impacts for the economy were determined more by changes in agricultural employment growth than by any slowdown in services employment growth. In the decade 1983-93, half of employment growth came from the primary sector, chiefly agriculture.

Table. Shares of Different Sectors in Increase of Employment (Million)

Sectors	1983	1993-94	Increase during 1983-93	Share in increase, %	1999-2000	Increase during 1994-2000	Share in increase, %
Primary	208.99	245.16	36.17	50.5	239.83	–5.33	–23.6
Secondary	41.66	55.53	13.87	19.3	66.91	11.38	50.4
Tertiary	52.11	73.76	21.65	30.2	90.26	16.50	73.2
Total	302.76	374.45	71.69	100.00	397.00	22.55	100.00

However, in the subsequent six years, primary sector employment actually shrank, while neither industry nor services could pick up the entire slack. Part of this phenomenon can be explained, as suggested by Joshi, by the possibility that the employment absorption capacity of agriculture has reached a saturation point, while employment growth in the high productivity industrial sector was sluggish in this latter period because of a combination of an industrial sector recession and continued use of relatively capital-intensive-technology.

Joshi goes on to emphasize the services sector as a key area for employment generation–however, the organized sector employment numbers quoted earlier in this part, do not give a clear indication that this is happening in any automatic way. On the other hand, the figures for organized sector employment miss over 90 per cent of employment in India.

In fact, the most recent National Sample Survey Organisation data, released in 2004, estimate that the employment growth rate from 1999-2000 to December 2002 averaged about 2 per cent: the same as that in the 1983-94 period, and double the growth rate in the 1994-2000 period. This translated into about 8 million jobs added per year, with growth coming chiefly in urban areas and particularly in the small-scale sector. Thus, unorganized sector employment growth outweighed job losses in the corporate sector. Sectoral employment data going back to 1951 emphasize the strikingly poor record of manufacturing employment growth over five decades, though the GDP growth rate was, of course, lower before the 1980s. This would support the view that the real problems in employment generation lie with long-run structural and policy constraints that inhibit employers from hiring, rather than more recent policy changes.

Employment elasticities for the 1980s and 1990s may be interpreted similarly. While there is some decrease in employment elasticities in the 1990s, they are low in the 1980s as well, supporting the long-run view of the employment problem. One is also tempted to conclude from the data that the employment problem is somewhat independent of the fact that employment has lagged GDP growth–the latter, as noted, is an indicator of rising productivity.

The cause for concern is that this rising productivity of labour has not translated into a stronger and wider demand for that factor. The answer to that may have something to do with India's pattern of skillintensive development, itself determined by educational patterns. Clearly, the pattern vis-à-vis agricultural employment is consistent with a Kaldorian or similar story of development, with manufacturing somewhat replaced, and definitely supplemented, by services that are organized more on industrial lines. However, both services and manufacturing in India are apparently more skill-intensive than is commensurate with India's level of income and development. This has implications for the pattern of development, in two ways.

First, since the scarcity of the requisite skills acts as an entry barrier to these sectors, rather than development drawing in new job seekers and increasing employment, the earnings of the skilled are being pushed up, often towards developed country levels. There may be trickle down demand effects, but the consequences for income distribution and social implications may be of concern. The second implication for development is on the demand side, with the pattern of goods and services being skewed towards the demand pattern of the upper end of the income distribution.

In this case, there may not be the kinds of spillovers that would occur in manufacturing, where expertise developed for mass produced goods for the middle classes in rich countries can be transferred to an array of goods that also satisfy wants of the masses in the developing country. The same degree of spillovers may not be available for call centres and BPO operations, which do not necessarily lead to efficiency benefits for the kinds of manufacturing that will employ lower-skilled workers. Of course there are some positive examples: in southern India, in particular, world-class manufacturing firms do seem to be emerging, partly driven by the business environment and culture created by IT and ITES firms. Some of the ideas can be incorporated in formal models, which typically assume full employment–the employment issues are then really about the quality of the jobs, and employment in high productivity sectors. New growth theories go beyond considering homogeneous investment as a driver of growth to emphasize the importance of technical progress, embodied in new varieties of capital and consumption goods, in driving long run or sustained economic growth. Those models typically assume homogeneity of consumers, but Sarkar, for example, allows heterogeneity of demands, and shows how demand thresholds can matter for growth, and how a sufficiently large middle class can be crucial in enabling growth.

In Sarkar's model, there are three classes of income earners: rich, middle class and poor. Having a large enough middle class is crucial for generating sufficient demand and profits to drive innovation, which in turn creates economic growth. In his formulation, the only feasible way to increase the growth rate is to promote the poor to the middle class by permanently increasing their productivity–through education, for example.

Thus, both theoretical and empirical analyses of the employment aspects of India's growth experience suggest that constraints on employment can be traced to the labour supply side, in the educational system, as well as to the more obvious labour demand side disincentives that are heavily built into the labour laws. The distortion of Indian public spending towards higher education and away from primary education is well known. A significant aspect of the 1990s and the years since has been that a relatively small proportion of Indian higher education graduates, either with professional or technical degrees, or with English communication skills, were able to take advantage of the rapid development of globally-oriented IT services and ITES in this period.

Financial and professional services have also started to come under this umbrella, as Indians provide a pool of managerial talent that is small relative to the population, but large in absolute numbers. The constraints on higher education in India create rents for this educated group, as they are now able to participate in an effectively global labour market. Among the many authors who have analysed the current state of India's higher education system, Kapur and Mehta and Kapur and Khilnani analyse the structural and institutional shortcomings of the organization of the sector.

Interestingly, the educational services sector itself does not figure explicitly in all the empirical analyses reviewed here, with the exception of Banga but it provides the underpinnings for all modern sectors of the economy through its outputs. Kapur and Mehta argue that the dismal overall state of higher education in India is a result of a withering away of public education funding support, because of the unsustainable subsidies required by the existing model.

At the same time, political interference and capture by vested interests have increased. The result has been a haphazard and uneven privatization, coupled with exit by those who can afford to send their children abroad. Kapur and Khilnani echo these points, and stress the need for removing subsidies to and controls on so-called elite institutions, allowing them to expand efficiently, and transferring resources to areas such as vocational education.

They point out that the vocational Industrial Training Institutes receive just 3 per cent of the higher education budget, and are in even worse shape than the rest of the higher education system. The policy measures that would correct the present quality and quantity constraints on the supply of higher education in India are well understood by economists, but political battles have instead been focused on dividing up the existing rents in the system, through controls on FDI in higher education and quotas for various societal groups.

Instead, free entry into higher education, coupled with a new and more effective system of regulation through certification, disclosure requirements, and media rankings would lead to transparent competition and an expansion of supply precisely where it is needed. Kapur and Mehta fault Indian industry for not being more proactive, since they would benefit, but one can see that in narrow areas such as IT services, firms have been quick to develop training programmes and push for their employees to acquire needed qualifications and skills. The problem is with more general skills, which give larger opportunities for benefits to be captured by non-training firms.

Even here, in areas such as ITES, firms have tried to develop collective action solutions through industry associations. Wider adoption of such approaches, as well as the alternative of private philanthropy to fund education, will require the government to overhaul its archaic regulatory system and legal frameworks for the provision of education services. Of course, many of these problems are endemic to primary education as well, and similar solutions are desirable.

In the end, what will matter for the sustainability of India's development will be its educational system, and not particular emphasis on manufacturing, services or any sub-sector among them, with the caveat that sub-sectors with greater labour intensities will obviously have more beneficial employment effects.

LESSONS FOR DEVELOPMENT POLICY

In reviewing India's experience with respect to service-sector-led development, we have noted policy implications for international trade, education, and employment generation. In many respects, these are traditional concerns of development policy, and a large theoretical and empirical literature exists on each of these aspects of economic development. While there is some degree of consensus on the importance of education, economic openness, and encouragement of labour-intensive activities, debate continues with respect to the degree and specificity of government targeting of particular sectors of a developing economy. The variety of views is considerable, even for a single country like India.

Dasgupta and Singh offer several policy prescriptions based on their examination of the Indian case. These include government support for the informal sector through financial and technical services, a Keynesian attention to maintaining aggregate demand, and a traditional industrial policy approach of identifying dynamic industries that have positive technological and pecuniary externalities for the rest of the economy.

ICT-related activities are emphasized in their discussion but they also reiterate the importance of encouraging knowledge-intensive industries more generally. Dahlman and Utz develop the latter point for India, and Dahlman provides a more general context and framework for this view. Rodrik makes a more general case for government intervention, based on the view that economic development is fundamentally driven by structural change in the economy, and that this change is "fraught with externalities and spillovers of all kinds." In doing so, he draws on China and India as examples of fast-growing countries with export profiles skewed towards high productivity goods.

Ocampo summarizes several areas where the Washington consensus has been insufficient. What concerns us here is "the role of productive development strategies." In this category, Ocampo emphasizes the need to build institutional capacity, the importance of Schumpeterian innovation and structural change, and the standard externality arguments with respect to markets such as those for long-term capital and technology. The Latin American case, in particular, is often used to illustrate the inadequacy of mere liberalization and policy neutrality.

One might add, however, that all these studies beg the question of political will and feasibility. In particular, the interplay of different interest groups may be the fundamental determinant of which policies are implemented and of the quality of implementation. Returning to the Indian case, one can argue that policy reforms that have enabled greater openness, more competition, and better government regulation have spurred growth but have not gone far enough.

Impediments to internal trade, labour market rigidities, and barriers to doing business all seem to be factors in keeping economic growth below potential. The Indian IT sector, as a major success story, has typically been highlighted as one where government policy made a difference. The key claim here is that the cluster of human and institutional capital in Bangalore, more general government investments in technology education, and government policies that promoted import-substituting industrialization all created the initial conditions that allowed the IT sector to flourish. On the other hand, there is a case to be made for the "benign neglect" interpretation of the IT sector's success. Government policy certainly did not pick a winner in this case, since there was little or no understanding of, or foresight with respect to, the market for software services. Many of those who were drawn into the sector came with general technical training, rather than skills specifically geared towards the markets that were being served from the 1990s onward. Nor is it the case that government investment in telecommunications infrastructure in India was based on any analysis or deep understanding of its potential role in facilitating or spurring development and growth.

Certainly, government made policy moves from the 1980s onward to improve telecommunications infrastructure and access, but in every case, the impetus came from outside the government and the slow pace of reform is evidenced in how much India lags behind China in telecommunications access.

Thus, the Indian case in the past hardly fits even the weak notion of industrial policy outlined in Rodrik:

- "The critics of industrial policy are correct when they argue that governments do not have adequate knowledge to pick "winners." Industrial policy is more appropriately conceived as a process whereby the state and the private sector jointly arrive at diagnoses about the sources of blockage in new economic activities and propose solutions to them. ... It simply requires to build the public-private institutional arrangements whereby information on profitable activities and useful instruments of intervention can be elicited".

Having cautioned against an overly rosy view of past "state-led" development in the Indian case, one can note that this does not preclude such a process from operating beneficially in the future, in the limited manner described by Rodrik. Numerous central and state government actions encouraged and supported IT and ITES once the success of these sectors became evident.

A similar dynamic is potentially under way with respect to financial services. However, the political realities of interest groups are evident in Indian policies that effectively ration access to education at all levels, and various other policies that impose unnecessary costs on the private sector, reduce efficiency and inhibit innovation.

We have suggested that broadening economic and institutional reforms, and extending them to government itself, may be more significant in terms of positive impacts than selective interventions in particular sub-sectors, provided that this process tackles emerging inequalities. In some respects, competition among state governments that has resulted from India's economic reforms may also shape India's political economy in a more favourable direction, ameliorating some of the conflicts highlighted in the abstract by Rajan and Zingales.

CONCLUSIONS

India's pattern of development, with relatively slow growth of manufacturing, and a more rapid increase in the size of the service sector than would be typical, has received considerable attention. The contribution of this paper has been to provide an integrated appraisal of India's experience and future potential along this growth path. It is straightforward to argue, as several authors have done, that manufacturing, services and agriculture are all important, and broad policy steps to improve growth and employment across the economy are desirable. Specific policy suggestions with respect to improving the tradability and productivity of particular services also emerge from various analyses.

Analyses of linkages suggest that certain service subsectors of the economy, such as trade, transportation and communications, may be particularly important, but this is also an intuitive conclusion. Several less obvious implications do emerge from this research. First, some of the dichotomy between services and manufacturing may be overdrawn, as certain kinds of services can be organized in ways that are closer to modern manufacturing.

Nevertheless, there are some differences in education requirements, and employment and social impacts, particularly in the skill intensity required by some of the services that have seen the highest growth in India in the last decade or two. Indeed, the constraints on appropriate skill acquisition that face the majority of the population in India represent the greatest barrier to any kind of sustained growth, and a major policy challenge in the politically charged arena of education.

Tackling the education bottleneck, and adding some labour market reform, may go a long way to allowing Indian industry and its services sector to draw on the large numbers of underemployed, poorly productive people in India's rural heartland. A few years, ago, the debate on the role of services in India's growth was couched in somewhat simplified terms, as services substituting for manufacturing.

Recognizing the blurring conceptual distinction between the modern components of the two sectors helps to refocus the issues on productivity, linkages and distributional concerns, rather than any simple dichotomous choice. China's recent major revision of its GDP figures upwards by onesixth, with most of that increase coming from a revaluation of services sector activity, is also significant in this context.

At a stroke, the estimated contribution of services to China's GDP went up by nine percentage points, crossing 40 per cent. This is a much more plausible figure than previous estimates, even though it is still short of the average for countries with similar per capita income levels. The difference between India and China in terms of services' contribution to the economy has therefore become much less stark. Just as China has focused on manufacturing exports, but seen a stimulation of services activity, in India's case, there may be positive spillovers from services growth to manufacturing, through income and demand, or through organizational learning.

Ultimately, the bland but appropriate conclusion may be that making the conditions right for enterprise and innovation throughout the economy is more important than any targeted intervention towards particular sectors of the economy.

5

Modern Issues

GRIEVANCES AND GRIEVANCE HANDLING PROCEDURE

RIGHTS AND RESPONSIBILITIES

A right can be considered as 'a just or legal claim to title', that which is due by law, tradition or nature. A responsibility is a duty, an obligation or a burden.

Trade union rights enjoyed by workers derive from a multitude of sources, including international conventions, national constitutions, statute law, the collective agreement, custom and practice, and the common law. At the same time, workers have responsibilities which derive mainly from the employment contract.

The main responsibilities of employees are summarized below:

- To perform his/her work with reasonable skill.
- To exercise reasonable care in the performance of his/her duties
- To serve his/her employer with good faith
- To protect his/her employer's confidential information.
- To account for his/her employer's property placed in his/her charge
- To be willing and ready to serve in his/her job function.
- To indemnify his/her employer for damage or injury for which the employer becomes liable to a third party as a result of the employee's failure to exercise reasonable skill or take reasonable care.

GRIEVANCES

Definition

Grievances are defined as breaches of the collective agreement, custom and practice, the statute law, common law, natural justice or as any problem of a sufficient nature to cause a disturbance of the workplace equilibrium. It is usually considered that a grievance moves to the dispute stage once a shop steward becomes involved in the process of grievance handling. Some grievances are individual, others are group grievances. Some are symptomatic, others are deeply-rooted. Some are rights grievances, others are interest grievances. Rights grievances speak to the breach of an established right; interest grievances relate to a dispute about an attempt at creating a new right.

Major Causes of Grievances

The major causes of grievances have been discovered to be:

- Loose, faulty or ambiguous contract language
- Management strategy to undermine the union
- Union strategies
- The prevailing social and political environment
- Historical factors
- Faulty systems
- Lack of appropriate codes and processes.

Investigating a Grievance

Grievance handling requires investigative skills and skills of advocacy. One of the major issues in the investigation is to determine what is the breach of the employee's right. Once it is established that a breach has occurred, then a report should be prepared based on the use of the five 'w's':

- Who were involved?
- When did the breach occur?
- Why did the breach occur?
- Where did the breach occur?
- What happened?

It is usually agreed that action will not be taken on any breach until the full grievance procedure is utilized, giving the person whose right has been breached, full opportunity to ventilate concerns. A grievance procedure should provide a formal framework, setting limits on the arbitrary exercise of management authority and power.

Grievance Handling Procedures:

- The person aggrieved raises the issue with the immediate supervisor;
- Failing settlement, the matter is referred to a manager;
- Failing settlement, the aggrieved workers can refer the issue to the shop steward;
- The shop steward or delegate can enter the case and request a meeting with the manager or someone from the personnel or human resource department;
- A senior trade union official can intervene;
- Failure at the domestic level can lead to a third party intervention eg an employers' federation;
- The final stage is conciliation or arbitration.

Grievance handling requires skills of advocacy and can be considered to be semi-judicial in nature. The grievance handler should try to set time limits for the resolution of grievances, should ensure that the person to make the decision on the grievance is competent to decide and free of bias, and should develop a menu of solutions- a variety of options to decide on the outcome.

Discipline

Discipline is a control mechanism employed to ensure compliance with organizational objectives. It is used to control those who deviate from performance and behaviourial standards.

There are three stages in the development of a disciplinary process:

1. Legislative
2. Administrative and
3. Interpretive.

Trade unions should be involved in the legislative stage, to ensure that the disciplinary code that is devised is acceptable. They must be involved at the administrative and interpretive stages to ensure that workers are treated fairly.

In developing a disciplinary code, there are usually two approaches. The code can be seen as punitive. Alternatively, it can emphasize a corrective and developmental approach. Most codes distinguish between infractions which constitute minor misconduct, and which will attract verbal or written warnings, as against gross or serious misconduct which may attract severe discipline including summary dismissal

Dismissal

Dismissal is the ultimate sanction and is seen as retributive. Dismissal can be with notice; it can also be summary, without notice or payment in lieu of notice; or instant, but may include pay in lieu of notice. Constructive dismissal relates to a situation where an employee is unable to perform a job function through employer obstruction.

Dismissal is considered to be fair where there is clear evidence that the employee:

- Is incapable of performing the job through lack of qualification, capability or health;
- Conducts himself/herself in such a way as to breach the contract of employment;
- Is redundant;
- Contravenes the law in such a way as to make continued employment untenable.

When addressing the 'fairness' of the punishment, questions should be raised on:

- Were proper procedures followed?
- Were similar breaches condoned in the past?
- Was all admissible evidence allowed?
- Was the dismissal for an admissible reason?
- Did the offence or the employee's record justify dismissal as a suitable sanction?

Punishments

Except for cases where the total sanction of dismissal is required –there are several lesser punishments such as warnings, transfers, demotions, fines and deductions from pay, which can help to keep the employee on the payroll. Where dismissals are shown to be unfair, demands can be made for reinstatement, or re-engagement, or for compensation.

Redundancy

Redundancy occurs where changes in the organization results in the displacement of labour or changes the nature of work significantly.

The legal definition of redundancy usually relates to situations where:

- The employer ceases to carry on the business, and the business closes in the place where the employee was employed
- Requirements of the business have ceased or diminished or are expected to cease or diminish for a variety of reasons-natural, economic or technological.

Some countries have provided legislation to deal with redundancies where others have not. Whether or not the law provides for redundancy, trade unions should negotiate such provisions within collective agreements. The modern period is witnessing mergers, amalgamations, buyouts and other strategies which create conditions for redundancies.

The trade union should try to create an environment where workers' employment is protected. At the same time, it should provide for those who do not wish their services to be transferred from employer to employer in a unilateral way.

There are three main phases for trade union involvement in redundancy situations:

- Where it is anticipated that redundancies will occur, it should be discussed, along with possible alternative approaches. There must be a determination of manpower needs.
- Once it is decided that redundancy is inevitable, there should be agreement on the selection of employees to be made redundant, the level of compensation to be paid, and the provision of assistance to redundant employees.
- Finally, the individual employee targeted for redundancy must be notified and counselled in a sensitive and mature manner.

Role of the Shop Steward

The union elected shop steward or delegate has a special role in terms of contract administration and grievance handling. By educating work colleagues about the contract, the shop steward can help to ensure that workers are aware of the terms and conditions under which they are employed. The shop steward also alerts union staff members of difficulties which are likely to lead to grievances at the workplace. The delegate should be highly trained in industrial relations matters as both a negotiator and an advocate. Trained, respected and effective shop stewards are able to solve grievances even before they reach the level of the union. Such shop stewards are usually effective communicators. They hold meetings with members at the workplace. They invite union staff to the workplace. They constantly seek training and re-training programmes offered by the union. Contractual clauses under which grievances constantly seem to arise usually need careful examination and correction.

Protection of the Shop Steward

ILO Convention No. 135, and ILO Recommendation No. 143 concern the Protection and Facilities to be afforded to workers' representatives in the undertaking.

Workers' representatives in the undertaking shall enjoy effective protection against any act prejudicial to them, including dismissal, based on their status or activities as a workers' representative or on union membership or participation in union activities, in so far as they act in conformity with existing laws or collective agreements or other jointly agreed arrangements.

It is usually agreed that a shop steward, while in a duly constituted meeting representing a member, is not subject to discipline, unless the shop steward behaves in a way that offends fundamental principles. The cut and thrust of advocacy will allow the use of vigorous debate, and strong language may be used, once they remain within the bounds of decorum and decency.

- Workers' representatives in the undertaking should be afforded the necessary time off from work, without loss of pay or social and fringe benefits for carrying out their representation functions in the undertaking.
- In order to enable them to carry out their functions effectively, workers' representatives should be afforded the necessary time off for attending trade union meetings, training courses, seminars, congresses and conferences.

Apart from the grievance handling process, other committees may be included in the agreement to assist with contract administration.

They include committees for:

- Safety and Health
- Works Council
- Productivity Enhancement Committees

INDUSTRIAL DISPUTES

An industrial dispute may be defined as a conflict or difference of opinion between management and workers on the terms of employment. It is a disagreement between an employer and employees' representative; usually a trade union, over pay and other working conditions and can result in industrial actions. When an industrial dispute occurs, both the parties, that is the management and the workmen, try to pressurize each other. The management may resort to lockouts while the workers may resort to strikes, picketing or gheraos. As per Section 2(k) of Industrial Disputes Act,1947, an industrial dispute in defined as any dispute or difference between employers and employers, or between employers and workmen, or between workmen and which is connected with the employment or non-employment or the terms of employment or with the conditions of labor, of any person.

This definition includes all the aspects of a dispute. It, not only includes the disagreement between employees and employers, but also emphasizes the difference of opinion between worker and worker. The disputes generally arise on account of poor wage structure or poor working conditions. This disagreement or difference could be on any matter concerning the workers individually or collectively. It must be connected with employment or non-employment or with the conditions of labor. From the point of view of the employer, an industrial dispute resulting in stoppage of work means a stoppage of production.

This results in increase in the average cost of production since fixed expenses continue to be incurred. It also leads to a fall in sales and the rate of turnover, leading to a fall in profits. The employer may also be liable to compensate his customers with whom he may have contracted for regular supply. Apart from the immediate economic effects, loss of prestige and credit, alienation of the labor force, and other non-economic, psychological and social consequences may also arise. Loss due to destruction of property, personal injury and physical intimidation or inconvenience also arises. For the employee, an industrial dispute entails loss of income. The regular income by way of wages and allowance ceases, and great hardship may be caused to the worker and his family.

Employees also suffer from personal injury if they indulge into strikes n picketing; and the psychological and physical consequences of forced idleness. The threat of loss of employment in case of failure to settle the dispute advantageously, or the threat of reprisal action by employers also exists. Prolonged stoppages of work have also an adverse effect on the national productivity, national income. They cause wastage of national resources. Hatred may be generated resulting in political unrest and disrupting amicable social/industrial relations or community attitudes.

CAUSES OF INDUSTRIAL DISPUTES

The causes of industrial disputes can be broadly classified into two categories: economic and non-economic causes. The economic causes will include issues relating to compensation like wages, bonus, allowances, and conditions for work, working hours, leave and holidays without pay, unjust layoffs and retrenchments. The non economic factors will include victimization of workers, ill treatment by staff members, sympathetic strikes, political factors, indiscipline etc.

- *Wages and allowances*: Since the cost of living index is increasing, workers generally bargain for higher wages to meet the rising cost of living index and to increase their standards of living. In 2002, 21.4% of disputes were caused by demand of higher wages and allowances. This percentage was 20.4% during 2003 and during 2004 increased up to 26.2%. In 2005, wages and allowances accounted for 21.8% of disputes.
- *Personnel and retrenchment*: The personnel and retrenchment have also been an important factor which accounted for disputes. During the year 2002, disputes caused by personnel were 14.1% while those caused by retrenchment and layoffs were 2.2% and 0.4% respectively. In 2003, a similar trend could be seen, wherein 11.2% of the disputes were caused by personnel, while 2.4% and 0.6% of disputes were caused by retrenchment and layoffs. In year 2005, only 9.6% of the disputes were caused by personnel, and only 0.4% were caused by retrenchment.
- *Indiscipline and violence*: From the given table, it is evident that the number of disputes caused by indiscipline has shown an increasing trend. In 2002, 29.9% of disputes were caused because of indiscipline, which rose up to 36.9% in 2003. Similarly in 2004 and 2005, 40.4% and 41.6% of disputes were caused due to indiscipline respectively. During the year 2003, indiscipline accounted for the highest percentage (36.9%) of the total time-loss of all disputes, followed by cause-groups wage and allowance and personnel with 20.4% and11.2% respectively. A similar trend was observed in 2004 where indiscipline accounted for 40.4% of disputes.
- *Bonus*: Bonus has always been an important factor in industrial disputes. 6.7% of the disputes were because of bonus in 2002 and 2003 as compared to 3.5% and 3.6% in 2004 and 2005 respectively.
- *Leave and working hours*: Leaves and working hours have not been so important causes of industrial disputes. During 2002, 0.5% of the disputes were because of leave and hours of work while this percentage increased to 1% in 2003. During 2004, only 0.4% of the disputes were because of leaves and working hours.
- *Miscellaneous*: The miscellaneous factors include:
  - Inter/Intra Union Rivalry
  - Charter of Demands
  - Work Load
  - Standing orders/rules/service conditions/safety measures
  - Non-implementation of agreements and awards etc.

Table. Percentage Distribution of Disputes by Causes

Cause Group	2002	2003	2004	2005
Wages and Allowances	21.3	20.4	26.2	21.8
Personnel	14.1	11.2	13.2	9.6
Retrenchment	2.2	2.4	0.2	0.4
Lay-off	0.4	0.6	-	0.2
Indiscipline	29.9	36.9	40.4	41.6
Violence	0.9	1	0.9	0.4
Leave and Hours of Work/shift Working	0.5	1	0.4	-
Bonus	6.7	6.7	3.5	3.6
Inter/Intra Union Rivalry	0.4	0.6	0.4	0.4
Non-implementation of Agreements and Awards etc.	3.1	1	1.1	0.9
Charter of Demands	10.5	8.8	5.7	7.1
Work Load	0.5	0.4	0.7	1.1
Standing orders/rules/service conditions/safety measures	1.8	1	2.4	0.2

ANALYSIS OF INDUSTRIAL DISPUTES

The number of industrial disputes in country has shown slow but steady fall over the past ten years. In 1998, the total number of disputes was 1097 which fell by more than half to 440 in 2006.It is being estimated that this trend will continue in 2007 as well. To support this, only 45 cases of disputes have been recorded during the first four months of 2007. This significant decline is attributed to the serious attempts made by industries to improve industrial relations with their workers. However, a deeper look at the data reveals that the number of mandays lost due to disputes has not come down as significantly. The country, on an average, lost 25.4 million mandays of work annually between 1998 and 2006, which might have affected its industrial output. More than 2.14 lakh mandays were lost due to work stoppages in 23 industrial disputes during January to March 2007. Though there has been a decline in the number of strikes, the country still witnessed some major strikes between 2004 and 2006, like those in Honda, Escorts, Apollo, and Skumars factories and in SBI bank.

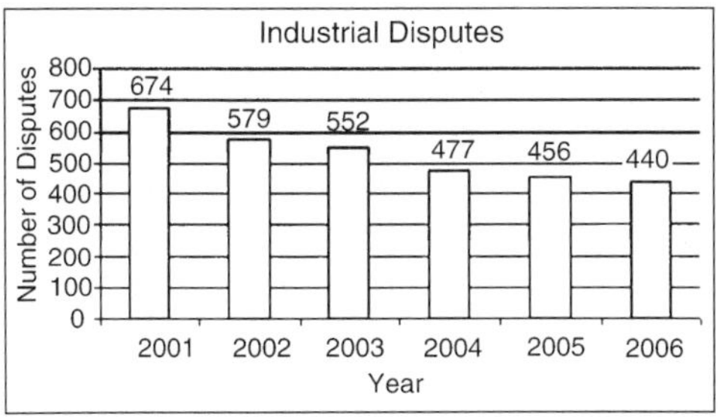

On analyzing the data sector wise, it is clear that the private sector has witnessed greater number of disputes as compared to the public sector. In 2005, only 57 disputes were recorded in public sector which resulted in a wage loss of 79 Crores. In contrast to this, 399 disputes were recorded in the private sector. In the recent past, maximum number of disputes has been recorded in the manufacturing, agriculture and mining and quarrying industries.

Sectors	2003	2004	2005
Public Sector			
No. of disputes	59	49	57
Workers involved ('000)	1099	1590	2039
Mandays lost ('000)	6856	1806	2322
Wages lost (₹in crores)	39.35	82.52	79.09
	–47	–41	–44
Value of production loss	22.47	36.97	59.8
(₹in crores)	–22	–22	–19
Private Sector			
No. of disputes	493	428	399
Workers involved ('000)	717	482	875
Mandays lost ('000)	23400	22061	27343
Wages lost (₹in crores)	26.79	25.64	37.02
	–144	–119	–102
Value of production loss	391.02	318.62	285.28
(₹in crores)	–127	–129	–102

STRIKES

A strike is a very powerful weapon used by trade unions and other labor associations to get their demands accepted. It generally involves quitting of work by a group of workers for the purpose of bringing the pressure on their employer so that their demands get accepted. When workers collectively cease to work in a particular industry, they are said to be on strike.

Industrial Disputes Act 1947, a strike is "a cessation of work by a body of persons employed in an industry acting in combination; or a concerted refusal of any number of persons who are or have been so employed to continue to work or to accept employment; or a refusal under a common understanding of any number of such persons to continue to work or to accept employment". This definition throws light on a few aspects of a strike. Firstly, a strike is a referred to as stoppage of work by a group of workers employed in a particular industry. Secondly, it also includes the refusal of a number of employees to continue work under their employer. In a strike, a group of workers agree to stop working to protest against something they think is unfair where they work. Labors withhold their services in order to pressurize their employment or government to meet their demands. Demands made by strikers can range from asking for higher wages or better benefits to seeking changes in the workplace environment. Strikes sometimes occur so that employers listen more carefully to the workers and address their problems.

Causes of strikes:

- *Strikes can occur because of the following reasons*:
  - Dissatisfaction with company policy
  - Salary and incentive problems
  - Increment not up to the mark
  - Wrongful discharge or dismissal of workmen
  - Withdrawal of any concession or privilege
  - Hours of work and rest intervals
  - Leaves with wages and holidays
  - Bonus, profit sharing, Provident fund and gratuity
  - Retrenchment of workmen and closure of establishment
  - Dispute connected with minimum wages

Types of Strike

- *Economic Strike*: Under this type of strike, labors stop their work to enforce their economic demands such as wages and bonus. In these kinds of strikes, workers ask for increase in wages, allowances like traveling allowance, house rent allowance, dearness allowance, bonus and other facilities such as increase in privilege leave and casual leave.
- *Sympathetic Strike*: When workers of one unit or industry go on strike in sympathy with workers of another unit or industry who are already on strike, it is called a sympathetic strike. The members of other unions involve themselves in a strike to support or express their sympathy with the members of unions who are on strike in other undertakings. The workers of sugar industry may go on strike in sympathy with their fellow workers of the textile industry who may already be on strike.
- *General Strike*: It means a strike by members of all or most of the unions in a region or an industry. It may be a strike of all the workers in a particular region of industry to force demands common to all the workers. These strikes are usually intended to create political pressure on the ruling government, rather than on any one employer. It may also be an extension of the sympathetic strike to express generalized protest by the workers.
- *Sit down Strike*: In this case, workers do not absent themselves from their place of work when they are on strike. They keep control over production facilities. But do not work. Such a strike is also known as 'pen down' or 'tool down' strike. Workers show up to their place of employment, but they refuse to work. They also refuse to leave, which makes it very difficult for employer to defy the union and take the workers' places. In June 1998, all the Municipal Corporation employees in Punjab observed a pen down strike to protest against the non-acceptance of their demands by the state government.

- *Slow Down Strike*: Employees remain on their jobs under this type of strike. They do not stop work, but restrict the rate of output in an organized manner. They adopt go-slow tactics to put pressure on the employers.
- *Sick-out (or sick-in)*: In this strike, all or a significant number of union members call in sick on the same day. They don't break any rules, because they just use their sick leave that was allotted to them on the same day. However, the sudden loss of so many employees all on one day can show the employer just what it would be like if they really went on strike.
- *Wild cat strikes*: These strikes are conducted by workers or employees without the authority and consent of unions. In 2004, a significant number of advocated went on wildcat strike at the City Civil Court premises in Bangalore. They were protesting against some remarks allegedly made against them by an Assistant Commissioner

LOCKOUTS

A lockout is a work stoppage in which an employer prevents employees from working. It is declared by employers to put pressure on their workers. This is different from a strike, in which employees refuse to work. Thus, a lockout is employers' weapon while a strike is raised on part of employees. Acc to Industrial Disputes Act 1947, lock-out means the temporary closing of a place of employment or the suspension of work or the refusal by an employer to continue to employ any number of persons employed by him.

A lockout may happen for several reasons. When only part of a trade union votes to strike, the purpose of a lockout is to put pressure on a union by reducing the number of members who are able to work. For example, if a group of the workers strike so that the work of the rest of the workers becomes impossible or less productive, the employer may declare a lockout until the workers end the strike. Another case in which an employer may impose a lockout is to avoid slowdowns or intermittent work-stoppages. Occupation of factories has been the traditional method of response to lock-outs by the workers' movement.

Picketing

When workers are dissuaded from work by stationing certain men at the factory gates, such a step is known as picketing. If picketing does not involve any violence, it is perfectly legal. Pickets are workers who are on strike that stand at the entrance to their workplace. It is basically a method of drawing public attention towards the fact that there is a dispute between the management and employees.

The purpose of picketing is:

- To stop or persuade workers not to go to work
- To tell the public about the strike
- To persuade workers to take their union's side

Gherao

Gherao in Hindi means to surround. It denotes a collective action initiated by a group of workers under which members of the management are prohibited from leaving the industrial establishment premises by workers who block the exit gates by forming human barricades. The workers may gherao the members of the management by blocking their exits and forcing them to stay inside their cabins. The main object of gherao is to inflict physical and mental torture to the person being gheraoed and hence this weapon disturbs the industrial peace to a great extent.

ANALYSIS OF STRIKES AND LOCKOUTS

In 1990, 1,825 strikes and lockouts were recorded. As a result, 24.1 million workdays were lost, from which 10.6 million were lost to strikes and 13.5 million to lockouts. More than 1.3 million workers were involved in these labor disputes. The number and seriousness of strikes and lockouts have varied from year to year. As can be seen from the below chart, there has been a steep decline in the number of strikes and lockouts. This continuous decline in strikes and lockouts indicates that the industrial relations in India are improving. There were 227 strikes in 2005, resulting in the loss of 10.81 million man-days, while the number of lockouts stood at 229 with a loss of 18.86 million man-days. In January-September 2006, there were only 154 strikes and 192 lockouts across the country, as compared to the statistics of 2005, which resulted in the time loss of 3.16 million man-days and 10.60 million man-days respectively.

	Strikes		Lockouts		Total	
	Number	Mandays lost	Number	Mandays lost	Number	Mandays lost
2000	426	11.96	345	16.8	771	28.76
2001	372	5.56	302	18.2	674	23.76
2002	295	9.66	284	16.92	579	26.58
2003	255	3.21	297	27.05	552	30.26
2004	236	4.83	241	19.04	477	23.87
2005	227	10.81	229	18.86	456	29.67
2006	154	3.16	192	10.6	346	13.76

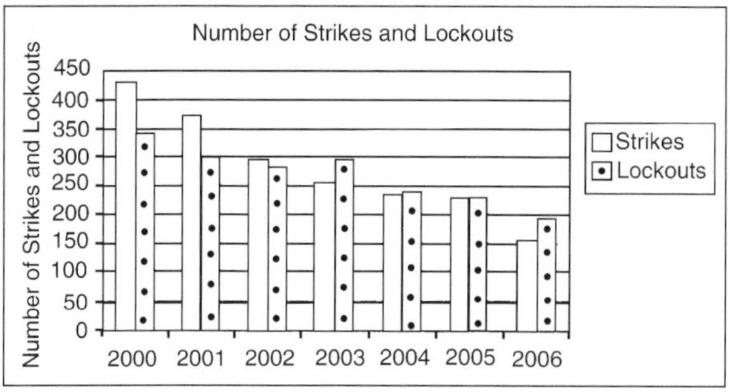

The number of strikes and lockouts, taken together, was down by 4.4 per cent in 2005. During 2005, West Bengal experienced the maximum instances of strikes and lockouts followed by Kerala and Rajasthan. Industrial disturbances were concentrated mainly in manufacturing, financial intermediation, agriculture and mining and quarrying industries during 2005.

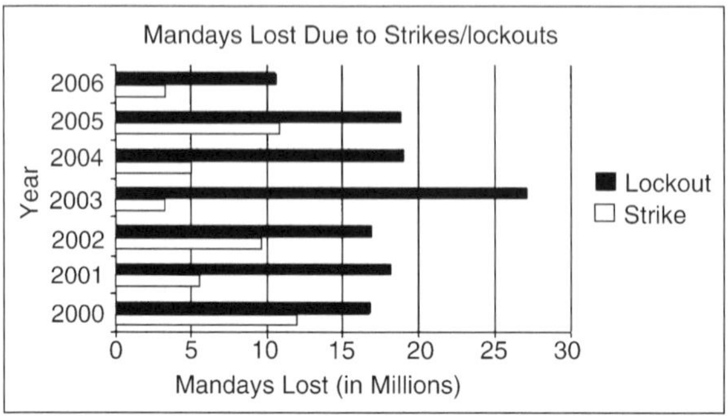

During 2000, 426 strikes and 325 lockouts were observed which resulted in total time-loss of 28.76 million mandays. Maximum time-loss was caused by 297 lockouts during 2003 which resulted in a time-loss of 27.05 million mandays. As compared to previous years, in 2006 only 13.76 million mandays were lost due to strikes and lockouts.

PROHIBITION OF STRIKES AND LOCK-OUTS

Employees are prohibited from striking according to the section 22 of Industrial Disputes Act 1947. Employees, who are working in a public utility service, cannot go on a strike without giving a notice of strike within the six weeks before striking. They can not go on strike either within fourteen days of providing the strike notice or before the expiry of the date of strike specified in any such notice. The same rule applies to the employers. Employers who are carrying on a public utility service can not lockout any of their employees without giving them a prior notice within six weeks before the lock out or within the fourteen days of giving such a notice. Moreover, the notice of strike or lockout is to be given in a prescribed manner showing the number of persons involved in the strike/lockout.

The notice of strike or lockout is not necessary when there is already a strike or lockout going on in the company. However, a notice should be issued on the day on which the lockout is declared just to intimate the appropriate authorities about the lockout. The employer is supposed to report the number of notices of strikes received by him to the appropriate Government or the authority prescribed by the government within the five days of receiving such notices.

Illegal Strikes and Lock-Outs

A strike or a lock-out is illegal if it is declared in noncompliance with the section 22 of Industrial Disputes Act 1947, that is, if the notice period is not served or if the strike is held within the fourteen days of issuing the notice of strike. If a strike or lockout has already taken place and is being referred to a Board, the continuance of such a strike or lock out is not illegal provided it is in compliance with the provisions of act. Moreover, a lockout declared in consequence of an illegal strike or a strike declared in consequence of an illegal lock-out shall not be deemed to be illegal.

Penalty for Illegal Strikes and Lock-outs

A workman who is involved in an illegal strike can be penalized with imprisonment for a term extendable to a month or with a fine or fifty rupees or both. In similar way, an employer who initiates and continues a lockout is punishable with imprisonment extendable to a month or with a fine of one thousand rupees or both. According to Section 25 of Industrial Disputes Act 1947, no person should provide any sort of financial aid to any illegal strike or lock-out. Any person who knowingly provides such a help in support of any illegal strike or lock-out is punishable with imprisonment for a term which may extend to six months, or with fine which may extend to one thousand rupees, or with both.

MEASURES FOR IMPROVING INDUSTRIAL RELATIONS

The following measures should be taken to achieve good industrial relations:

- *Strong and Stable Union*: A strong and stable union in each industrial enterprise is essential for good industrial relations. The employers can easily ignore a weak union on the plea that it hardly represents the workers. The agreement with such a union will hardly be honored by a large part of workforce. Therefore, there must be strong and stable unions in every enterprise to represent the majority of workers and negotiate with the management about the terms and conditions of service.
- *Mutual Trust*: Both management and labor should help in the development of an atmosphere of mutual cooperation, confidence and respect. Management should adopt a progressive outlook and should recognize the rights of workers. Similarly, labor unions should persuade their members to work for the common objectives of the organization. Both the management and the unions should have faith in collective bargaining and other peaceful methods of settling disputes.
- *Workers' Participation in Management*: The participation of workers in the management of the industrial unit should be encouraged by making effective use of works committees, joint consultation and other methods. This will improve communication between managers and workers, increase productivity and lead to greater effectiveness.

- *Mutual Accommodation*: The employers must recognize the right of collective bargaining of the trade unions. In any organization, there must be a great emphasis on mutual accommodation rather than conflict or uncompromising attitude. One must clearly understand that conflicting attitude does not lead to amicable labor relations; it may foster union militancy as the union reacts by engaging in pressure tactics. The approach must be of mutual "give and take rather than "take or leave." The management should be willing to co-operate rather than blackmail the workers.
- *Sincere Implementation of Agreements*: The management should sincerely implement the settlements reached with the trade unions. The agreements between the management and the unions should be enforced both in letter and spirit. If the agreements are not implemented then both the union and management stop trusting each other. An environment of uncertainty is created. To avoid this, efforts should be made at both ends to ensure the follow up of the agreements.
- *Sound Personnel Policies*: The following points should be noted regarding the personnel policies. The policies should be:
  - Formulated in consultation with the workers and their representatives if they are to be implemented effectively.
  - Clearly stated so that there is no confusion in the mind of anybody.
  - Implementation of the policies should be uniform throughout the organization to ensure fair treatment to each worker.
- *Government's Role*: The Government should play an active role for promoting industrial peace. It should make law for the compulsory recognition of a representative union in each industrial unit. It should intervene to settle disputes if the management and the workers are unable to settle their disputes. This will restore industrial harmony.
- *Progressive Outlook*: There should be progressive outlook of the management of each industrial enterprise. It should be conscious of its obligations and responsibilities to the owners of the business, the employees, the consumers and the nation. The management must recognize the rights of workers to organize unions to protect their economic and social interests.

LABOR COURT

A labor court is a governmental judiciary body which rules on labor or employment-related matters and disputes. In a number of countries, labor cases are often taken to separate national labor high courts. Other states, such as the United States, possess general non-judiciary labour relations boards which govern union certifications and elections.

INDUSTRIAL TRIBUNALS

Industrial Tribunals are independent judicial bodies that hear and determine claims to do with employment matters. These include a range of claims relating to unfair dismissal, breach of contract, wages/other payments, as well as discrimination on the grounds of sex, race, disability, sexual orientation, age, part time working or equal pay.

CODE OF DISCIPLINE

To maintain harmonious relations and promote industrial peace, a Code of Discipline has been laid down which applies to both public and private sector enterprises. It specifies various obligations for the management and the workers with the objective of promoting cooperation between their representatives.

The basic objectives of Code of Discipline are to:

- Maintain peace and order in industry.
- Promote constructive criticism at all levels of management and employment.
- Avoid work stoppage in industry
- Secure the settlement of disputes and grievances by a mutually agreed procedure
- Avoiding litigations
- Facilitate a free growth of trade unions
- Eliminate all forms of coercion, intimidation and violations of rules and regulations governing industrial relations.

The Code is based on the following principles:

- There should be no strike or lockout without prior notice.
- No unilateral action should be taken in connection with any industrial matter.
- Employees should follow go slow tactics
- No deliberate damage should be caused to a plant or property
- Acts of violations, intimidation and coercion should not be resorted
- The existing machinery for the settlement of disputes should be utilized.
- Actions that disturb cordial relationships should be avoided.

To ensure better discipline in industry, management and unions agree on not indulging into various actions. These actions can b summarized as follows.

- *Management and Union(s) agree*:
  - That no unilateral action should be taken in connection with any industrial matter and that should be settled at appropriate level
  - That the existing machinery for settlement of disputes should be utilized with the utmost efficiency
  - That there should be no strike or lock-out without prior notice

  - That neither party will have recourse to coercion, intimidation, victimization or go –slow tactics
  - That they will avoid litigation, sit-down and stay-in strikes and lock-outs
  - That they will promote constructive co-operation between their representatives at all levels and as between workers themselves
  - That they will establish upon a mutually agreed grievance procedure which will ensure a speedy and full investigation leading to settlement;
  - That they will abide by various stages in the grievance procedure and take no arbitrary action which would by-pass this procedure; and
- *Management Agrees*:
  - Not to increase work-loads unless agreed upon or settled otherwise
  - Not to support or encourage any unfair labor practice such as discrimination and victimization of any employee
  - To take prompt action for settlement of grievances and implementation of settlements, awards, decision and orders
  - To take appropriate disciplinary action against its officers and members in cases where enquiries reveal that they were responsible for precipitate action by workers leading to indiscipline
- *Union agrees*:
  - Not to engage in any form of physical duress
  - Not to permit demonstrations which are not peaceful
  - That their members will not engage or cause other employees to engage in any union activity during working hours
  - To discourage unfair labor practices such as negligence of duty, damage to property and insubordination
  - To take prompt action to implement awards, agreements, settlements and decisions

6

Industrial Psychology

INDUSTRIAL PSYCHOLOGY

Industrial psychology is a relatively new branch of psychology that was created for corporations and organizations that needed more structure. Industrial psychology is able to provide this structure by evaluating employee behaviour for the good of the company. It is often referred to as *organizational* psychology because of its emphasis on analyzing individuals who work for various organizations. Essentially, industrial psychologists study the behaviour of employees in a work setting. Although industrial psychology didn't begin until the 1920's, the discipline has evolved rapidly and revolutionized the workplace within the last century.

Because the workplace is a social system, the application of industrial psychology is useful in understanding its complexity. For years, psychologists have studied how human beings have interacted with their environments and each other, but industrial psychology begins to evaluate the interaction between people and their jobs. Industrial psychologists can be used to improve job satisfaction as well as company productivity and is becoming vital to the success of many organizations.

There are certain things that industrial psychologists focus on when evaluating the relationship a person has with their work. They analyse the way a person works, their skills, duties, obligations, and general satisfaction with their job on a day-to-day basis. This information is extremely helpful to human resources departments and company overseers who must create training programmes, feedback and rewards systems, and make hiring decisions as well as engage in recruitment practices. Most companies use industrial psychologists to train their own staff so that the organizations can run smoothly and at peak capacity.

One of the most interesting aspects of industrial psychology is how employee behaviour affects others individuals on the job and organization in general. Industrial psychology can be used to reduce counterproductive behaviour, enhance team effectiveness, and boost morale. It is also vital in conflict resolution. Many individuals find the brunt of their work dissatisfaction rooted in their relationships with managers and colleagues. Fortunately, industrial psychology provides solutions for this. Although industrial psychology is a mixture of anthropology, counseling, sociology and industrial management, there are key components used in this type of psychology.

Some of the key components include the evaluation of employee's personalities, perceptions, as well the biological side of their behaviour. By documenting these key points, industrial psychologists have the ability to help organizations improve their functionality and set up a system that promotes growth for the company and employees. Industrial psychology also helps CEOs and executives adjust their way of thinking and their management style, which can impact the stress levels of the employees that they manage. By using psychology, many companies are able to retain their employees because they understand how to keep them happy. Organizations with a low retention rate and employee dissatisfaction benefit from the work and assessment of industrial psychologists.

AIMS

Industrial psychology aims at reaching industrial efficiency, it has no claims on the worker outside the factory, foundry, or workshop, although the worker's leisure is undoubtedly coloured by work shop or factory conditions. In America where standardisation is synonymous with workshop practice the Daily Mail Trade Mission noted that the workers enjoyed their leisure to the full despite the heavy demands on their energy by the work they performed. The evidence gathered showed that it was the scientific direction of effort in work rather than a multitude of labour saving devices which increased production without unduly fatiguing the workers.

FORCES AND FUNDAMENTAL CONCEPTS

JOB ANALYSIS

Job analysis is often described as the cornerstone of successful employee selection efforts and performance management initiatives. A job analysis involves the systematic collection of information about a job. Job-analytic methods are often described as belonging to one of two approaches. One approach, the task-oriented job analysis, involves an examination of the duties, tasks, and/or competencies required by a job. The second approach, a worker-oriented job analysis, involves an examination of the knowledge, skills, abilities, and other characteristics required to successfully perform the work. These two approaches are not mutually exclusive. Various adaptations of job-analytic methods include competency modeling, which examines large groups of duties and tasks related to a common goal or process, and practice analysis, which examines the way work is performed in an occupation across jobs. Job-analytic data are often collected using a variety of quantitative and qualitative methods. The information obtained from a job analysis is then used to create job-relevant selection procedures, performance appraisals and criteria, or training programmes. Additional uses of job-analytic information include job evaluations for the purpose of determining compensation levels and job redesign.

PERSONNEL RECRUITMENT AND SELECTION

I-O psychologists typically work with HR specialists to design:

- Recruitment processes and
- Personnel selection systems.

Personnel recruitment is the process of identifying qualified candidates in the workforce and getting them to apply for jobs within an organization. Personnel recruitment processes include developing job announcements, placing ads, defining key qualifications for applicants, and screening out unqualified applicants. Personnel selection is the systematic process of hiring and promoting personnel. Personnel selection systems employ evidence-based practices to determine the most qualified candidates. Personnel selection involves both new hires and individuals who can be promoted from within the organization.

Common selection tools include ability tests (*e.g.*, cognitive, physical, or psychomotor), knowledge tests, personality tests, structured interviews, the systematic collection of biographical data, and work samples. I-O psychologists must evaluate evidence regarding the extent to which selection tools predict job performance, evidence that bears on the validity of selection tools. Personnel selection procedures are usually validated, *i.e.*, shown to be job relevant, using one or more of the following types of validity: content validity, construct validity, and/or criterion-related validity. I-O psychologists adhere to professional standards, such as the Society for Industrial and Organizational Psychology's (SIOP) Principles for Validation and Use of Personnel Selection Procedures and the Standards for Educational and Psychological Testing. The Equal Employment Opportunity Commission's Uniform Guidelines are also influential in guiding personnel selection although they have been criticized as outdated when compared to the current state of knowledge in I-O psychology.

PERFORMANCE APPRAISAL/MANAGEMENT

Performance appraisal or performance evaluation is the process of measuring an individual's work behaviours and outcomes against the expectations of the job. Performance appraisal is frequently used in promotion and compensation decisions, to help design and validate personnel selection procedures, and for performance management. Performance management is the process of providing performance feedback relative to expectations and improvement information (*e.g.*, coaching, mentoring). Performance management may also include documenting and tracking performance information for organization-level evaluation purposes. An I-O psychologist would typically use information from the job analysis to determine a job's performance dimensions, and then construct a rating scale to describe each level of performance for the job.

Often, the I-O psychologist would be responsible for training organizational personnel how to use the performance appraisal instrument, including ways to minimize bias when using the rating scale, and how to provide effective performance feedback.

Additionally, the I-O psychologist may consult with the organization on ways to use the performance appraisal information for broader performance management initiatives.

INDIVIDUAL ASSESSMENT AND PSYCHOMETRICS

Individual assessment involves the measurement of individual differences. I-O psychologists perform individual assessments in order to evaluate differences among candidates for employment as well as differences among employees.

The constructs measured pertain to job performance. With candidates for employment, individual assessment is often part of the personnel selection process. These assessments can include written tests, physical tests, psychomotor tests, personality tests, work samples, and assessment centers. Psychometrics is the science of measuring psychological variables, such as knowledge, skills, and abilities. I-O psychologists are generally well-trained in psychometric psychology.

REMUNERATION AND COMPENSATION

Compensation includes wages or salary, bonuses, pension/retirement contributions, and perquisites that can be converted to cash or replace living expenses. I-O psychologists may be asked to conduct a job evaluation for the purpose of determining compensation levels and ranges. I-O psychologists may also serve as expert witnesses in pay discrimination cases when disparities in pay for similar work are alleged.

TRAINING AND TRAINING EVALUATION

Most people hired for a job are not already versed in all the tasks required to perform the job effectively. Similar to performance management, an I-O psychologist would employ a job analysis in concert with principles of instructional design to create an effective training programme. A training programme is likely to include a summative evaluation at its conclusion in order to ensure that trainees have met the training objectives and can perform the target work tasks at an acceptable level. Training programmes often include formative evaluations to assess the impact of the training as the training proceeds. Formative evaluations can be used to locate problems in training procedures and help I-O psychologist make corrective adjustments in the while the training is ongoing.

MOTIVATION IN THE WORKPLACE

Motivation is a positive drive that forces a person to reach the goal. In a workplace the manager or supervisor has to know the needs or drive of individual and motivate according to it. In an organization, when an employee is doing good job or production is increased by him, he must be rewarded with respect to his needs.

ORGANIZATIONAL CULTURE

Organizational culture can be described as a set of assumptions shared by the individuals in an organization that directs interpretation and action by defining appropriate behaviour for various situations. There are three levels of organizational culture: artifacts, shared values, and basic beliefs and assumptions.

Artifacts comprise the physical components of the organization that relay cultural meaning. Shared values are individuals' preferences regarding certain aspects of the organization's culture. Basic beliefs and assumptions include individuals' impressions about the trustworthiness and supportiveness of an organization, and are often deeply ingrained within the organization's culture. In addition to an overall culture, organizations also have subcultures. Examples of subcultures include corporate culture, departmental culture, local culture, and issue-related culture.

While there is no single "type" of organizational culture, some researchers have developed models to describe different organizational cultures. Organizational culture has been shown to have an impact on important organizational outcomes such as performance, attraction, recruitment, retention, employee satisfaction, and employee well-being. Also, organizations with an adaptive culture tend to perform better than organizations with an unadaptive culture.

GROUP BEHAVIOUR

Group behaviour is the interaction between individuals of a collective and the processes such as opinions, attitudes, growth, feedback loops, and adaptations that occur and change as a result of this interaction. The interactions serve to fulfill some need satisfaction of an individual who is part of the collective and helps to provide a basis for his interaction with specific members of the group. A specific area of research in group behaviour is the dynamics of teams. Team effectiveness refers to the system of getting people in a company or institution to work together effectively. The idea behind team effectiveness is that a group of people working together can achieve much more than if the individuals of the team were working on their own.

JOB SATISFACTION AND COMMITMENT

Job satisfaction reflects an employee's overall assessment of their job particularly their emotions, behaviours, and attitudes about their work experience. It is one of the most heavily researched topics in industrial/ organizational psychology with several thousand published studies. Job satisfaction has theoretical and practical utility for the field of psychology and has been linked to important job outcomes including attitudinal variables, absenteeism, employee turnover, and job performance. For instance, job satisfaction is strongly correlated with attitudinal variables such as job involvement, organizational commitment, job tensions, frustration, and feelings of anxiety.

Job satisfaction also has a weak correlation with employee's absentee behaviours and turnover from an organization with employees more likely to miss work or find other jobs if they are not satisfied. Finally, research has found that although a positive relationship exists between job satisfaction and performance, it is moderated by the use of rewards at an organization and the strength of employee's attitudes about their job.

PRODUCTIVE BEHAVIOUR

Productive behaviour is defined as employee behaviour that contributes positively to the goals and objectives of an organization. When an employee begins a new job, there is a transition period during which he or she is not contributing positively to the organization.

To successfully transition from being an outsider to a full-fledged member of an organization, an employee typically needs job-related training as well as more general information about the culture of the organization. In financial terms, productive behaviour represents the point at which an organization begins to achieve some return on the investment it has made in a new employee. There are three common forms of productive behaviour in organizations: job performance, organizational citizenship behaviour (OCB), and innovation.

Job Performance

Job performance represents behaviours employees engage in while at work which contribute to organizational goals. These behaviours are formally evaluated by an organization as part of an employee's responsibilities. In order to understand and ultimately predict job performance, it is important to be precise when defining the term.

Job performance is about behaviours that are within the control of the employee and not about results (effectiveness), the costs involved in achieving results (productivity), the results that can be achieved in a period of time (efficiency), or the value an organization places on a given level of performance, effectiveness, productivity, or efficiency (utility). To model job performance, researchers have attempted to define a set of dimensions that are common to all jobs. Using a common set of dimensions provides a consistent basis for assessing performance and enables the comparison of performance across jobs. While there is disagreement about the exact dimensions of job performance, there is agreement on two major categories of job performance: in-role (technical aspects of a job) and extra-role (non-technical abilities such as communication skills and being a good team member). To assess job performance, reliable and valid measures must be established.

The most commonly used measures are ratings of employee performance on specific tasks and on overall job performance. While there are many sources of error with performance ratings, error can be reduced through rater training and through the use of behaviorally anchored ratings scales. Such scales can be used to clearly define the behaviours that constitute poor, average, and superior performance.

Additional factors that complicate the measurement of job performance include the instability of job performance over time and the restriction of variation in individual performance by organizational forces. The determinants of job performance consist of factors having to do with the individual worker as well as environmental factors in the workplace. Campbell's Model of The Determinants of Job Performance, job performance is a result of the interaction between declarative knowledge (knowledge of facts or things), procedural knowledge (knowledge of what needs to be done and how to do it), and motivation (reflective of an employee's choices regarding whether to expend effort, the level of effort to expend, and whether to persist with the level of effort chosen).

Regardless of the job, three determinants stand out as predictors of performance:

- General mental ability (especially for jobs higher in complexity),
- Job experience (although there is a law of diminishing returns), and
- The personality trait of conscientiousness (people who are dependable and achievement oriented, who plan well).

These determinants appear to influence performance largely through the acquisition and usage of job knowledge and the motivation to do well.

Organizational Citizenship Behaviour

Organizational citizenship behaviour (OCB) refers to productive behaviours that are not part of an employees' formal job description.

There are five categories of organizational citizenship behaviours:

- Altruism,
- Courtesy,
- Sportsmanship,

- Conscientiousness, and
- Civic virtue.

There are three different explanations for why employees engage in organizational citizenship behaviour. The first has to do with positive affect, an overall positive mood increases the frequency of helping behaviour. The second explanation, which stems from the equity theory, is that employees reciprocate fair treatment that they have received from the organization. The third explanation is that some employees have personality traits that predispose them to participate in organizational citizenship behaviour. There are also employees who will perform organizational citizenship behaviour to influence how they are viewed within the organization. While these behaviours are not formally part of the job description, performing them can certainly influence performance appraisals.

Innovation

Innovation is a form of productive behaviour that employees exhibit when they come up with novel ideas that further the goals of the organization. Innovation at an individual level is dependent on task-relevant skills (general mental ability and job specific knowledge), creativity-relevant skills (ability to concentrate on a problem for long periods of time, to abandon unproductive searches, and to temporarily put aside stubborn problems), and task motivation (internal desire to perform task and level of enjoyment).

There are things that organizations can do in order to breed innovation in the workplace. Some of these items include providing creativity training, having leaders encourage and model innovation, allowing employees to question current procedures and rules, seeing that the implementation of innovations had real consequences, documenting innovations in a professional manner, allowing employees to have autonomy and freedom in their job roles, reducing the number of obstacles that may be in the way of innovation, and giving employees access to resources (whether these are monetary, informational, or access to key people inside or outside of the organization).

COUNTERPRODUCTIVE BEHAVIOUR

Counterproductive behaviour can be defined as employee behaviour that goes against the goals of an organization. These behaviours can be intentional or unintentional and result from a wide range of underlying causes and motivations.

It has been proposed that a person-by-environment interaction can be utilized to explain a variety of counter-productive behaviours. For instance, an employee who steals from the company may do so because of lax supervision (environment) and underlying psychopathology (person) that work in concert to result in the counterproductive behaviour. The forms of counter-productive behaviour with the most empirical examination are ineffective job performance, absenteeism, job turnover, and accidents. Less common but potentially more detrimental forms of counterproductive behaviour have also been investigated including theft, violence, substance use, and sexual harassment.

LEADERSHIP

Leadership is a process of influencing and supporting and motivating others to work enthusiastically or effectively towards achieving the objectives or goal. A leader acts as a catalyst, who identifies the potential of a worker and tries to put that into reality. A leader can be a positive leader or a negative leader. A leader's influence within an organization or group has been said to stem from two primary sources, that person's personal characteristics and their position within the organization. Personal power, also made up of two factors called expert power and referent power, is derived from elements like an individual's personality, their knowledge base, their ability to effectively interact with others, and their demonstrated level of effort.

Positional power, also often referred to as legitimate power, is derived from the leader's position within the organization, and the authority imbued in them either directly or indirectly by the organization's controlling parties to provide either rewards or sanctions for performance. The leader's role is to use this influence to encourage those within the organization to focus their actions towards the accomplishment of the organization's goals. Distinction should be noted between management v.

leadership. Managers process administrative tasks that organize work environments. Leaders conduct those same tasks while also inspiring and motivating the workforce for which they oversee. Managers cope with complexity, leaders cope with change. Managers participate in stepwise tasks of planning and budgeting, organizing and staffing, and controlling and problem solving. In contrast, leaders approach these stages of business development through equivalent tasks of setting a direction or vision, aligning people or communication, and motivating and inspiring, respectively.

NATURE OF PEOPLE AND ORGANIZATIONS

Imagine you went to sleep and woke up to a work day in 1970. How different is your work life today, compared to what it was 40 years ago? Clearly, there would not be a Starbucks on every corner or a cell phone in every pocket—but what else has changed and why? In today's world, the structure, content, and process of work have changed.

Work is now:

- More cognitively complex
- More team-based and collaborative
- More dependent on social skills
- More dependent on technological competence

- More time pressured
- More mobile and less dependent on geography.

In today's world, you will also be working for an organization that is likely to be very different due to competitive pressures and technological breakthroughs.

Organizations today are:

- Leaner and more agile
- More focused on identifying value from the customer perspective
- More tuned to dynamic competitive requirements and strategy
- Less hierarchical in structure and decision authority
- Less likely to provide lifelong careers and job security
- Continually reorganizing to maintain or gain competitive advantage.

This Resource Page explores the changing nature of organizations and work, the drivers behind the changes, and the consequences for workers and the workplace.

DESCRIPTION

The Key Drivers for Changing Nature of Work

Although many factors ultimately contribute to the changing patterns of work, organizational theorists point to two key drivers:

- Increasing pressures on organizations to be more competitive, agile, and customer focused—to be a "lean enterprise."
- Communication and information technology breakthroughs, especially mobile technologies and the Internet that enable work to be separated from time and space.

Changes in Organizational Focus: What does it Mean to be Lean?

The Lean Enterprise model was introduced to the world by Toyota in the 1970s. Since then, it has fueled changes in organizations across the globe, particularly—but not exclusively—in manufacturing and product development.

The key principles of Lean Enterprise (or "lean thinking", as it is sometimes called) are:

- Define value from the customer's perspective.
- Identify internal activities and processes that add value for the customer and identify linkages between them (the "value chain").
- Eliminate non-value added activities (or "waste") across the organization.
- Reduce waste and inefficiencies in support (*e.g.*, overhead) functions.

The lean enterprise principles enabled many organizations to respond more rapidly to the marketplace by reducing cycle time, developing mass customization processes, and supporting continual change and innovation.

Creating the Lean Machine: Changes in Organizational Structure and Relationships

Adopting lean principles and lean thinking has led to numerous changes in organizational structure to improve the efficiency of internal processes, with a goal of eliminating waste and defining customer value. These changes have been supported and enabled by transformations in information and communications technology, especially the Internet and mobile computing and communication devices.

Key organizational changes include:

- *Reduced hierarchical structure*: Hierarchies are cumbersome and cannot respond quickly to changing market demands, such as pressures for reduced cycle time and continuous innovation. Hierarchies are being replaced by cross unit organizational groupings with fewer layers and more decentralized decision making.
- *Blurred boundaries*: As organizations become more laterally structured, boundaries begin to breakdown as different parts of the organization need to work more effectively together. Boundaries between departments as well as between job categories (manager, professional, technical) become looser and there is a greater need for task and knowledge sharing.
- *Teams as basic building blocks*: The move towards a team-based organizational structure results from pressures to make rapid decisions, to reduce inefficiencies, and to continually improve work processes.
- *New management perspective*: Workers are no longer managed to comply with rules and orders, but rather to be committed to organizational goals and mission. The blurring of boundaries also affects organizational roles. As employees gain more decision authority and latitude, managers become more social supporters and coaches rather than commanders.
- *Continuous change*: Organizations are expected to continue the cycles of reflection and reorganization. However, changes may be both large and small and are likely to be interspersed with periods of stability. Kling and Zmuidzinas identify three types of change—"metamorphosis" (far reaching, fundamental change), "migration" (shifts towards a new form), and "elaboration" (changes that enhance some aspect of work).

How Work is Changing for Individuals and Groups

Over the past two decades, a new pattern of work is emerging as the knowledge economy realises the full potential of both new technologies and new organizational models.

The changes fall into the following domains:

- Cognitive competence
- Social and interactive competence
- The new "psychological contract" between employees and employers
- Changes in process and place

Although these domains are discussed separately, they overlap. We briefly discuss the overlaps, where they exist, and point to the benefits and concerns the new work patterns present for workers and managers.

Cognitive Competence

Cognitive workers are expected to be more functionally and cognitively fluid and able to work across many kinds of tasks and situations.

The broader span of work, brought about by changes in organizational structure, also creates new demands, including:

- *Increased complexity of work*: Workers need to know more, not only to do their jobs and tasks, but also to work effectively with others on teams. Many knowledge-based tasks require sound analytical and judgment skills to carry out work that is more novel, extemporaneous, and context based, with few rules and structured ways of working. Although demand for high cognitive skills are especially prominent in professional, technical, and managerial jobs, even administrative tasks require more independent decision making and operational decision making.
- *Continuous competency development*: Not only do workers need to keep their technology skills up to date, they need to be continuous learners in their knowledge fields and to also be more conversant with business strategy. Time to read and attend training classes is no longer a perquisite of only a few, it is essential for all workers.
- *Different ways of thinking*: Rosabeth Kantor argues that cross-functional and cross boundary teams require "kaleidoscope thinking," the ability to see alternative angles and perspectives and to create new patterns of thinking that propel innovation. Workers also need to be able to synthesize disparate ideas in order to make the cognitive leaps that underlie innovation.

Cognitive Overload: The Cost of Complexity

Vastly increased access to information has made work both easier and more difficult. The ease comes from ability to rapidly locate and download information from diverse web sites. The difficulty comes with the need to consume and make sense of new information in a timely fashion. Information overload, coupled with time pressures and increased work complexity, lead to what psychologists call "cognitive overload syndrome (COS)." Symptoms of COS include stress, inability to concentrate, multitasking, task switching, and a tendency to focus on what is easy to do quickly rather than what is important.

Social and Interactive Competence

In a 2001 report on the changing nature of work, the National Research Council called attention to the importance of relational and interactive aspects of work. As collaboration and collective activity become more prevalent, workers need well-developed social skills—what the report calls "emotional labor."

Good social skills are necessary for:

- *Team work and collaboration*: Conflict resolution and negotiation skills are essential to collaborative work. Conflicts often occur about group goals, work methods, assignments, workloads, and recognition. Team members with good conflict and negotiation skills are better equipped to deal openly with problems, to listen and understand different perspectives, and to resolve issues in mutually beneficial ways.
- *Relationship development and networking*: Sharing important information, fulfilling promises, willingness to be influenced, and listening are building blocks of reciprocity and the development of trust. When workers trust one another, they are more committed to attaining mutual goals, more likely to help one another through difficulties, and more willing to share and develop new ideas.
- *Learning and growth*: Many organizations strive to be learning centers—to create conditions in which employees learn not only through formal training but through relationships with coworkers. Learning relationships build on joint problem solving, insight sharing, learning from mistakes, and working closely together to aid transmission of tacit knowledge. Learning also develops from mentoring relationships between newcomers and those with experience and organizational know-how.

The Costs of Collaborative Environments

In a collaborative work setting, the fate of individuals is inextricably bound to collective success. Dependence on others for one's own success is often uncomfortable. As Susan Mohrman and Susan Cohen write in a stage from the Changing Nature of Work:

- "We have been socialized to value individual responsibility and individual achievement, and feel discomfort with the thought of relying on others."

Comments about the fear of not having individual efforts recognized are common in the literature on team work. Collaboration and relationship development also take time and effort. Understanding coworkers' perspectives and "thought worlds" requires time spent listening, integrating, and synthesizing. For those workers recognized as both knowledgeable and approachable, the demands of interaction may be especially high.

The New Psychological Contract

As work changes, so does the nature of the relationships between employees and employers. In the new work context, the informal, "psychological contract" between workers and employers—what each expects of the other—focuses on competency development, continuous training, and work/life balance. In contrast, the old psychological contract was all about job security and steady advancement within the firm. As already discussed, few workers expect, or desire, lifelong employment in a single firm.

As job security declines, many management scientists see clouds on the horizon, including:

- *Corporate indifference*: Shoshana Zuboff and James Maxmin, in The Support Economy, describe a new individualism among U.S. workers. These new individuals are invested in "psychological self determination." They desire participation, expression, identity, and quality of life—all values which are espoused by organizations, but largely ignored in practice as organizations continue to focus on reducing fixed labor costs.
- *Reduced loyalty and commitment*: With little expectation for advancement, workers feel less committed to organizational goals and more committed to their own learning and development. The knowledge and technological skills that employees bring with them to the workplace are transportable and are not lost when a new job is taken.
- *Increased time burdens*: Years of downsizing and outsourcing have produced what Lesie Perlow calls a "time famine"—the feeling of having too much to do and too little time to do it. In order to keep up with workloads, many workers are spending longer hours at work, according to reports by the Bureau of Labor Statistics and the Center for Workforce Development.
- *Flexible work arrangements do not keep up with employee preferences*: The Work Trends 2000 report found that 74% of workers were not allowed flexible hours and work arrangements (such as telecommuting). Those with flex hours have limited freedom regarding when and where to work. The vast majority of workers have to commit to a specific day to work at home or a specific day to take off if they work four10-hour days.

The Changing Workplace

The changing workplace is driven by the organizational issues and enabled by technologies that support mobility and easy access to information.

These pressures and opportunities, however, have not resulted in a specific new workplace model. Many models and ideas exist concurrently, with designs depending upon the organization, its work practices, culture, and customers. Table highlights key drivers, solutions, and potential issues raised by the solution.

HISTORICAL DEVELOPMENT

The "industrial" side of I-O psychology has its historical origins in research on individual differences, assessment, and the prediction of performance. This branch of the field crystallized during World War I, in response to the need to rapidly assign new troops to duty stations.

After the War the growing industrial base in the US added impetus to I-O psychology. Walter Dill Scott, who was elected President of the American Psychological Association (APA) in 1919, was arguably the most prominent I-O psychologist of his time, although James McKeen Cattell and Hugo Münsterberg (1898) were influential in the early development of the field. Organizational psychology gained prominence after World War II, influenced by the Hawthorne studies and the work of researchers such as Kurt Lewin and Muzafer Sherif.

TIME AND MOTION STUDIES

The idea of a Time and Motion Study is often still associated with production lines and manufacturing industry. It gained a bad reputation as a source of disagreement between "management" and "workers". However if used properly it can be of benefit to modern companies and their workforce.

SCIENTIFIC MANAGEMENT

Time and Motion studies have their roots in the work of Frederick Winslow Taylor who in 1911 published his famous article "The Principles of Scientific Management". Essentially this involved getting the best person for each job and training them to do it the best way possible. Although Taylor believed in cooperation between management and workers, "Taylorism" can be seen as formalising the management/worker divide. Management would be responsible for deciding how things were done with workers simply doing what they were told. It was seen as dehumanising, reducing skilled workers to the status of mechanical parts and resources.

GILBRETHS

Time and Motion study was refined in the early twentieth century by Frank and Lillian Gilbreth. The Gilbreths' preferred "motion study" to Taylor's "time study", however the term "Time and Motion" has tended to stick in popular terminology. The Gilbreths studied the actions taken by workers at certain task with the aim of streamlining the processes involved. One of their most famous experiments involved analysing the work of bricklayers and significantly reducing the number of "operations" involved. This change benefited both employer (increased productivity) and employee (decreased fatigue).

THERBLIGS

The Gilbreths developed a categorisation system for the different basic activities which went to make up a task. These were called Therbligs (an anagram of "Gilbreths"). The basic Therbligs numbered around 15 (the system developed over time) and included such actions as "find", "select" and "rest". Each of these was represented by an icon, for example an eye for "find". The activity of a worker could then be plotted on a Simo Chart ("Simultaneous Motion Chart") for optimisation.

HAWTHORNE EFFECT

One problem for Time and Motion studies is what is known as the Hawthorne Effect (named after a factory not a person). This in essence says that employees change their behaviour when they know that they are being measured-the mere act of performing a study can improve performance. It's a form of "observer effect" akin to a productivity placebo. The Hawthorne Effect also showed that productivity tends to improve whatever changes are made, then return to normal over time. This recognises that workers are human beings and that knowing they are valued can in itself inspire better performance. The Hawthorne Effect doesn't undermine the value of Time and Motion studies but does emphasise that people are the most significant element of any workplace.

MTM

The original Time and Motion Study concepts led during the twentieth century to the development of Predetermined Motion Time Systems (PMTS) such as Methods-Time-Measurement (MTM). This was released in 1948 by Maynard, Stegemerten, and Schwab and is today found in three versions: MTM-1, MTM-2 and MTM-3

MUTUAL BENEFITS

In the"bad old days" of industrial relations, Time and Motion studies were often seen as a tool for the management to exploit the workers. The Time and Motion study-sometimes carried out in secret-could be used to pressurise people to work harder or lose their jobs. It's not surprising that many workers came to resent the whole concept of time and motion. It needn't be that way. Modern analysis methodologies and software packages have little in common with the old image of a "Motion Man" timing workers with a stopwatch. A Time and Motion study carried out openly with full buy-in from all concerned can be of mutual benefit. Improvements can be made to working conditions and methods that both improve productivity and make working less stressful or reduce fatigue. Perhaps the best way to ensure full cooperation is to ensure that any benefits of the study are shared between company and workforce. If efficiency improvements are identified then the gains can be shared between shareholders and workers, with the latter benefiting from greater wages or shorter hours. Unfortunately too many companies today still see a Time and Motion study as simply a way to increase profits with no benefit returning to the workforce who are ultimately responsible for those profits.

7

Workplace Affordances and Individual Engagement at Work

MOTIVATION

Motivation is the activation or energization of goal-orientated behaviour. Motivation is said to be intrinsic or extrinsic. The term is generally used for humans but, theoretically, it can also be used to describe the causes for animal behaviour as well. This object refers to human motivation. Motivation may be rooted in the basic need to minimize physical pain and maximize pleasure, or it may include specific needs such as eating and resting, or a desired object, hobby, goal, state of being, ideal, or it may be attributed to less-apparent reasons such as altruism, selfishness, morality, or avoiding mortality.

Conceptually, motivation should not be confused with either volition or optimism. Motivation is related to, but distinct from, emotion. Intrinsic motivation refers to motivation that is driven by an interest or enjoyment in the task itself, and exists within the individual rather than relying on any external pressure. Intrinsic motivation has been studied by social and educational psychologists since the early 1970s. Research has found that it is usually associated with high educational achievement and enjoyment by students.

Intrinsic motivation has been explained by Fritz Heider's attribution theory, Bandura's work on self-efficacy, and Deci and Ryan's cognitive evaluation theory. Extrinsic motivation comes from outside of the individual. Common extrinsic motivations are rewards like money and grades, coercion and threat of punishment. Competition is in general extrinsic because it encourages the performer to win and beat others, not to enjoy the intrinsic rewards of the activity. A crowd cheering on the individual and trophies are also extrinsic incentives. Social psychological research has indicated that extrinsic rewards can lead to overjustification and a subsequent reduction in intrinsic motivation. In one study demonstrating this effect, children who expected to be rewarded with a ribbon and a gold star for drawing pictures spent less time playing with the drawing materials in subsequent observations than children who were assigned to an unexpected reward condition and to children who received no extrinsic reward. Self-determination theory proposes that extrinsic motivation can be internalised by the individual if the task fits with their values and beliefs and therefore helps to fulfill their basic psychological needs. Internalised extrinsic motivation has been shown to lead to more positive outcomes, such as wellbeing, increased productivity and task satisfaction.

The self-control of motivation is increasingly understood as a subset of emotional intelligence; a person may be highly intelligent according to a more conservative definition, yet unmotivated to dedicate this intelligence to certain tasks. Yale School of Management professor Victor Vroom's "expectancy theory" provides an account of when people will decide whether to exert self control to pursue a particular goal.

Drives and desires can be described as a deficiency or need that activates behaviour that is aimed at a goal or an incentive. These are thought to originate within the individual and may not require external stimuli to encourage the behaviour.

Basic drives could be sparked by deficiencies such as hunger, which motivates a person to seek food; whereas more subtle drives might be the desire for praise and approval, which motivates a person to behave in a manner pleasing to others. By contrast, the role of extrinsic rewards and stimuli can be seen in the example of training animals by giving them treats when they perform a trick correctly. The treat motivates the animals to perform the trick consistently, even later when the treat is removed from the process.

MODEL

Over the years many psychologists have attempted to define and categorise what motivates people. This became particularly important after the Second World War as the Western nations attempted to rebuild their drained industrial economies, and during the '50s and '60s much was researched and written about Human Relations. It was recognised that people who worked in organisations were more than just numbers and, if properly managed, could not only produce more, but also contribute more.

This is not the place to cover the work of every motivational theorist: we've simply chosen a couple that have entered the mainstream management vocabulary:

- Theory X/ Theory Y
- Herzberg's Motivation-Hygiene Theory

Theory X/ Theory Y

Douglas McGregor published "The Human Side of Enterprise" in 1960, in which he suggested that traditional management methods might not be the only way to get people motivated. Instead, you could take a different approach and achieve the same if not more.

Theory X is the traditional view of direction and control, based on these assumptions:

- The average person inherently dislikes work and will avoid it if at all possible.
- As a result, most people have to be coerced, controlled and threatened if they are to put in enough effort to achieve the organisation's goals.
- In fact the average person prefers to be directed, avoids responsibility, isn't ambitious and simply seeks security.

Theory Y, based on the integration of individual and organisational goals, assumes:

- The physical and mental effort of work is as natural as play or rest, so the average person doesn't inherently dislike work.
- We are capable of self-direction and self-control, so those factors don't necessarily have to come from elsewhere.
- Our commitment to an objective is a function of the rewards for its achievement.
- The average person learns not only to accept but to seek responsibility.
- Most people have a capacity for imagination, ingenuity and creativity.
- The intellectual potential of most people is under-used in modern industrial life.

Theory Y is not a soft option. In fact it can take as much management effort as Theory X, but the effects of a Theory Y approach will last longer. The Theory X manager is a dying breed and Theory Y lies behind most modern approaches to motivation. Nowadays the terminology is used as a polite way of referring to the old command-and-control approach to management: the trouble is the diehard Theory X manager won't pick up the subtle criticism!

Herzberg's Motivation-Hygiene Theory

Frederick Herzberg studied and practised clinical psychology in Pittsburgh, where he researched the work-related motivations of thousands of employees. His findings were published in "The Motivation to Work" in 1959.

He concluded that there were two types of motivation:

- *Hygiene Factors that can demotivate if they are not present*: Such as supervision, interpersonal relations, physical working conditions, and salary. Hygiene Factors affect the level of dissatisfaction, but are rarely quoted as creators of job satisfaction.
- *Motivation Factors that will motivate if they are present*: Such as achievement, advancement, recognition and responsibility. Dissatisfaction isn't normally blamed on Motivation Factors, but they are cited as the cause of job satisfaction.

So, once you've satisfied the Hygiene factors, providing more of them won't generate much more motivation, but lack of the Motivation Factors won't of themselves demotivate. There are clear relationships to Maslow here, but Herzberg's ideas really shaped modern thinking about reward and recognition in major companies.

ACHIEVEMENT MOTIVATION

Over the years, behavioral scientists have noticed that some people have an intense desire to achieve something, while others may not seem that concerned about their achievements. This phenomenon has attracted a lot of discussions and debates. Scientists have observed that people with a high level of achievement motivation exhibit certain characteristics. Achievement motivation is the tendency to endeavor for success and to choose goal oriented success or failure activities. Achievement motivation forms to be the basic for a good life. People who are oriented towards achievement, in general, enjoy life and feel in control. Being motivated keeps people dynamic and gives them self-respect.

They set moderately difficult but easily achievable targets, which help them, achieve their objectives. They do not set up extremely difficult or extremely easy targets. By doing this they ensure that they only undertake tasks that can be achieved by them. Achievement motivated people prefer to work on a problem rather than leaving the outcome to chance. It is also seen that achievement motivated people seem to be more concerned with their personal achievement rather than the rewards of success. It is generally seen that achievement motivated people evidenced a significantly higher rate of advancement in their company compared to others. Programmes and courses designed, involves seven "training inputs."

The first step refers to the process through which achievement motivation thinking is taught to the person. The second step helps participants understand their own individuality and goals. The third assist participants in practicing achievement-related actions in cases, role-plays, and real life. A fourth refers to practicing of achievement-related actions in business and other games. A fifth input encourages participants to relate the achievement behaviour model to their own behaviour, self-image, and goals. The sixth programme facilitates participants to develop a personal plan of action. Finally, the course provides participants with feedback on their progress towards achieving objectives and targets. Achievement motivation as a branch of study has greatly established its prominence. A number of companies are now training their employees in the same.

Effects of Achievement Motivation on Behaviour

Motivation is the basic drive for all of our actions. Motivation refers to the dynamics of our behaviour, which involves our needs, desires, and ambitions in life. Achievement motivation is based on reaching success and achieving all of our aspirations in life. Achievement goals can affect the way a person performs a task and represent a desire to show competence. These basic physiological motivational drives affect our natural behaviour in different environments. Most of our goals are incentive-based and can vary from basic hunger to the need for love and the establishment of mature sexual relationships. Our motives for achievement can range from biological needs to satisfying creative desires or realizing success in competitive ventures. Motivation is important because it affects our lives everyday. All of our behaviours, actions, thoughts, and beliefs are influenced by our inner drive to succeed.

Implicit and Self-Attributed Motives

Motivational researchers share the view that achievement behaviour is an interaction between situational variables and the individual subject's motivation to achieve. Two motives are directly involved in the prediction of behaviour, implicit and explicit. Implicit motives are spontaneous impulses to act, also known as task performances, and are aroused through incentives inherent to the task. Explicit motives are expressed through deliberate choices and more often stimulated for extrinsic reasons. Also, individuals with strong implicit needs to achieve goals set higher internal standards, whereas others tend to adhere to the societal norms. These two motives often work together to determine the behaviour of the individual in direction and passion. Explicit and implicit motivations have a compelling impact on behaviour. Task behaviours are accelerated in the face of a challenge through implicit motivation, making performing a task in the most effective manner the primary goal. A person with a strong implicit drive will feel pleasure from achieving a goal in the most efficient way.

The increase in effort and overcoming the challenge by mastering the task satisfies the individual. However, the explicit motives are built around a person's self-image. This type of motivation shapes a person's behaviour based on their own self-view and can influence their choices and responses from outside cues. The primary agent for this type of motivation is perception or perceived ability. Many theorists still can not agree whether achievement is based on mastering one's skills or striving to promote a better self-image. Most research is still unable to determine whether these different types of motivation would result in different behaviours in the same environment.

The Hierarchal Model of Achievement Motivation

Achievement motivation has been conceptualized in many different ways. Our understanding of achievement-relevant effects, cognition, and behaviour has improved. Despite being similar in nature, many achievement motivation approaches have been developed separately, suggesting that most achievement motivation theories are in concordance with one another instead of competing. Motivational researchers have sought to promote a hierarchal model of approach and avoidance achievement motivation by incorporating the two prominent theories: the achievement motive approach and the achievement goal approach. Achievement motives include the need for achievement and the fear of failure. These are the more predominant motives that direct our behaviour towards positive and negative outcomes. Achievement goals are viewed as more solid cognitive representations pointing individuals towards a specific end. There are three types of these achievement goals: a performance-approach goal, a performance-avoidance goal, and a mastery goal. A performance-approach goal is focused on attaining competence relative to others, a performance-avoidance goal is focused on avoiding incompetence relative to others, and a mastery goal is focused on the development of competence itself and of task mastery. Achievement motives can be seen as direct predictors of achievement-relevant circumstances.

Thus, achievement motives are said to have an indirect or distal influence, and achievement goals are said to have a direct or proximal influence on achievement-relevant outcomes. These motives and goals are viewed as working together to regulate achievement behaviour. The hierarchal model presents achievement goals as predictors for performance outcomes. The model is being further conceptualized to include more approaches to achievement motivation. One weakness of the model is that it does not provide an account of the processes responsible for the link between achievement goals and performance. As this model is enhanced, it becomes more useful in predicting the outcomes of achievement-based behaviours.

Achievement Goals and Information Seeking

Theorists have proposed that people's achievement goals affect their achievement-related attitudes and behaviours. Two different types of achievement-related attitudes include task-involvement and ego-involvement. Task-involvement is a motivational state in which a person's main goal is to acquire skills and understanding whereas the main goal in ego-involvement is to demonstrate superior abilities. One example of an activity where someone strives to attain mastery and demonstrate superior ability is schoolwork. However situational cues, such as the person's environment or surroundings, can affect the success of achieving a goal at any time. Studies confirm that a task-involvement activity more often results in challenging attributions and increasing effort than in an ego-involvement activity. Intrinsic motivation, which is defined as striving to engage in activity because of self-satisfaction, is more prevalent when a person is engaged in task-involved activities. When people are more ego-involved, they tend to take on a different conception of their ability, where differences in ability limit the effectiveness of effort.

Ego-involved individuals are driven to succeed by outperforming others, and their feelings of success depend on maintaining self-worth and avoiding failure. On the other hand, task-involved individuals tend to adopt their conception of ability as learning through applied effort. Therefore less able individuals will feel more successful as long as they can satisfy an effort to learn and improve. Ego-invoking conditions tend to produce less favorable responses to failure and difficulty.

Competence moderated attitudes and behaviours are more prevalent in ego-involved activities than task-involved. Achievement does not moderate intrinsic motivation in task-involving conditions, in which people of all levels of ability could learn to improve. In ego-involving conditions, intrinsic motivation was higher among higher achievers who demonstrated superior ability than in low achievers who could not demonstrate such ability. These different attitudes towards achievement can also be compared in information seeking. Task- and ego-involving settings bring about different goals, conceptions of ability, and responses to difficulty. They also promote different patterns of information seeking. People of all levels of ability will seek information relevant to attaining their goal of improving mastery in task-involving conditions. However they need to seek information regarding self-appraisal to gain a better understanding of their self-capacity. On the other hand people in ego-involving settings are more interested in information about social comparisons, assessing their ability relative to others.

Self-Worth Theory in Achievement Motivation

Self-worth theory states that in certain situations students stand to gain by not trying and deliberately withholding effort. If poor performance is a threat to a person's sense of self-esteem, this lack of effort is likely to occur. This most often occurs after an experience of failure. Failure threatens self-estimates of ability and creates uncertainty about an individual's capability to perform well on a subsequent basis. If the following performance turns out to be poor, then doubts concerning ability are confirmed. Self-worth theory states that one way to avoid threat to self-esteem is by withdrawing effort. Withdrawing effort allows failure to be attributed to lack of effort rather than low ability which reduces overall risk to the value of one's self-esteem. When poor performance is likely to reflect poor ability, a situation of high threat is created to the individual's intellect.

On the other hand, if an excuse allows poor performance to be attributed to a factor unrelated to ability, the threat to self-esteem and one's intellect is much lower. A study was conducted on students involving unsolvable problems to test some assumptions of the self-worth theory regarding motivation and effort. The results showed that there was no evidence of reported reduction of effort despite poorer performance when the tasks were described as moderately difficult as compared with tasks much higher in difficulty. The possibility was raised that low effort may not be responsible for the poor performance of students in situations which create threats to self-esteem. Two suggestions were made, one being that students might unconsciously withdraw effort, and the other stating that students may reduce effort as a result of withdrawing commitment from the problem. Regardless of which suggestion is true, self-worth theory assumes that individuals have a reduced tendency to take personal responsibility for failure.

Avoidance Achievement Motivation

In everyday life, individuals strive to be competent in their activities. In the past decade, many theorists have utilized a social-cognitive achievement goal approach in accounting for individuals striving for competence. An achievement goal is commonly defined as the purpose for engaging in a task, and the specific type of goal taken on creates a framework for how individuals experience their achievement pursuits. Achievement goal theorists commonly identify two distinct ideas towards competence: a performance goal focused on demonstrating ability when compared to others, and a mastery goal focused on the development of competence and task mastery. Performance goals are hypothesized to produce vulnerability to certain response patterns in achievement settings such as preferences for easy tasks, withdrawal of effort in the face of failure, and decreased task enjoyment. Mastery goals can lead to a motivational pattern that creates a preference for moderately challenging tasks, persistence in the face of failure, and increased enjoyment of tasks.

Most achievement goal theorists conceptualize both performance and mastery goals as the "approach" forms of motivation. Existing classical achievement motivation theorists claimed that activities are emphasized and oriented towards attaining success or avoiding failure, while the achievement goal theorists focused on their approach aspect. More recently, an integrated achievement goal concep-tualization was proposed that includes both modern performance and mastery theories with the standard approach and avoidance features. In this basis for motivation, the performance goal is separated into an independent approach component and avoidance component, and three achievement orientations are conceived: a mastery goal focused on the development of competence and task mastery, a performance-approach goal directed towards the attainment of favorable judgments of competence, and a performance-avoidance goal centered on avoiding unfavorable judgments of competence.

The mastery and performance-approach goals are characterized as self-regulating to promote potential positive outcomes and processes to absorb an individual in their task or to create excitement leading to a mastery pattern of achievement results. Performance-avoidance goals, however, are characterized as promoting negative circumstances. This avoidance orientation creates anxiety, task distraction, and a pattern of helpless achievement outcomes. Intrinsic motivation, which is the enjoyment of and interest in an activity for its own sake, plays a role in achievement outcomes as well. Performance-avoidance goals undermined intrinsic motivation while both mastery and performance-approach goals helped to increase it. Most achievement theorists and philosophers also identify task-specific competence expectancies as an important variable in achievement settings. Achievement goals are created in order to obtain competence and avoid failure. These goals are viewed as implicit or self-attributed and direct achievement behaviour. Competence expectancies were considered an important variable in classical achievement motivation theories, but now appear to only be moderately emphasized in contemporary perspectives.

Approach and Avoidance Goals

Achievement motivation theorists focus their research attention on behaviours involving competence. Individuals aspire to attain competence or may strive to avoid incompetence, based on the earlier approach-avoidance research and theories. The desire for success and the desire to avoid failure were identified as critical determinants of aspiration and behaviour by a theorist named Lewin. In his achievement motivation theory, McClelland proposed that there are two kinds of achievement motivation, one oriented around avoiding failure and the other around the more positive goal of attaining success.

Atkinson, another motivational theorist, drew from the work of Lewin and McClelland in forming his need-achievement theory, a mathematical framework that assigned the desire to succeed and the desire to avoid failure as important determinants in achievement behaviour. Theorists introduced an achievement goal approach to achievement motivation more recently. These theorists defined achievement goals as the reason for activities related to competence. Initially, these theorists followed in the footsteps of Lewin, McClelland, and Atkinson by including the distinction between approach and avoidance motivation into the structure of their assumptions. Three types of achievement goals were created, two of which being approach orientations and the third an avoidance type.

One approach type was a task involvement goal focused on the development of competence and task mastery, and the other being a performance or ego involvement goal directed towards attaining favorable judgments of competence. The avoidance orientation involved an ego or performance goal aimed at avoiding unfavorable judgments of competence. These new theories received little attention at first and some theorists bypassed them with little regard. Motivational theorists shifted away and devised other conceptualizations such as Dweck's performance-learning goal dichotomy with approach and avoidance components or Nicholls' ego and task orientations, which he characterized as two forms of approach motivation.

Presently, achievement goal theory is the predominant approach to the analysis of achievement motivation. Most contemporary theorists use the frameworks of Dweck's and Nicholls' revised models in two important ways. First, most theorists institute primary orientations towards competence, by either differentiating between mastery and ability goals or contrasting task and ego involvement. A contention was raised towards the achievement goal frameworks on whether or not they are conceptually similar enough to justify a convergence of the mastery goal form with the performance goal form. Secondly, most modern theorists characterized both mastery and performance goals as approach forms of motivation, or they failed to consider approach and avoidance as independent motivational tendencies within the performance goal orientation.

The type of orientation adopted at the outset of an activity creates a context for how individuals interpret, evaluate, and act on information and experiences in an achievement setting. Adoption of a mastery goal is hypothesized to produce a mastery motivational pattern characterized by a preference for moderately challenging tasks, persistence in the face of failure, a positive stance towards learning, and enhanced task enjoyment. A helpless motivational response, however, is the result of the adoption of a performance goal orientation. This includes a preference for easy or difficult tasks, effort withdrawal in the face of failure, shifting the blame of failure to lack of ability, and decreased enjoyment of tasks.

Some theorists include the concept of perceived competence as an important agent in their assumptions. Mastery goals are expected to have a uniform effect across all levels of perceived competence, leading to a mastery pattern. Performance goals can lead to mastery in individuals with a high perceived competence and a helpless motivational pattern in those with low competence. Three motivational goal theories have recently been proposed based on the tri-variant framework by achievement goal theorists: mastery, performance-approach, and performance-avoidance. Performance-approach and mastery goals both represent approach orientations according to potential positive outcomes, such as the attainment of competence and task mastery. These forms of behaviour and self-regulation commonly produce a variety of affective and perceptual-cognitive processes that facilitate optimal task engagement. They challenge sensitivity to information relevant to success and effective concentration in the activity, leading to the mastery set of motivational responses described by achievement goal theorists. The performance-avoidance goal is conceptualized as an avoidance orientation according to potential negative outcomes.

This form of regulation evokes self-protective mental processes that interfere with optimal task engagement. It creates sensitivity to failure-relevant information and invokes an anxiety-based preoccupation with the appearance of oneself rather than the concerns of the task, which can lead to the helpless set of motivational responses. The three goal theories presented are very process oriented in nature. Approach and avoidance goals are viewed as exerting their different effects on achievement behaviour by activating opposing sets of motivational processes.

Intrinsic Motivation and Achievement Goals

Intrinsic motivation is defined as the enjoyment of and interest in an activity for its own sake. Fundamentally viewed as an approach form of motivation, intrinsic motivation is identified as an important component of achievement goal theory. Most achievement goal and intrinsic motivational theorists argue that mastery goals are facilitative of intrinsic motivation and related mental processes and performance goals create negative effects. Mastery goals are said to promote intrinsic motivation by fostering perceptions of challenge, encouraging task involvement, generating excitement, and supporting self-determination while performance goals are the opposite.

Performance goals are portrayed as undermining intrinsic motivation by instilling perceptions of threat, disrupting task involvement, and creating anxiety and pressure. An alternative set of predictions may be derived from the approach-avoidance framework.

Both performance-approach and mastery goals are focused on attaining competence and foster intrinsic motivation. More specifically, in performance-approach or mastery orientations, individuals perceive the achievement setting as a challenge, and this likely will create excitement, encourage cognitive functioning, increase concentration and task absorption, and direct the person towards success and mastery of information which facilitates intrinsic motivation. The performance-avoidance goal is focused on avoiding incompetence, where individuals see the achievement setting as a threat and seek to escape it. This orientation is likely to elicit anxiety and withdrawal of effort and cognitive resources while disrupting concentration and motivation.

Personal Goals Analysis

In recent years, theorists have increasingly relied on various goal constructs to account for action in achievement settings. Four levels of goal representation have been introduced: task-specific guidelines for performance, such as performing a certain action, situation-specific orientations that represent the purpose of achievement activity, such as demonstrating competence relative to others in a situation, personal goals that symbolize achievement pursuits, such as getting good grades, and self-standards and future self-images, including planning for future goals and successes.

These goal-based achievement motivation theories have focused almost exclusively on approach forms behaviour but in recent years have shifted more towards avoidance. Motivation is an important factor in everyday life. Our basic behaviours and feelings are affected by our inner drive to succeed over life's challenges while we set goals for ourselves. Our motivation also promotes our feelings of competence and self-worth as we achieve our goals. It provides us with means to compete with others in order to better ourselves and to seek out new information to learn and absorb. Individuals experience motivation in different ways, whether it is task- or ego-based in nature. Some people strive to achieve their goals for personal satisfaction and self-improvement while others compete with their surroundings in achievement settings to simply be classified as the best.

Motivation and the resulting behaviour are both affected by the many different models of achievement motivation. These models, although separate, are very similar in nature and theory. The mastery and performance achievement settings each have a considerable effect on how an individual is motivated.

Each theorist has made a contribution to the existing theories in today's achievement studies. More often than not, theorists build off of each other's work to expand old ideas and create new ones. Achievement motivation is an intriguing field, and I find myself more interested after reviewing similar theories from different perspectives.

AFFILIATION MOTIVATION

Affiliation motivation is the need for human relationships and for meaningful social contact. It was studied by David McClelland developed scales to measure it. Those with a high need for affiliation need harmonious relationships with other people and need to feel accepted by other people. They tend to conform to the norms of their work group. High nAff individuals prefer work that provides significant personal interaction. They enjoy being part of groups and when not anxious make excellent team members, though sometimes are distractible into social interaction. They can perform well in customer service and client interaction situations.

COMPETENCE MOTIVATION

Hull's motivational theory dominated the psychology of motivation during the late 1930s and the 1940s. Hull's last great work was published in 1952, shortly before he died. Already psychologists were questioning Hull's exclusive emphasis on drive-reduction. Hull portrayed all motivation as a matter of reducing uncomfortable drive or tension states. It is true that hunger and thirst are uncomfortable, but this conception of motivation leaves out many of the factors that energize and direct human behaviour.

As Hull's dominance in the field weakened, psychologists began to explore different types of motives not directly aimed at satisfying biological needs. In 1959 Robert W. White wrote a classic article for Psychological Review titled, "Motivation Reconsidered: The Concept of Competence." In it, White proposed a new concept: effectance motivation. Effectance was described as a "tendency to explore and influence the environment." White suggested that the "master reinforcer" for humans is personal competence. He defined competence as "the ability to interact effectively with the environment." White pointed out several ways competence motives were different from Hullian motives.

Unlike biological motives such as hunger and thirst, competence motives are never really satisfied. They serve to enhance the abilities of the organism, rather than to regulate a biological process. They are not based on a state of biological deprivation. Rather, they help an organism improve itself. Competence motivation is visible in children. Toddlers try to act powerful and capable, big and grown up, almost as soon as they understand the concepts. Children of all ages try to exercise control over some domain of objects.

Healthy, normal children commonly wish to be regarded as knowledgeable and capable beyond their years. In general, people who have a special talent love to exercise it. People like a subject or a game that "plays to their strengths" because it makes them feel competent. Competency motivation emerges as a critical factor in career success. A survey of successful entrepreneurs—people who started their own businesses—showed two factors that were even more important than competitiveness or grades in school.

The important factors were:

- An appetite for hard work, and
- An enjoyment of mastering skills.

They were powerful predictors of financial success.

MASLOW'S HIERARCHY OF NEEDS

Psychologist Abraham Maslow first introduced his concept of a hierarchy of needs in his 1943 paper "A Theory of Human Motivation" and his subsequent book, Motivation and Personality. This hierarchy suggests that people are motivated to fulfill basic needs before moving on to other needs. Maslow's hierarchy of needs is most often displayed as a pyramid. The lowest levels of the pyramid are made up of the most basic needs, while the more complex needs are located at the top of the pyramid.

Needs at the bottom of the pyramid are basic physical requirements including the need for food, water, sleep and warmth. Once these lower-level needs have been met, people can move on to the next level of needs, which are for safety and security.

As people progress up the pyramid, needs become increasingly psychological and social. Soon, the need for love, friendship and intimacy become important. Further up the pyramid, the need for personal esteem and feelings of accomplishment take priority. Like Carl Rogers, Maslow emphasized the importance of self-actualization, which is a process of growing and developing as a person to achieve individual potential.

Types of Needs

Maslow believed that these needs are similar to instincts and play a major role in motivating behaviour. Physiological, security, social, and esteem needs are deficiency needs, meaning that these needs arise due to deprivation. Satisfying these lower-level needs is important in order to avoid unpleasant feelings or consequences. Maslow termed the highest-level of the pyramid as growth needs. Growth needs do not stem from a lack of something, but rather from a desire to grow as a person.

Five Levels of the Hierarchy of Needs

There are five different levels in Maslow's hierarchy of needs:

1. *Physiological Needs*: These include the most basic needs that are vital to survival, such as the need for water, air, food and sleep. Maslow believed that these needs are the most basic and instinctive needs in the hierarchy because all needs become secondary until these physiological needs are met.
2. *Security Needs*: These include needs for safety and security. Security needs are important for survival, but they are not as demanding as the physiological needs. Examples of security needs include a desire for steady employment, health insurance, safe neighborhoods and shelter from the environment.
3. *Social Needs*: These include needs for belonging, love and affection. Maslow considered these needs to be less basic than physiological and security needs. Relationships such as friendships, romantic attachments and families help fulfill this need for companionship and acceptance, as does involvement in social, community or religious groups.
4. *Esteem Needs*: After the first three needs have been satisfied, esteem needs becomes increasingly important. These include the need for things that reflect on self-esteem, personal worth, social recognition and accomplishment.
5. *Self-actualizing Needs*: This is the highest level of Maslow's hierarchy of needs. Self-actualizing people are self-aware, concerned with personal growth, less concerned with the opinions of others and interested fulfilling their potential.

Self-Actualization

What exactly is self-actualization? Located at the peak of Maslow's hierarchy, he described this high-level need in the following way:

- "What a man can be, he must be. This need we may call self-actualization...It refers to the desire for self-fulfillment, namely, to the tendency for him to become actualized in what he is potentially.

> This tendency might be phrased as the desire to become more and more what one is, to become everything that one is capable of becoming."

While Maslow's theory is generally portrayed as a fairly rigid hierarchy, Maslow noted that the order in which these needs are fulfilled does not always follow this standard progression. For example, he notes that for some individuals, the need for self-esteem is more important than the need for love. For others, the need for creative fulfillment may supersede even the most basic needs.

HERZBERG'S MOTIVATION-HYGIENE THEORY

To better understand employee attitudes and motivation, Frederick Herzberg performed studies to determine which factors in an employee's work environment caused satisfaction or dissatisfaction. He published his findings in the 1959 book The Motivation to Work. The studies included interviews in which employees where asked what pleased and displeased them about their work.

Herzberg found that the factors causing job satisfaction were different from those causing job dissatisfaction. He developed the motivation-hygiene theory to explain these results. He called the satisfiers motivators and the dissatisfiers hygiene factors, using the term "hygiene" in the sense that they are considered maintenance factors that are necessary to avoid dissatisfaction but that by themselves do not provide satisfaction. The following table presents the top six factors causing dissatisfaction and the top six factors causing satisfaction, listed in the order of higher to lower importance.

Factors Affecting Job Attitudes

Leading to Dissatisfaction	Leading to Satisfaction
• Company policy	• Achievement
• Supervision	• Recognition
• Relationship w/Boss	• Work itself
• Work conditions	• Responsibility
• Salary	• Advancement
• Relationship w/Peers	• Growth

Herzberg reasoned that because the factors causing satisfaction are different from those causing dissatisfaction, the two feelings cannot simply be treated as opposites of one another. The opposite of satisfaction is not dissatisfaction, but rather, no satisfaction. Similarly, the opposite of dissatisfaction is no dissatisfaction. While at first glance this distinction between the two opposites may sound like a play on words, Herzberg argued that there are two distinct human needs portrayed. First, there are physiological needs that can be fulfilled by money, for example, to purchase food and shelter. Second, there is the psychological need to achieve and grow, and this need is fulfilled by activities that cause one to grow. From the table of results, one observes that the factors that determine whether there is dissatisfaction or no dissatisfaction are not part of the work itself, but rather, are external factors. Herzberg often referred to these hygiene factors as "KITA" factors, where KITA is an acronym for Kick In The A..., the process of providing incentives or a threat of punishment to cause someone to do something. Herzberg argues that these provide only short-run success because the motivator factors that determine whether there is satisfaction or no satisfaction are intrinsic to the job itself, and do not result from carrot and stick incentives.

Implications for Management

If the motivation-hygiene theory holds, management not only must provide hygiene factors to avoid employee dissatisfaction, but also must provide factors intrinsic to the work itself in order for employees to be satisfied with their jobs. Herzberg argued that job enrichment is required for intrinsic motivation, and that it is a continuous management process.

Herzberg:

- The job should have sufficient challenge to utilize the full ability of the employee.
- Employees who demonstrate increasing levels of ability should be given increasing levels of responsibility.
- If a job cannot be designed to use an employee's full abilities, then the firm should consider automating the task or replacing the employee with one who has a lower level of skill. If a person cannot be fully utilized, then there will be a motivation problem.

Critics of Herzberg's theory argue that the two-factor result is observed because it is natural for people to take credit for satisfaction and to blame dissatisfaction on external factors. Furthermore, job satisfaction does not necessarily imply a high level of motivation or productivity. Herzberg's theory has been broadly read and despite its weaknesses its enduring value is that it recognizes that true motivation comes from within a person and not from KITA factors.

STRESS

Employees stress is a growing concern for organizations today. Stress can be defined as a lively circumstance in which people face constraints, opportunities, or loss of something they desire and for which the consequence is both unpredictable as well as crucial. Stress is the response of people to the unreasonable/excessive pressure or demands placed on them. Stress is not always negative. It may also bring out the best in individuals at times. It may induce an individual to discover innovative and smarter way of doing things. This positive dimension of stress is called as enstress. But usually, the term stress has a negative implication and this negative aspect of stress is termed as distress. For instance-When a subordinate is harassed or warned by his superior, unhappiness of unsuitable job, etc. We can say that "Stress causes some people to break, and other to break records."

SYMPTOMS OF STRESS

Some of the symptoms of stress at workplace are as follows:

- Absenteeism, escaping from work responsibilities, arriving late, leaving early, etc.
- Deterioration in work performance, more of error prone work, memory loss, etc.
- Cribbing, over-reacting, arguing, getting irritated, anxiety, etc.
- Deteriorating health, more of accidents, etc.
- Improper eating habits, excessive smoking and drinking, sleeplessness, etc.

It is thus very essential to have effective stress management strategies in an organization so that the detrimental repercussions of stress on the employees as well as their performance can be reduced and controlled.

CAUSES OF STRESS

The factors leading to stress among individual are called as stressors. *Some of the factors/stressors acting on employees are*:

- Organizational factors- With the growth in organizational stress and complexity, there is increase in organizational factors also which cause stress among employees. Some of such factors are:
  - Discrimination in pay/salary structure
  - Strict rules and regulations
  - Ineffective communication
  - Peer pressure
  - Goals conflicts/goals ambiguity
  - More of centralized and formal organization structure
  - Less promotional opportunities
  - Lack of employees participation in decision-making
  - Excessive control over the employees by the managers
- *Individual factors*: There are various expectations which the family members, peer, superior and subordinates have from the employee. Failure to understand such expectations or to convey such expectations lead to role ambiguity/role conflict which in turn causes employee stress. Other individual factors causing stress among employees are inherent personality traits such as being impatient, aggressive, rigid, feeling time pressure always, etc. Similarly, the

family issues, personal financial problems, sudden career changes all lead to stress.

- *Job concerning factors*: Certain factors related to job which cause stress among employees are as follows:
  - Monotonous nature of job
  - Unsafe and unhealthy working conditions
  - Lack of confidentiality
  - Crowding
- *Extra-organizational factors*: There are certain issues outside the organization which lead to stress among employees. In today's modern and technology savvy world, stress has increased. Inflation, technological change, social responsibilities and rapid social changes are other extra-organizational factors causing stress.

STRATEGIES FOR MANAGING STRESS

Stress experienced by the employees in their job has negative impact on their health, performance and their behaviour in the organization. Thus, stress needs to be managed effectively so as to set off these harmful consequences.

Strategies for managing stress are as follows:

- *Organizational strategies for managing stress*:
  - Encouraging more of organizational communication with the employees so that there is no role ambiguity/conflict. Effective communication can also change employee views. Managers can use better signs and symbols which are not misinterpreted by the employees.
  - Encourage employees' participation in decision-making. This will reduce role stress.
  - Grant the employees greater independence, meaningful and timely feedback, and greater responsibility.
  - The organizational goals should be realistic, stimulating and particular. The employees must be given feedback on how well they are heading towards these goals.
  - Encourage decentralization.
  - Have a fair and just distribution of incentives and salary structure.
  - Promote job rotation and job enrichment.
  - Create a just and safe working environment.
  - Have effective hiring and orientation procedure.
  - Appreciate the employees on accomplishing and over-exceeding their targets.
- *Individual strategies for managing stress*:
  - The employees should make a "to-do" list daily, prioritize the acts in the list and plan the acts accordingly. Take regular breaks

during work to relax you. By effective time management, the employees can achieve their targets timely and can meet work pressures and, thus, avoid stress.

- Do hard work. Strive to achieve your goals but do not do it to the harm of family, health, or peer.
- Indulge in physical exercises. It helps in effective blood circulation, keeps you fit, diverts mind from work pressures.
- Encourage a healthy lifestyle. Take a regular sleep, have plenty of water, have healthy eating habits. Promote relaxation techniques such as yoga, listening music and meditation.
- The employees should have optimistic approach about their work. They should avoid connections with negative approach employees.
- The employees should have emotional intelligence at workplace. They should have self-awareness, self-confidence and self-control at workplace.
- The employees should build social support. They should have close connections with trustworthy peer who can listen to their problems and boost their confidence level. This social network will help the employees to overcome stress.
- Employee counselling is a very good strategy to overcome employee stress. Through counselling, employees can become aware of their strengths and how to develop those strengths; their weaknesses and how to eliminate them; and they can develop strategies for changing their behaviour. Employees are also given career counselling which helps in reducing their ambiguities with regard to career.
- Find a fun way to release stress, such as, cracking jokes, playing tennis, golf, etc.
- Do not remain pre-occupied with yourself. Turn your focus outwards. Help others. This will release some stress.

JOB RELATED CAUSES OF STRESS: FRUSTRATION

Frustration is a common emotional response to opposition. Related to anger and disappointment, it arises from the perceived resistance to the fulfillment of individual will. The greater the obstruction, and the greater the will, the more the frustration is likely to be. Causes of frustration may be internal or external. In people, internal frustration may arise from challenges in fulfilling personal goals and desires, instinctual drives and needs, or dealing with perceived deficiencies, such as a lack of confidence or fear of social situations. Conflict can also be an internal source of frustration; when one has competing goals that interfere with one another, it can create cognitive dissonance.

External causes of frustration involve conditions outside an individual, such as a blocked road or a difficult task. While coping with frustration, some individuals may engage in passive-aggressive behaviour, making it difficult to identify the original cause(s) of their frustration, as the responses are indirect. A more direct, and common response, is a propensity towards aggression.

Symptoms

Frustration can be considered a problem-response behaviour, and can have a number of effects, depending on the mental health of the individual. In positive cases, this frustration will build until a level that is too great for the individual to contend with, and thus produce action directed at solving the inherent problem. In negative cases, however, the individual may perceive the source of frustration to be outside of their control, and thus the frustration will continue to build, leading eventually to further problematic behaviour. Stubborn refusal to respond to new conditions affecting the goal, such as removal or modification of the barrier, sometimes occurs. As pointed out by J.A.C. Brown, severe punishment may cause individuals to continue nonadaptive behaviour blindly: "Either it may have an effect opposite to that of reward and as such, discourage the repetition of the act, or, by functioning as a frustrating agent, it may lead to fixation and the other symptoms of frustration as well. It follows that punishment is a dangerous tool, since it often has effects which are entirely the opposite of those desired".

Causes of Frustration

To the individual experiencing frustration, the emotion is usually attributed to external factors which are beyond their control. Although mild frustration due to internal factors is often a positive force, it is more often than not a perceived uncontrolled problem that instigates more severe, and perhaps pathological, frustration.

An individual suffering from pathological frustration will often feel powerless to change the situation they are in, leading to frustration and, if left uncontrolled, further anger. Frustration can be a result of blocking motivated behaviour. An individual may react in several different ways. He/She may respond with rational problem-solving methods to overcome the barrier. Failing in this, he/she may become frustrated and behave irrationally. An example of blockage of motivational energy would be the case of a worker who wants time off to go fishing but is denied permission by his/her supervisor. Another example would be the executive who wants a promotion but finds he/she lacks certain qualifications. If, in these cases, an appeal to reason does not succeed in reducing the barrier or in developing some reasonable alternative approach, the frustrated individual may resort to less adaptive methods of trying to reach the goal. He/She may, for example, attack the barrier physically, verbally or both.

VULNERABILITY STRESS

In the diathesis–stress model, a biological or genetic vulnerability or predisposition interacts with the environment and life events to trigger behaviours or psychological disorders. The greater the underlying vulnerability, the less stress is needed to trigger the behaviour or disorder. Conversely, where there is a smaller genetic contribution greater life stress is required to produce the particular result. Even so, someone with a diathesis towards a disorder does not necessarily mean they will ever develop the disorder. Both the diathesis and the stress are required for this to happen.

This theory was created by Holmes and Rahe. Holmes and Rahe conducted a study into life events as stressors, marriage was given an arbitory rating of 50 in their life events scale, participants were asked to rate other life events such as imprisonment, change in financial state and death of a spouse as needing more or less re-adjustment. Ratings were based on the participants' own experiences or the perception of how others had adjusted to given life events. Holmes and Rahe found that the more life events were experienced the more stress was experienced-this could be linked to a person becoming ill. The study of life events carries western views of success, materialism and conformism, it would not be suitable to generalise across many different cultures.

LEADERSHIP

Leadership is stated as the "process of social influence in which one person can enlist the aid and support of others in the accomplishment of a common task." Definitions more inclusive of followers have also emerged. Alan Keith stated that, "Leadership is ultimately about creating a way for people to contribute to making something extraordinary happen." Tom DeMarco says that leadership needs to be distinguished from posturing. The following parts discuss several important aspects of leadership including a description of what leadership is and a description of several popular theories and styles of leadership. This object also discusses topics such as the role of emotions and vision, as well as leadership effectiveness and performance, leadership in different contexts, how it may differ from related concepts and some critiques of leadership as generally conceived.

TYPES OF LEADERSHIP

Autocratic Leadership

Autocratic leadership is a classical leadership style with the following characteristics:

- Manager seeks to make as many decisions as possible
- Manager seeks to have the most authority and control in decision making

- Manager seeks to retain responsibility rather than utilise complete delegation
- Consultation with other colleagues in minimal and decision making becomes a solitary process
- Managers are less concerned with investing their own leadership development, and prefer to simply work on the task at hand.

The autocratic leadership style is seen as an old fashioned technique. It has existed as long as managers have commanded subordinates, and is still employed by many leaders across the globe. The reason autocratic leadership survives, even if it is outdated, is because it is intuitive, carries instant benefits, and comes natural to many leaders. Many leaders who start pursuing leadership development are often trying to improve upon their organisations autocratic leadership style.

The Benefits of the Autocratic Leadership Style

Despite having many critics, the autocratic leadership styles offer many advantages to managers who use them.

These include:

- *Reduced stress due to increased control*: Where the manager ultimately has significant legal and personal responsibility for a project, it will comfort them and reduce their stress levels to know that they have control over their fate.
- *A more productive group 'while the leader is watching'*: The oversight that an autocratic manager exerts over a team improves their working speed and makes them less likely to slack. This is ideal for poorly motivated employees who have little concern or interest in the quality or speed of work performed.
- *Improved logistics of operations*: Having one leader with heavy involvement in many areas makes it more likely that problems are spotted in advance and deadlines met. This makes autocratic leadership ideal for one-off projects with tight deadlines, or complicated work environments where efficient cooperation is key to success.
- *Faster decision making*: When only one person makes decisions with minimal consultation, decisions are made quicker, which will allow the management team to respond to changes in the business environment more quickly.

Disadvantages of the Autocratic Leadership Style

- *Short-termistic approach to management*: While leading autocratically will enable faster decisions to be made in the short term, by robbing subordinates of the opportunity to gain experience and start on their own leadership development, and learn from their mistakes, the manager is actually de-skilling their workforce which will lead to poorer decisions and productivity in the long run.

- *Manager perceived as having poor leadership skills*: While the autocratic style has merits when used in certain environments, autocratic leadership style is easy yet unpopular. Managers with poor leadership skills with often revert to this style by default.
- *Increased workload for the manager*: By taking on as much responsibility and involvement as possible, an autocratic leader naturally works at their full capacity, which can lead to long term stress and health problems and could damage working relationships with colleagues. This hyper-focus on work comes at the expense of good leadership development.
- *People dislike being ordered around*: They also dislike being shown very little trust and faith. As a result, the autocratic leadership style can result in a demotivated workforce. This results in the paradox that autocratic leadership styles are a good solution for demotivated workers, but in many cases, it is the leadership style alone that demotivates them in the first place. Generation Y employees particularly dislike this style.
- *Teams become dependent upon their leader*: After becoming conditioned to receive orders and act upon them perfectly, workers lose initiative and the confidence to make decisions on their own. This results in teams of workers who become useless at running operations if they loose contact with their leader. This is the result of a lack of time dedicated to leadership development on the employees part.

Autocratic Leadership Style Effective

Following on from the merits and drawbacks, the autocratic leadership style is useful in the following work situations:

- Short term projects with a highly technical, complex or risky element.
- Work environments where spans of control are wide and hence the manager has little time to devote to each employee.
- Industries where employees need to perform low-skilled, monotonous and repetitive tasks and generally have low levels of motivation.
- Projects where the work performed needs to be completed to exact specifications and/or with a tight deadline.
- Companies that suffer from a high employee turnover, *i.e.* where time and resources devoted to leadership development would be largely wasted. Although one could argue that a lack of leadership development in the first place caused the high turnover.

DEMOCRATIC LEADERSHIP

Democratic Leadership is the leadership style that promotes the sharing of responsibility, the exercise of delegation and continual consultation.

The style has the following characteristics:

- Manager seeks consultation on all major issues and decisions.
- Manager effectively delegate tasks to subordinates and give them full control and responsibility for those tasks.
- Manager welcomes feedback on the results of intiatives and the work environment.
- Manager encourages others to become leaders and be involved in leadership development.

The Benefits of the Democratic Leadership Style

- *Positive work environment*: A culture where junior employees are given fair amount of responsibility and are allowed to challenge themselves is one where employees are more enthused to work and enjoy what they do.
- *Successful initiatives*: The process of consultation and feedback naturally results in better decision making and more effective operations. Companies run under democratic leadership tend to run into fewer grave mistake and catastrophes. To put it simply–people tell a democratic leader when something is going badly wrong, while employees are encouraged to simply hide it from an autocrat.
- *Creative thinking*: The free flow of ideas and positive work environment is the perfect catalyst for creative thinking. The benefits of this aren't just relevant for creative industries, because creative thinking is required to solve problems in every single organisation, whatever it's nature.
- *Reduction of friction and office politics*: By allowing subordinates to use their ideas and even more importantly–gain credit for them, you are neatly reducing the amount of tension employees generate with their manager. When autocratic leaders refuse to listen to their workers, or blatantly ignore their ideas, they are effectively asking for people to talk behind their back and attempt to undermine or supercede them.
- *Reduced employee turnover*: When employees feel empowered through leadership development, a company will experience lower rates of employee turnover which has numerous benefits. A company that invests in leadership development for its employees, is investing in their future, and this is appreciated by a large majority of the workforce.

The Disadvantages of the Democratic Leadership Style

- *Lengthy and 'boring' decision making*: Seeking consultation over every decision can lead to a process so slow that it can cause opportunities to be missed, or hazards avoided too late.
- *Danger of pseudo participation*: Many managers simply pretend to

follow a democratic leadership style simply to score a point in the eyes of their subordinates. Employees are quick to realise when their ideas aren't actually valued, and that the manager is merely following procedure in asking for suggestions, but never actually implementing them. In other words, they're simply exerting autocratic leadership in disguise.

The Democratic Leadership Style Effective

Now you've heard about the benefits and drawbacks of this leadership style, let's look at where its actually implemented in the business world.

- Democratic leadership is applied to an extent in the manufacturing industry, to allow employees to give their ideas on how processes can become leaner and more efficient. While 'Fordism' is still applied in some factories across the country, truth is that production managers are now really starting to harness the motivational bonuses associated with not treating employees like robots anymore.
- Democratic leadershp is effective in proffessional organisations where the emphasis is clearly on training, professional and leadership development and quality of work performed. Democratic procedures are simply just one cog in the effective leadership mechanisms firms like The Big Four have created over the years.
- Non profit organisations also tremendously benefit from drawing upon the creative energies of all their staff to bring about cost cutting techniques or fund raising ideas.
- As previously mentioned, creative industries such as advertising and television enjoy a lot of benefits from the free flow of ideas that democratic leadership brings.

BUREAUCRATIC LEADERSHIP

The bureaucratic leadership style is concerned with ensuring workers follow rules and procedures accurately and consistently.

Bureaucratic leadership normally has the following characteristics:

- Leaders expect a employees to display a formal, business-like attitude in the workplace and between each other.
- Managers gain instant authority with their position, because rules demand that employees pay them certain priveledges, such as being able to sign off on all major decisions. As a result, leaders suffer from 'position power'. Leadership development becomes pointless, because only titles and roles provide any real control or power.
- Employees are rewarded for their ability to adhere to the rules and follow procedure perfectly.
- Bureaucratic systems usually gradually develop over a long period of time, and hence are more commonly found in large and old businesses.

The Benefits of the Bureaucratic Leadership Style:

- *Increased safety*: In dangerous workplaces where procedures save lives, a bureaucratic management style can help enforce health and safety rules.
- *Quality work*: Some tasks, such as completing proffessional work or medical examinations, need to be done in a meticulous fashion to be done correctly. Laziness can result in poor work, and hence one solution is to enforce the rules via the bureacratic leadership style.
- *Ultimate control*: An environment whereby employees are intrinsically motivated to follow rules in order to be promoted and succeed results in the tightest control management can ever assume over a company. This control can be used to cut costs or improve productivity.

The Disadvantages of the Bureaucratic Leadership Style:

- *Dehumanises the business*: Bureacratic companies tend to remove as much potential for 'human error' out of the picture as possible. Unfortunately this also has the effect of removing all the enjoyment and reward that comes from deciding how to do a task and accomplishing it.
- *Lack of self-fulfillment*: The bureaucratic way of working hampers employees efforts to become successful and independent, because the system becomes too contraining.
- *Parkinson's Law*: Cyril Northcote Parkinson made the scientific observation that the number of staff in bureaucracies increased by an average of 5%-7% per year "irrespective of any variation in the amount of work to be done."". He explains this growth by two forces:

Parkinson's findings suggest that bureaucratic leadership encourages inefficiency and waste of internal resources in the long run.

- *'Position power' obessession*: After working in an environment that reinforces the idea that authority is created by rules which in turn support senior positions. Employees become attached to the idea that simply being in a job position creates authority. This can lead to intense office politics, arrogant leaders and little incentive to perform well once an employee has landed a top job.
- *Lack of creativity*: It goes without saying that a rule-based culture hinders creativity and encourages workers to simply perform puppet-like work rather than think independently. This may result in a lack of growth in the business due to employees simply not thinking out of the box or looking for new areas to develop.
- *Poor communication*: A common feature of a bureaucratic system is a complicated network of communication lines. Managers who don't

want to be 'bothered' by junior staff simply create procedures that allow them to avoid communicating with those below them. 'Go through the formal process', 'Talk to my secretary' and 'My schedule is full' are common rule-based excuses for blocked contact. Barriers to communication can hinder the success of any company. For example, the board may be charging ahead with a doomed product simply because their shop floor workers cannot pass on the message that customers are giving very negative feedback.

When is the Bureaucratic Leadership Style Effective?

Bureaucratic leadership is found in extremely large corporations such as General Electric, Daimler and General Motors. However these cultures have evolved due to the age and size of these companies, and are generally blamed for the slow growth and recent failures at these companies.

- Governmental bodies often have bureaucratic systems, and while these are often despised by the public, they ensure accountability to the tax payer and fair treatment for all. Excessive form-filling also serves the purpose of passing effort from the government authority onto the individual, helping to save costs.
- Dangerous workplaces such as mines, oil rigs, construction sites and film sets all benefit from the tight control over health and safety that rules offer.

OTHER LEADERSHIP STYLES

What Different Leadership Types are there?

These 3 key management leadership styles are by no means a comprehensive list. Different leadership styles include laissez faire leadership, where the leader sets tasks and leaves workers up to their own devices to complete it. To help you discover which leadership style you possess, try our new Leadership Style Questionnaire.

Leadership Development

Leadership development is a complicated area, and thus countless styles have been theorised and researched. Good leadership development often involves using resources such as Leadership Expert to be 'sift' through these different leadership development tips and ideas.

Once you've been able to pull together a solid leadership development plan for yourself, you can start to really engage your employees–and maybe even set them off on their own leadership development quest! To further their leadership education, people often check the online MBA rankings to see whether MBA online is a match for them. Leadership Expert also has articles on another leadership style: charismatic leadership.

POSITIVE LEADER

Positive Leadershi

At Positive Leadership Solutions, positive psychological principles are used to help leaders, teams and organizations successfully meet goals, increase profitability, and enhance effectiveness. By focusing on strengths, people take responsibility for creating exceptional teams and organizations.

Central to understanding positive leadership is the positive psychology movement. Positive Psychology is a branch of psychology that uses scientific principles to understand what makes people healthy and helps them thrive. Positive Psychologists research positive emotions such as happiness or hope and positive individual traits such as wisdom or social intelligence.

They might also focus on how groups or organizations build better communities and healthy places to work; often referred to as Positive Organizational Scholarship or Positive Organizational Behaviour. A central element of Positive Psychology is that it is research-based, not simply a set of "feel good" ideas.

Positive Leadership Focuses on Relationships, not Roles

Every person has the potential to be a positive force in the workplace or community. Positive Leaders consistently match their values and beliefs to building something that improves their world. A high tide raises all boats. People in organizations can work towards building a truly exceptional workplace, but often miss the opportunity. This oversight costs the organization, the employees and the community. Through assessment, self-reflection and executive coaching, you can learn to improve and create a workplace that attracts great employees, managers and clients.

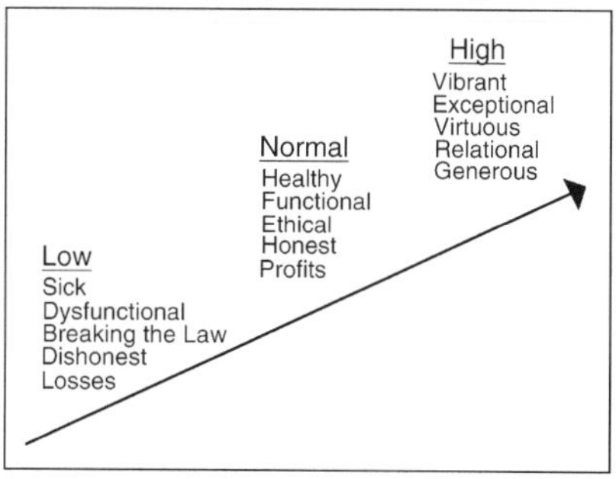

Characteristics of a Great Leader

There is a saying that great leaders are made not born. This should give you hope that once you understand the characteristics of a great leader you can become one yourself. Here are a few things that every great leader does or possesses within themselves to inspire people around them.

- Leaders are always improving. They understand that things are changing around them and for them to be great leader they must be changing too!
- Great leaders inspire people around them to become better. People want to do their best because of their leadership.
- Leaders know how to concentrate on people's strengths and not their weaknesses. Everyone has things that they are good at and leaders know how to bring this out in a person.
- Leaders are pro active and not reactive. They understand the importance of leading their people and not waiting for somebody else to get started.
- Leaders treat people with respect and importance. They know that to get a person to do something they need to want to do it. Treating people with respect and importance is a technique that works for this.
- Great leaders are self-motivated. They understand there will be ups and downs in their life and in their business, but they stay positive and do not let outside influences affect their attitudes.
- Leaders are well spoken. They know how to say the right thing at the right time.
- Leaders are always prepared. They don't leave things to chance but rather they control situations through preparation.
- Great leaders do not have big egos. They care about others as opposed to being a self centered individual.
- Great leaders are great mentors. They know how to pass on the knowledge that they themselves have personally already attained.
- Leaders are people who write down goals and strive to achieve them. They understand the importance of goal setting and the example that they are teaching by doing this.
- Great leaders are ambitious hard workers. They never expect more out of the people around them then they are willing to give themselves. This type of attitude is contagious and leads to everybody working harder.

NEGATIVE LEADER

Negative leaders act domineering and superior with people. They believe the only way to get things done is through penalties, such as loss of job, days off without pay, reprimanding employees in front of others, etc. They believe their authority is increased by frightening everyone into higher levels of productivity.

Yet what always happens when this approach is used wrongly is that morale falls; which of course leads to lower productivity. Also note that most leaders do not strictly use one or another, but are somewhere on a continuum ranging from extremely positive to extremely negative. People who continuously work out of the negative are bosses while those who primarily work out of the positive are considered real leaders.

ORGANISATIONAL CULTURE

A single definition of organizational culture has proven to be very elusive. No one definition of organizational culture has emerged in the literature. One of the issues involving culture is that it is defined both in terms of its causes and effect. For example, these are the two ways in which cultures often defined.

- *Outcomes*: Defining culture as a manifest pattern of behaviour- Many people use the term culture to describe patterns of cross individual behavioral consistency For example, when people say that culture is "The way we do things around here," they are defining consistent way is in which people perform tasks, solve problems, resolve conflicts, treat customers, and treat employees.
- *Process*: Defining culture as a set of mechanisms creating cross individual behavioral consistency- In this case culture is defined as the informal values, norms, and beliefs that control how individuals and groups in an organization interact with each other and with people outside the organization.

Both of these approaches are relevant to understanding culture. It is important to know on what types of behaviour culture has greatest impact and how culture works to control the behaviour of organizational members. As suggested, address these two questions later in the module.

Functions of organizational culture:

- Behavioral control
- Encourages stability
- Provides source of identity

Draw backs of culture:

- Barrier to change and improvement
- Barrier to diversity
- Barrier to cross departmental and cross organizational cooperation
- Barrier to mergers and acquisitions

WHAT TYPES OF BEHAVIOUR DOES CULTURE CONTROL

Using the outcome approach, cultures are described in terms of the following variables:

- *Innovation versus Stability*: The degree to which organizational members are encouraged to be innovative, creative and to take risks.
- *Strategic versus Operational Focus*: The degree to which the members of the management team focus on the long term big picture versus attention to detail.
- *Outcome versus Process Orientation*: The degree to which management

focuses on outcomes, goals and results rather than on techniques, processes, or methods used to achieve these results.

- *Task Versus Social Focus*: The relative emphasis on effect of decisions on organizational members and relationships over task accomplishment at all costs
- *Team versus Individual orientation*: The degree to which work activities are organized around teams rather than individuals
- *Customer Focus versus Cost Control*: The degree to which managers and employees are concerned about customer satisfaction and Service rather than minimizing costs
- *Internal verses External Orientation*: The degree to which the organization focuses on and is adaptive to changes in its environment

CULTURAL CONTROL MECHANISMS

How does organizational culture control the behaviour of organizational members? If consistent behavioral patterns are the outcomes or products of a culture, what is it that causes many people to act in a similar manner? There are four basic ways in which a culture, or more accurately members of a reference group representing a culture, creates high levels of cross individual behavioral consistency.

There are:

- *Social Norms*: Social norms are the most basic and most obvious of cultural control mechanisms. In its basic form, a social norm is simply a behavioral expectation that people will act in a certain way in certain situations. Norms are enforced by other members of a reference group by the use of social sanctions. Norms have been categorized by level.
  - Peripheral norms are general expectations that make interactions easier and more pleasant. Because adherence of these norms is not essential to the functioning of the group, violation of these norms general results in mild social sanctions.
  - Relevant norms encompass behaviours that are important to group functioning. Violation of these norms often results in non-inclusion in important group functions and activities
  - Pivotal norms represent behaviours that are essential to effective group functioning. Individuals violating these norms are often subject to expulsion from the group.
- *Shared Values*: As a cultural control mechanism the keyword in shared values is shared. The issue is not whether or not a particular individual's behaviour can best be explained and/or predicted by his or her values, but rather how widely is that value shared among organizational members, and more importantly, how responsible was

the organization/culture in developing that value within the individual. What is a value? Any phenomenon that is some degree of worth to the members of giving groups: The conception of the desirable that establishes a general direction of action rather than a specific objective. Values are the conscious, affective desires or wants of people that guide their behaviour How are values formed/ developed within individuals? We like to think that our values are unique to us and an essential part of who we are. The critical question here is, how much of our values are derived from our reference group affiliation? We find that for most people, their values are generally consistent with the values of the reference group in which they were socialized.

There are two kinds of values:

1. Instrumental values represent the "means" an individual prefers for achieving important "ends."
2. Terminal values are preferences concerning "ends" to be achieved. When an individual can no long answer the question of"

These components of culture have a well–defined linkage with each other which binds a culture and makes change in any one of the components difficult. However, change in any one of these components causes chain reactions amongst others.

Culture is a very powerful force at the workplace, which is consciously and deliberately cultivated and is passed on to the incoming employees. It reflects the true nature and personality of an organisation. There are various myths about organisational culture. Some of them are presented here along with the counter arguments.

- *Organisational culture is same as organisational climate*: In management literature there is often ambiguity about the two concepts–organisational culture and organisational climate. As explained earlier, organisational culture is a macro phenomenon which refers to the patterns of beliefs, assumptions, values, and behaviours reflecting commonality in people working together. However, organisational climate is a micro phenomenon and reflects how employees in an organisation feel about the characteristics and quality of culture like morale, goodwill, employee relations, job satisfaction, commitmrnt at the organisational, department or unit level. It refers to the psychological enviornment in which behaviour of organisational members occurs. It is a relatively persistent set of perceptions held by organisational members about the organisational culture. Another viewpoint about climate is that various variables get subsumed under the concept of climate, whereas has unique indicators like symbols, rites, myths, and stories.

- *Culture is same as 'groupthink'*: Since culture refers to shared assumptions and beliefs, it is likely to cause confusion. Groupthink refers to group members hiding any differences in how they feel and think and behave in a certain way. The phenomenon of groupthink is mostly used in a face–to–face situation when dealing with small groups. Culture, on the other hand, is a much larger phenomenon characterised by historical myths, symbols, beliefs, and artifacts.
- *Culture is same as organisation*: Culture is a result of sustained interaction among people in organisations and exists commonly in thoughts, feelings, and behaviour of people. Organisations on the other hand, consist of a set of expectations and a system of reward and punishment substained by rules, regulations, and norms of behaviour.
- *Culture is a social structure*: Social structures in various collectives exhibit tangible and specific ways in which people relate to one another overtly. However, culture operates on a system of unseen, abstract, and emotionally loaded forms which guide organisational members to deal with their physical and social needs.

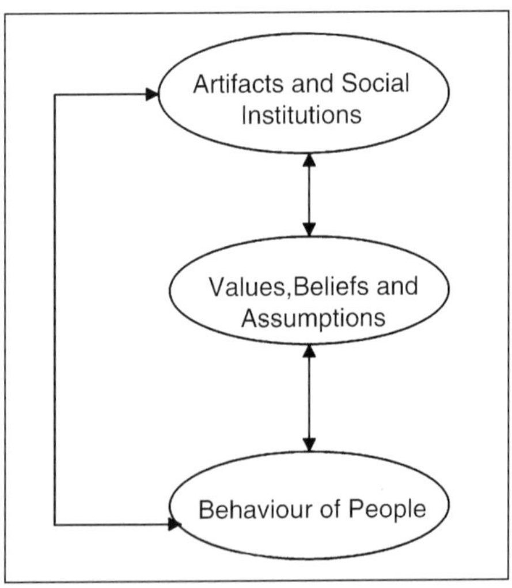

Fig. Relationship Among Components of Culture

Culture: Conceptual Framework

Basic Concepts and Definitions

Culture has been defined differently by various scholars. According to Kroeber and Kluckholn culture consists of patterns, explicit and implicit, of and for behaviour acquired and transmitted by symbols, constituting the distinctive achievement of human groups, including their embodiment in artifacts. The essential core of culture consists of traditional ideas and especially their attached values. Culture systems may, on the one hand, be considered as products of action, and as conditioning elements of future action. In the words of Hofstede culture is, " The collective programming of the mind which distinguishes the members of one human group from another .... The interactive aggregate of common characteristics that influences a human group's response to its environment."

Anthropologist Symington has defined culture as, "... that complex whole which includes knowledge, belief, art, law, morals, customs and capabilities and habits acquired by a man as a member of society." The Indian perspective of culture given by Sinha suggests that "Culture consists of totality of assumptions, beliefs, values, social systems and institutions, physical artifacts and behaviour of people, reflecting their desire to maintain continuity as well as to adapt to external demands."

What these descriptions suggest is a set of value systems that are equally shared by all the members. They take a long time to evolve and are sustained over a long period of time. They form a common core which binds people together. Work culture, on the other hand, is a totality of various levels of interaction among organisational factors and organismic factors interact among themselves at various levels. Over a period of time they develop roles, norms and values focusing work and is called work culture.

NATURE OF ORGANISATIONAL CULTURE

The culture of an organisation may reflect in various forms adopted by the organisation.

These could be:

- The physical infrastructure
- Routine behaviour, langauge, ceremonies
- Gender equality, equity in payment
- Dominant values such as quality, efficiency and so on
- Philosophy that guides the organisation's policies towards it employees and customers like 'customer first' and 'customer is king', and the manner in which employees deal with customers.

Individually none of these connote organisational culture, however, together, they reflect organisational culture. Although organisational culture has common properties, it is found that large organisations have a dominant culture and a number of sub–cultures. The core values shared by the majority of the organisational members constitute the dominant culture. Therefore, whenever one refers to the culture of an organisation one actually talks about the dominant culture of an organisation one actually talks about the dominant culture. Subcultures within an organisation are a set of shared understandings among members of one group/department/geographic operations. For example, the finance department of an organisation may have a sub–culture which is unique to this department vis–a–vis other departments. This means that this department will not only have the core values of the organisation's dominant culture but also some unique values.

If an organisation does not have a dominant culture and is comprised only of various sub–cultures, its effectiveness would be difficult to judge and there will be no consistency of behaviour among departments. Hence, the aspect of common or shared understanding is an essential component of organisational culture. Also, organisational culture exists at various levels.

LEVELS OF ORGANISATIONAL CULTURE

One comes across a number of elements in the organisation which depict its culture. Organisational culture can be viewed at three levels based on manifestations of the culture in tangible and intangible forms.

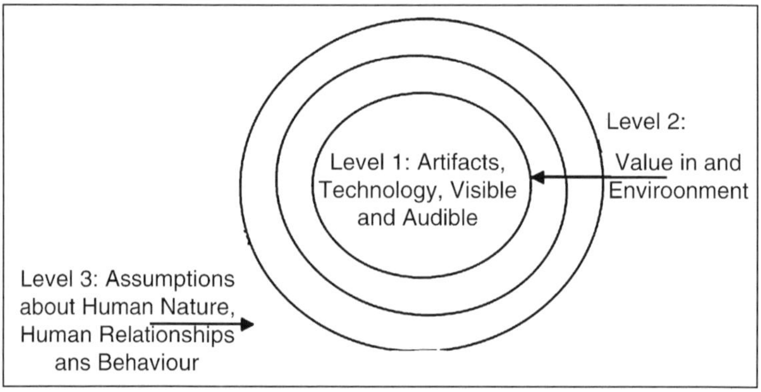

Fig. Levels of Organisational Culture

- At Level One the organisational culture can be observed in the form of physical objects, technology and other visible forms of behaviour like ceremonies and rituals. Though the culture would be visible in various forms, it would be only at the superficial level. For example, people may interact with one another but what the underlying feelings are or whether there is understanding among them would require probing.
- At Level Two there is greater awareness and internalisation of cultural values. People in the organisation try solutions of a problem in ways which have been tried and tested earlier. If the group is successful there will be shared perception of that 'success', leading to cognitive changes turning perception into values and beliefs.
- Level Three represents a process of conversion. When the group repeatedly observes that the method that was tried earlier works most of the time, it becomes the 'preferred solution' and gets converted into underlying assumptions or dominant value orientation. The

conversion process has both advantages. The advantages are that the dominant value orientation guides behaviour, however at the same time it may influence objective and rational thinking.

These three levels range on a scale of superficial to deeply embedded. As cultural symbols get converted to shared assumptions, they move from a superficial level to a real internationalised level as shown in Figure.

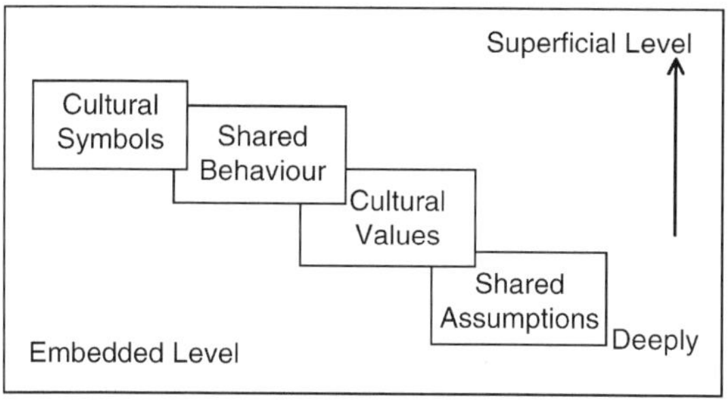

Fig. Levels of Organisational Culture

PATTERNS OF ORGANISATIONAL CULTURE

Types of Organizational Culture

Organisational culture can vary in a number of ways. It is these variances that differentiate one organisation from the others.

Some of the bases of the differentiation are presented below:

- *Strong vs weak culture*: Organisational culture can be labelled as strong or weak based on sharedness of the core values among organisational members and the degree of commitment the members have to these core values. The higher the sharedness and commitment, the stronger the culture increases the possibility of behaviour consistency amongst its members, while a weak culture opens avenues for each one of the members showing concerns unique to themselves.
- *Soft vs hard culture*: Soft work culture can emerge in an organisation where the organisation pursues multiple and conflicting goals. In a soft culture the employees choose to pursue a few objectives which serve personal or partal interests. A typical example of soft culture can be found in a number of public sector organisations in India where the management feels constrained to take action against employees to maintain high productivity. The culture is welfare oriented; people are held accountable for their mistakes but are not rewarded for good performance. Consequently, the employees consider work to be less important than personal and social obligations. Sinha has presented a case study of a public sector fertilizer company which was established in an industrially backward rural area to promote employment generation and

industrial activity. Under pressure from local communities and the government, the company succumbed to overstaffing, converting mechanised operations into manual operations, payment of overtime, and poor discipline. This resulted in huge financial losses to the company.

- *Formal vs informal culture*: The work culture of an organisation, to a large extent, is influenced by the formal components of organisational culture. Roles, responsibilities, accountability, rules and regulations are components of formal culture. They set the expectations that the organisation has from every member and indicates the consequences if these expectations are not fulfilled.

Table. Presents some of the Components of Formal Culture and their Implication for Organisations.

S. No	Description	Effect on Organisational Culture	
1	Mission/Vision	The milestones to be reached	Could be unrealistic
2	Policies	Statements designed to be guidelines to bahavioural decision	Policies, if not drafted properly can provide leeway
3	Procedures	Methods of providing specific guidelines	Can facilitate or create obstacles in smooth functioning
4	Rules	Specific instructions for performing a task	Rules could be a means or an end in themselves
5	State of Organisational Development	Organisation at young, growing, maturing, or mature stage of development	State of organisational development has direct impact on work culture

Informal culture on the other hand has tangible and intangible, specific and non–specific manifestations of shared values, beliefs, and assumptions. This part of organisational culture comprising of artifacts, symbols, ceremonies, rites, and stories is highlighted in almost all the definitions of organisational culture.

8

Design of Social Security Benefits for the Unorganised Workers

INTRODUCTION

Social security is the protection which society provides for its members against the economic and social distress that otherwise would be caused by substantial reduction or ceasing of earnings resulting from sickness, maternity, employment injury, unemployment, invalidity, old age, and death; the provision of medical care; and the provision of subsidies for families and children. The strategies for providing social security include the preventive, mitigating, and coping aspects.

India is the most populous country in the world, next to China. If one looks at the characteristics of Indian population it reveals the interesting dimension about the existence of unorganised sector, which is the dominant sector and could not be properly attended to under the social security measures initiated so for. As per the 2001 census, the total work force in our country is 402 million, of which 313 million are main workers and 89 million are marginal workers. Out of the 313 million main workers, about 285 million is in the unorganised sector, accounting 91 per cent.

The estimates provided by the National Sample Survey Organisation also reveal the similar pattern. As per the NSSO estimates for the year 2004-05, India had population of 1093 million, with a workforce of about 385 million. Of these, about 7 per cent belong to organised and the rest 93 per cent of the workforce include those self employed and employed in unorgnaised sector. As far as social security measures are concerned, India has a long history of providing securities to all, inclusive of unemployed, aged, children, weaker parts and vulnerable groups. However, the social security system prevailed for the unorganised sector got run-down and that of the organised sector gained momentum. In the present context of globalisation, the unorganised sector warrants greater attention and protection to safeguard themselves from the evils of globalisation. In this context, the present study attempts to examine the social security measures for the unorganised sectors in India.

The discussion in this paper is organised in four parts. In the first part, the basic characteristics of unorganised sectors and the trends in the magnitude of workers in this sector are analysed. The second part discusses the Indian experience in social security measures initiated for organised and unorganised sectors. The efforts initiated by the Centre, State and other agencies towards unorganised sector are also discussed. In the third part, the areas of attention needed for social security of unorganised workers are discussed. The last part summarises the main findings.

TRENDS IN UNORGANISED LABOUR AND THEIR CHARACTERISTICS IN INDIA

Indian economy is characterised by the existence of high level of informal or unorganised labour employment. The workers in the organised sector constitute about 7 per cent of the country's total work force and the rest comprises of subsistence farmers, agricultural workers, fisherfolk, dairy workers and those working in traditional manufacturing like handlooms are grouped under unorganised sector. The term 'unorganised labour' has been defined as those workers who have not been able to organise themselves to pursuit of their common interests due to certain constraints like casual nature of employment, ignorance and illiteracy, small and scattered size of establishments, etc. Ministry of Labour has categorised the unorganised labour force under four groups in terms of occupation, nature of employment, specially distressed categories and service categories. In terms of occupation, it included small and marginal farmers, landless agricultural labourers, share croppers, fishermen and those engaged in animal husbandry, beedi rolling, labeling and packing, building and construction workers, leather workers, weavers, artisans, salt workers, workers in brick kilns and stone quarries, workers in saw mills, oil mills etc..

In terms of nature of employment, they are attached agricultural labourers, bonded labourers, migrant workers, contract and casual labourers. Toddy tappers, scavengers, carriers of head loads, drivers of animal driven vehicles, loaders and unloaders, belong to the specially distressed category while midwives, domestic workers, fishermen and women, barbers, vegetable and fruit vendors, newspaper vendors etc. come under the service category. In addition to the categories, there exists a large part of urorganised labour force such as cobblers, hamals, handicraft artisans, handloom weavers, lady tailors, physically handicapped self-employed persons, rikshaw pullers/ auto drivers, sericulture workers, carpenters, leather and tannery workers, powerloom workers and urban poor. The extent of unorganised workers is significantly high among agricultural workers, building and other construction workers, and among home based workers. But, the availability of statistical information on its intensity and accuracy vary significantly. Agricultural workers constitute the largest segment of workers in the unorganised sector.

The NSSO estimates for the year 2004-05, 52 per cent of the total workers are found in agriculture. Many small and marginal farmers, because of their small and uneconomical holdings and low yield, also work on the land of others and hence qualify as agricultural laborers. Further a significant number, are engaged in rearing livestock, forestry, fishery, orchard and allied activities. Construction workers constitute the second largest category of workers in the unorganised sector. The NSSO estimates, about 5.57 percentage of workers are engaged in building and other construction works in 2004-05. The construction industry covers a vast field of activity in the civil, mechanical, electrical and public health area processes. A large number of multinational, national and local companies employ lakhs of such workers. More over, a large number of self employed individuals are engaged in actual construction works and allied activities like white washing, painting, plumbing and fixing of mechanical or electrical fixtures etc.

Home Based Workers are those who are engaged in the production of goods or services for an employed or contractor in an arrangement whereby the work is carried out at the place of the worker's own choice, often the worker's own home. In India, there is no authentic data on home based workers. Official data sources such as Census of India do not recognise these workers as an independent category but have included them in the broad category of those working in house-hold industries. Home based workers are mainly engaged in beedi rolling, garment making, agarbati making, gem cutting, preparation of food items like papad, pickle, etc., handloom, lace and chikan work etc. The beedi rolling industry, which is generally family based, employs about 45 lakh workers out of which 90 per cent are home based workers.

The major characteristics of unorganised workers could be listed as below:

- The unorganised labour is overwhelming in terms of its number range and therefore, they are omnipresent throughout India.
- As the unorganised sector suffers from cycles of excessive seasonality of employment, majority of the unorganised workers does not have stable and durable avenues of employment. Even those who appear to be visibly employed are not gainfully and substantially employed, indicating the existence of disguised unemployment.
- The workplace is scattered and fragmented. The workers do the same kind of job in different habitations and may not work and live together in compact geographical areas.
- There is no formal employer-employee relationship between small and marginal farmers, share croppers and agricultural labourers as they work together in situations which may be marginally favourable to one category but may be broadly described as identical.
- In rural areas, the unorganised labour force is highly stratified on caste and community considerations. In urban areas while such

considerations are much less, it cannot be said that it is altogether absent as the bulk of the unorganised workers in urban areas are basically migrant workers from rural areas.

- Workers in the unorganised sector are usually subject to a lot of fads, taboos, and outmoded social customs like child marriage, excessive spending on ceremonial festivities etc. which lead to indebtedness and bondage.
- The unorganised workers are subject to exploitation significantly by the rest of the society. The unorganised workers receive poor working conditions, especially wages much below that in the formal sector, even for closely comparable jobs *i.e.*, where labour productivity are no different. The work status is of inferior quality of work and inferior terms of employment, both remuneration and employment.
- Primitive production technologies and feudal production relations are rampant in the unorganised sector, and they do not permit or encourage the workmen to imbibe and assimilate higher technologies and better production relations. Large scale ignorance and illiteracy and limited exposure to the goings on in the outside world are also responsible for such poor absorption.
- The unorganised workers do not receive sufficient attention from the trade unions.

In general, unorganised workers are observed to be large in numbers, suffering from cycles of excessive seasonality of employment, scattered and fragmented work place, poor in working conditions, and lack of attention from the trade unions. The extent of workforce in the organised and unorganised sectors, and their changes over time could be understood by the information provided by the Ministry of Labour and Employment, Director General of Employment and Training, Government of India and published in the Economic Surveys. The share of organised workforce was about 8.per cent by 1983, which declined to 7.54 per cent by 2004-2005. The corresponding share of urorganised workforce was about 92.07 per cent by 1983, which increased to 92.46 per cent by 2004-2005.

SOCIAL SECURITY MEASURES: THE EXPERIENCE

India has a long tradition of social security and social assistance directed particularly towards the more vulnerable parts of society. The institution of self sufficient village communities, the system of common property resources, the system of joint families and the practice of making endowments for religious and charitable provided the required social security and assistance to the needy and poor of the nation. In fact, the caste and religion based institutions also played significant role in providing the needed support to the weaker parts of the selected castes and group of people. These informal arrangements of social security measures underwent steady and inevitable erosion in the wake of industrialisation and urbanisation. During the British rule the policy was to provide assistance only to the employees of the company or the government, basically to promote the commitment and loyalty of the workforce and as a part of non-union strategy. Only during the postindependent period, the welfare dimension gained relevance and importance. However, even after independence, the State was concerned more with the problems of industrial work force and neglected the rural labour force on social security matters to a greater extent, till recent past.

It is rightly true that when independent India's Constitution was drafted, social security was specially included in List III to Schedule VII of the Constitution and it was made as the concurrent responsibility of the Central and State Governments. A number of Directive Principles of State Policy relating to aspects of social security were incorporated in the Indian Constitution. The initiatives in the form of Acts such as, the Workmen's Compensation Act (1923), the Industrial Dispute Act (1947), the Employees State Insurance Act (1948), the Minimum Wages Act (1948), the Coal Mines Provident Funds and Miscellaneous Provisions Act (1948), the Employees Provident Fund and Miscellaneous Provisions Act (1952), the Assam Tea Plantations Provident Funds/Scheme Act (1955), the Maternity Benefit Act (1961), the Seamen's Provident Fund Act (1966), the Contract Labour Act (1970), the Payment of Gratuity Act (1972), the Building and Construction Workers Act (1996), etc reveal the attention given to the organised workers to attain different kinds of social security and welfare benefits.

Needless to state that the benefits arising through these initiatives are meant for:

- Employees of the Central and State Governments, local bodies, including universities and aided educational institutions,
- Public sector establishments, under both the Centre and States, including mines, railways, ports and docks, air corporations, banks, insurance companies, electricity Boards, road transport undertakings, manufacturing units, trading concerns, service industries, etc.
- Employees in organised private sector establishments in industries as in cotton textiles, jute, silk and art silk, cement, engineering, chemical, electronics, transport, construction, services and so on.

Though it has been argued that the Acts are directly and indirectly applicable to the workers in the unorganised sector also, their contribution is negligible to the unorganised workers. Although not much has been done in providing social security cover to the rural poor and the unorganised labour force, the country has made some beginning in that direction. Both the Central and State Governments have formulated certain specific schemes to support unorganised workers. The Old Age Pension Scheme (OAPS) was introduced in all the States and Union Territories. Kerala was the First State to experiment with the pension scheme for the agricultural workers in the year 1982, followed by Tamilnadu (1982). Andhra Pradesh (1983) introduced the OAPS to the landless agricultural workers. The Government of Karnataka introduces the Asha Kiran Scheme (1983) to provide relief against death or loss of limbs due to accident to agricultural labourers and other labourers (aged 16-65) such as fishermen, beedi workers, washerman, cobblers, masions, goldsmiths, drivers of animal drawn vehicles, riksha pullers, etc.

The Government of Maharashtra introduced a pension scheme in 1980 to support the physically handicapped and economically weaker parts of the society. In addition to pension schemes, there were initiatives to provide death and retirement benefits for the artisans and skilled workers and insurance benefits to the unorganised sectors initiated in state level. In order to evolve comprehensive legislation for workers in the unorganised sectors, various commissions and study groups were appointed. The First National Commission on Labour (1969) defined the unorganised workers and recommended the Minimum Wages Act to cover unorganised workers too. In 1984, the Economic Administration Reforms Commission constituted a 6-member working group on social security. The Working Group could not carry out detailed investigation.

In August 1987, Government of India appointed a National Commission on Rural Labour to examine the national and regional problems pertaining rural labour in India. The Commission submitted its report in July 1991 and recommended old age pension, life insurance, maternity benefit, disability benefits and minimum health care and sickness benefits to all rural workers. The Second National Labour Commission constituted in 1999 submitted its report in 2002 and recommended an umbrella type legislation and drafted an indicative Bill also to provide protection to the workers in the unorganised sector. Based on the Commission's recommendations, the Government launched the 'Unorganised Sector Workers' Social Security Scheme, 2004' on pilot basis in 50 districts.

The scheme provided three benefits such as, old age pension, medical insurance and accidental insurance. However, the scheme was not found viable as it had no statutory backing, it was voluntary in nature and the contribution from the employers was not forthcoming. Moreover, given the size of the unorganised sector the magnitude of the problem is huge and the resource requirements are quite large. The National Common Minimum Programme (NCMP) of the present government highlights the commitment of the government towards the welfare and wellbeing of all workers, particularly in the unorganised sector. The government constituted a National Commission for the Enterprises in the Unorganised Sector (NCEUS) under Chairmanship of Dr. Arjun Sen Gupta to examine the problems of enterprises in the unorganised sector and make recommendations to provide technical, marketing and credit support to these enterprises.

The Commission was also to review the social security system available for the unorganised workers and make recommendations for expanding their coverage. The Commission presented its report on the Social Security for the unorganised sector workers in May 2006. Based on the committee's recommendations the government is in the process of enactment of Legislation (Bill) and formulation of social security schemes. Poverty Alleviation Programmes (PAP) and Employment Oiented Programmes initiated in India are primarily focused on developing rural labour and unorganised workers. These programmes improve the access of the poor to developmental programmes, use surplus labour for community asset formation and strengthen the position of the poor by providing assets and income.

The first PAPs introduced were Small Farmers Development Agency (SFDA) and Marginal Farmers and Agricultural Labour Agency (MFAL). In 1980, Integrated Rural Development Programme (IRDP) was launched with the aim of helping the poor families to cross poverty line and enabling them to achieve sustain poverty eradication. Productive assets and inputs were provided through financial assistance by government subsidy and term credit from financial institutions. The programme covered small and marginal farmers, agricultural labourers and rural artisans.

In 1979, Training for Rural Youth for Self-Employment was introduced to provide technical and entrepreneurial skills to rural youth from families below poverty line to enable them to take up income generating activities. To develop women and children in rural areas with a cooperation of UNICEF a special programme named Development of Women and Children in Rural Areas (DWCRA) was started during 1982-83. As an effort towards employment security National Rural Employment Programme (NREP) was launched during the sixth plan (1982-85).

In 1983, Rural Landless Employment Guarantee Programme (RLEGP) was introduced to ensure employment generation of hundred days in a year in the rural landless households. By replacing the NREP and RLEGP Jawahar Rozgar Yojana (JRY) was launched in 1989. In the same year Nehru Rozgar Yojana (NRY) also got launched with a target towards persons living below the poverty line in Urban areas. There are several other programme such as Drought Prone Area Programme (DPAP), Desert Development Programme (DDP), Hill Area Development Programme (HADP) and North-East Council (NEC) were also launched with similar objectives of developing weaker parts of selected areas. In addition to the Central assisted programmes, State-level initiatives for poverty alleviation and employment generation were initiated towards unorganised workers.

For instance in Tamil Nadu old age pension is available to:

- Aged poor who are 65 year and above
- Destitute and physically handicapped,
- Destitute widows

- Destitute agricultural labourers and
- Destitute/ deserted wives.

Under the Annapurna Scheme, food grains are distributed to the destitute/ senior citizens covered under the National Old Age Pension Scheme. The beneficiaries are given 10 kgs. of rice per month at free of cost. The State of Goa has enacted the Goa Employment (Condiitons of Service) and Retirement Benefit Act, 2005. This act the employers is required to issue social security cards to the workers engaged by him in both the organised and unorganised sectors.

West Bengal Government introduced a State Assisted Scheme of Provident Fund for unorganised workers in 2001. Tripura Government also introduced the similar Provident Fund programme in 2001. In the State of Punjab, in addition to old age pension scheme, financial assistance to women and destitute women, dependent children and disabled persons are also made available. Similar such State level initiatives are carried out in Kerala, Bihar, Uttar Prades, Madhya Pradesh, Haryana, Gujarat and other states. The involvement of Non-Governmental Organisations (NGOs) in the social security of unorganised workers could not be ignored. A large number of voluntary and people's organisations are directly involved in providing protective social security to workers and their families in the unorganised sector.

The services provided by the NGO's include access to microcredit, housing, preventive health care and employment. The NGO's support to unorganised workers is carried out in two ways. Firstly, the NGO's use their own funds and the aids obtained from other agencies (domestic and international donors) and implement several projects and schemes to the targeted people who are basically weaker and vulnerable parts of the community. Secondly, they serve as an intermediary between the formal provider (say, Government) and the community, and help in routing the services to the needy. In both the ways, it is expected that the services are reaching to the community with no delay, less cost and to the right ones. It is estimated that the NGO's could cover only 3 to 4 per cent of the total workforce in the unorganised sector.

SOCIAL SECURITY FOR THE UNORGANISED WORKERS: THE NEEDS

The foregoing discussion about the growing unorganised labourforce, their characteristics and the social security initiatives of the Centre, State and NGO's indicated that the needs are much more than the supports provided and the efforts must be targeted and vast enough to cover the growing unorganised workers. In this context, it is worthwhile to list out the major security needs of the unorganised workers.

They are:

- *Food Security*: Food security is considered as an important component of social security. The rural workers and weaker parts of the community are badly affected during times of drought, flood and famine, and due to similar natural calamities. The DPAP largely confines itself in the provision of employment through rural works programme. What is required is to provide security for food in times of difficulty and during normal times. The Public Distribution System (PDS) implemented in Indian States stand as a model attempt in this direction. It is through the PDS that the government endeavors to protect the real purchasing power of the poorer parts by providing them an uninterrupted supply of foodgrains at prices far below market prices. It is to be noted that the PDS was introduced only to the urban areas initially, but since 1970s rural areas are also covered

- *Nutritional Security*: It is not just 'food', but the nutrition is very important. The weaker parts of the community and the unorganised workers are not conscious about the nutrient intake. Particularly, the children and women, pregnant women and aged do not receive adequate nutrient requirements. Lack of nutrient leads to poor growth, poor health and sickness, poor performance and shorter life. There are certain initiatives by the states, local bodies and NGO's to create awareness on health and nutrition and to ensure adequate nutrient intake for the targeted groups, particularly to children and women.
- *Health Security*: Health security can be described as ensuring low exposure to risk and providing access to health care services along with the ability to pay for medical care and medicine. Such health security should be made available to all citizens. Several studies that examined rural health conditions and health care needs highlight that the inadequate and poor rural health infrastructure, growing health care needs and health care expenses. Establishing hospitals with required infrastructure in all the villages is a question of feasibility, viability and availability of inputs and resources. However, it is a matter of concern to consider the needs of the 70 per cent of the people living in villages. The poor do not treat for common illness and sometimes to major diseases that are unidentified by them, causing higher level of untreated morbidity. Similarly, the cost and burden of treatments are ever increasing and leading to difficulty for the poor and weaker parts of the community.
- *Housing Security*: Housing is one of the basic needs of every individual and family. The housing needs of the unorganised workers and the poor are ever increasing in the context of the decay of joint family system, migration and urbanisation. In urban areas, though housing is a major issue, the organised workers are

supported by providing House Rent Allowances (HRA) or by providing houses through Housing Boards and by provising accommodation in the Quarters. There are several financing companies and commercial banks offering loans to organised workers to construct or purchase houses. These facilities are normally not available and could not be enjoyed by the unorganised workers. More over, the housing conditions of the rural poor are 'really poor' and there is scope for reconditioning, modification and reconstruction, in many. The rural housing programme implemented in Tamilnadu namely Samathuvapuram and construction of houses under Slum Clearance Board stand as examples for steps towards housing security.

- *Employment Security*: Unorganised workers are greatly affected by the seasonal nature of the employment opportunities. The problem of under-employment and unemployment persist to a large extent among unorganised sectors. There are several schemes such as Swarnajayanti Gram Swaeozgar Yojna (SGSY), Pradhan Manntri Gran Sadak Yojana (PMGSY), Sampoorna Gramin Rozgar Yojana (SGRY), National Food For Work Programme (NFFWP), Indra Awass Yojna (JAY), Integrated Wastelands (IWDP), Drought Prone Areas Programme (DPAP) and Desert Development Programme (DDP) initiated to generate employment opportunities in rural India. Further, the Government has recently enacted the National Rural Employment Guarantee Act to provide 100 days guaranteed employment to rural households. Though these initiatives have contributed in reducing the rural unemployment problem, the problem of employment insecurity needs to be addressed in a wider context and solved at.
- *Income Security*: Though income and number of days of employment are positively related, this relationship holds good mainly for organised workers. As for as unorganised workers are concerned, their income is highly influenced by nature of job, nature and type of products produced quantum of value addition, market value, competition, etc. To protect from the crop loss, Crop Insurance Scheme is available. But for various other self-employed enterprises and other jobs, there is no security available to realise income for the efforts.
- *Life and Accident Security*: The death of a worker in a family is a great loss to the entire family and it adds burden too. The death of a worker raises the question of survival of the family left behind due to the permanent loss of income to the family. Similarly, an accident is a major problem for an informal worker since it leads to loss of income and cost of treatment. If the accident leads to permanent or partial disability, the financial loss will be severe and

unimaginable. By covering the unorganized workers under the Insurance schemes of individual, family and group could alone provide security for life and accident.

- *Old Age Security*: The workers of the unorganised sector face the problem of insecurity when they reach to the life stage of aged when they could not work for themselves. The question of dependency is a major threat to the old age unorganised workers in the context of disappearing joint family system.

CONCLUSION

In the discussion, an attempt has been made to understand the nature and growth of unorganised workers, the initiatives of social security towards unorganised workers and to highlight the needs of the unorganised workers on social security aspects. The analysis of secondary information available from the Census and National Sample Survey Organisation revealed that the unorganised workers account for about 93 per cent of the total workforce and there is a steady growth in it over years. It was also observed that the unorganised workers would expand further due to globalisation. It was argued that India had a long tradition of social security and social assistance system directed particularly towards the more vulnerable parts of society.

The institution of self sufficient village communities, the system of common property resources, the system of joint families and the practice of making endowments for religious and charitable provided the required social security and assistance to the needy and poor of the nation. These informal arrangements of social security measures underwent steady and inevitable erosion. It was argued that even after independence, the State was concerned more with the problems of industrial and organised work force and neglected the rural and unorganized labour force on social security matters to a greater extent, till recent past. The social security initiatives of the Centre, State and NGO's indicated that the needs are much more than the supports provided and the efforts must be targeted and vast enough to cover the growing unorganised workers. In this context, it is argued that the major security needs of the unorganised workers are food security, nutritional security, health security, housing security, employment security, income security, life and accident security, and old age security. In sum, the study calls for a Comprehensive, Universal and Integrated Social Security System for the unorganised workers in India.

9

Expanding Women's Employment Opportunities

INTRODUCTION

Employment is critical for poverty reduction and for enhancing women's status. However, it is potentially empowering and liberating only if it provides women an opportunity to improve their well being and enhance their capabilities. On the other hand, if it is driven by distress and is low-paying then it may only increase a woman's drudgery. To understand women's work status in India's rural areas and to examine the trends and nature of women's employment, this paper analyses the data from large scale national surveys. The National Sample Survey Organisation carries out quinquennial surveys on employment and unemployment and covers more than 100,000 households and 500,000 individuals throughout the country.

The survey covers socio-economic and demographic characteristics, employment and unemployment charac-teristics, and provides information on wages. The latest year for which data is available for both surveys is 2004-05. The National Family Health Survey covers households with women in the reproductive age group of 15-49 and in the latest survey carried out in 2005-06; it covered 63,896 women in this age group. The authors' estimates from the NSS surveys of 1983, 1993-94, and 2004-05 and the NFHS survey of 2005-06 are based on analysis of unit level data. In addition, we have also drawn on data on women's control on agricultural holdings from the agricultural census, a large scale survey conducted by the Ministry of Agriculture, Government of India, as well as other sources of information such as national income data from the Central Statistical Organisation. The paper is organised in six parts.

The next part analyses work participation rates for women by socio economic characteristics such as caste, religion, education, and economic status. The participation of women in the agricultural and nonagricultural sectors and their categorisation by employment status. Some of the correlates of workforce participation including education and poverty. The determinants of women's work participation and the factors that influence their participation in different kinds of employment are explored by means of regression. The last section concludes with an overview and suggestions for improving the position of women workers in rural areas.

WORKFORCE PARTICIPATION BY SOCIO-ECONOMIC CHARACTERISTICS

The notion of work and employment, especially for women, is complex. The reasons why women work in gainful activity, or whether they work part time or full time, can be diverse and may be rooted in a complex interplay of economic, cultural, social, and personal factors. In developing economies, workers combine multiple activities over different parts of the year. The NSSO defines a person who is employed for a major part of the year as being "Principal Status" employed. If gainfully employed only for a part of the year, she is described as being employed in the "Subsidiary Status". A person employed either in "Usual Principal Status" or "Usual Subsidiary Status" is enumerated as being employed in the "Usual Status".

Unless otherwise stated, the reference is to UPSS employment throughout this paper. The industry associated with her employment is the one which she is associated for a major part of the employment. We focus for the most part on rural employment, but also provide data on urban employment in order to highlight the contrasts. As in most other parts of the world, fewer women participate in employment in India compared to men. In 2004-05, while in urban areas, 16.6 per cent women and 54.9 per cent men were employed, in rural areas, these percentages were 32.7 and 54.6 respectively.

More women are employed only in the subsidiary status, than men, especially in rural areas. This can be explained by factors from the supply side as well as the demand side. Taking the former first, the rural economy has been largely stagnant over the years and employment opportunities have not grown. Most women, therefore, are able to get work for only a few months in the year. This keeps them employed only in the 'subsidiary status'. On the supply side, women's primary duties are supposed to be in the household. For economic reasons they have to work, but must do so in addition to their domestic responsibilities, and are therefore only able to enter the labour force as subsidiary workers.

Over a thirty-two year span, the workforce participation rate of males and females shows no systematic variation despite a larger percentage of persons in the younger age groups joining education. The only notable changes appear to be a small increase in male WPR after 1987-88 and that urban females recorded a higher employment rate in 2004-05 over all preceding rounds of the survey. This also shows that globalisation appears to have enlarged work opportunities for women in urban areas, but has had no impact in rural areas. Yet, there are large variations in women's participation in work across socio-economic groups and across regions and states in India which we shall presently discuss. While mainly economic factors determine a man's participation in employment, the forces that influence a woman's participation in work are many and diverse and include demographic, reproductive, social, religious and cultural factors. Figure shows that WPR is highest for scheduled tribe and scheduled caste women and lowest for women from the 'other' caste. The SCs and STs are the most marginalised parts in the economy and the most impoverished.

Women from these groups have higher WPRs because extreme poverty leaves them with little choice but to work, and because they do not face social taboos that disapprove of work. The converse is true for women from 'other' castes. When religious background is considered, Muslim women in rural areas have a significantly low WPR–nearly half the national rate for women of all religions. Once again it is social norms that restrict women's mobility and entry into the workforce that keep more Muslim women tied to hearth and home.

Does education propel women into employment? The gender differences in this respect are interesting and stark. For male workers, higher levels of education are indeed associated with higher WPR, both in rural and urban areas. But for women, WPR is higher for illiterate women than for women with higher levels of school education–a trend which reverses itself only for women with technical/vocational education or graduates. This again is a pattern which reveals itself both in rural and urban areas. Thus 51 per cent of illiterate men are employed but this percentage goes up to 71 per cent among men who have passed their higher secondary.

On the other hand, 39 per cent illiterate women are employed, but this percentage declines to just 25 per cent among women who have passed higher secondary. Why? Multiple factors such as the compulsion for men to earn, the greater availability of jobs for men, and the restrictive social norms operating for women, appear to explain this pattern. It is interesting that in urban areas by contrast, women's employment goes up at higher educational levels and shows a pattern similar to that for men showing the narrowing of gender gaps in urban areas. How does economic status of women influence their participation in work? Indeed, the relationship between workforce participation and economic status of the household is critical for policy and programme interventions.

While the NSSO does not collect data on incomes, it provides data on monthly per capita consumption expenditure; a measure that is widely used as a proxy for the economic status of households. In this paper the authors have computed participation in employment across MPCE deciles groups from NSS unit records. These results are presented in Fig 4. Workforce participation shows a consistently declining trend with rising economic status for rural women, clearly reflecting on the economic distress that compels poor women to work. In contrast, for urban women, work participation shows a skewed v-shape, declining as economic status improves, but rises again with the highest consumption decile. The latter reflects on higher educational attainments of women associated with higher incomes, and the greater availability of employment opportunities in urban areas.

To conclude, women's participation in gainful work is lower compared to men; it is higher for scheduled caste and scheduled tribe women who are less restricted by social norms; among religious groups, work participation is lowest for Muslim women; education impacts differentially for men and women, with level of participation increasing with educational levels for men, but declining for rural women; as economic status improves, work participation declines for rural women suggesting that when there are no compelling economic reasons to earn, social taboos on women's mobility and participation in work exercise a strong influence. In general, while the gaps in work participation between men and women are clear and well recognised, the gaps between different classes of women hailing from different social and economic backgrounds are less well known and need to be understood for effective policy measures.

WOMEN'S EMPLOYMENT IN THE AGRICULTURAL AND NON-AGRICULTURAL SECTORS BY EMPLOYMENT STATUS

Within rural areas, work may be classified along two dimensions:

1. By sector, *viz.*, agriculture or non-agriculture, and
2. By employment status, that is whether a person is in regular employment, is self employed or is casually employed.

An analysis of women's employment by sector and employment status can tell us a great deal about the outcomes for women and if the work they do promotes their well being or is low-end, low paying and driven by distress. The distribution of workers by these cross cutting categories. What is the significance of this classification and what does it tell us about the nature and disparities in women's employment? This becomes clear that provides the percentage distribution of male and female workers in agriculture and non agriculture by employment status as well as the wages per day. It illustrates vividly the more disadvantaged position of women in the rural labour market. Firstly, wages are higher for men in all categories of employment.

The disparity is highest for regular workers in non-agriculture. Second, women are concentrated in agriculture where the wages are lowest. Thus 90 per cent women are in agriculture and only 10 per cent are in non-agriculture among casual labourers. Thirdly, there is a very low proportion of women in regular work where the wage rates are the highest, employment is more secure and working conditions are relatively better. This is the case both in agriculture and in non-agriculture. How does economic status relate to the nature of work that men and women do? Fig 5 makes this very clear. Along expected lines, the percentage of casual labourers among both male and female workers declines sharply with rising household MPCE deciles. The percentage of self-employed among workers shows an increasing trend with MPCE deciles, except for the highest deciles, where it dips. The share of regular workers is low throughout showing the scarcity of regular work; is negligible in the lower consumption deciles but rises in the highest deciles. For rural female workers, the share of the self-employed remains higher for each MPCE decile compared to male workers.

On the other hand women remain disadvantaged when it comes to regular work and as figure shows their access to regular work remains lower even as the economic status of households improves. Although the structure of employment by employment status has been remarkably constant across the years, previous NSS surveys showed some increase in casual labour in the rural male and female workforce and a decline in the share of the selfemployed. But during 1999/00-2004/05, there was a change in the trend; the share of selfemployed workers increased among both female and male workers, while the share of casual work declined. Why this has happened is difficult to say, but it is likely that the overall stagnation in agriculture and the rural economy may have led to this shift. The growth rate in agriculture and allied sectors was only little more than 2 per cent per annum in this period, registering a negative growth in some years.

This may have led to shrinking availability of wage work and compelled workers to eke out subsistence from self employment. The next part discusses women's employment in agriculture, while the subsequent part takes up women's employment in non-agriculture. In each, the three broad status of employment are analysed.

AGRICULTURE

In rural areas, nearly 84 per cent women workers are engaged in agriculture, either as cultivators or labourers as compared to 67 per cent male workers.The decline in the proportion of men as well as women in agriculture; but the decline is much sharper for men. There has been a kind of 'creeping feminisation' of agriculture; male workers have steadily moved out of agriculture while for women workers, this movement has been extremely tardy. Men have entered into more diversified occupations in non-agriculture, while women have largely tended to remain in agriculture that has been largely stagnant.

In 1972-93, 83.2 per cent male workers and 89.7 per cent female workers were engaged in agriculture. By 2004-05, only 66.5 per cent male workers were in agriculture compared to 83.3 per cent female workers. This has to be seen in the context of the fact that returns to labour are, on average, higher in non-agriculture than in agriculture, although the size of assets operated and type of employment, among other factors, are also relevant. One implication of the above slow change is that a significant proportion of the incremental female workforce gets engaged in agriculture. Between 1983 and 2004-05, nearly 72 per cent of the incremental rural female workforce was absorbed in agriculture, compared to 40 per cent for the male workforce.

Casual Workers

Compared to 23.2 per cent male rural workers, 29.2 per cent female rural workers were engaged as casual agricultural labourers in 2004-05. There is a disproportionate concentration of the most deprived social groups in this form of labour. Half of the female casual labourers and 43 per cent of male casual labourers in India belong to SCs and STs, nearly twice their share in population. Women agricultural casual workers form a distinct category: they are disadvantaged in many ways. There is significant gender segmentation of operations in agriculture. While men predominate in activities such as ploughing and harvesting, women predominate in weeding, transplanting and inter-culture. The wages are uniformly lower in all female dominant operations.

Overall women's wages are estimated at 69 per cent of male wages in 2004-05. Moreover, women also get fewer days of work. Further, women workers rarely get the minimum wages stipulated by the government: more than 95 per cent of female agricultural wage workers received wages lower than the minimum wage. The deprivation of casual workers is aggravated by the fact that not only are their lower than wages in non-agriculture; they have also grown at a lower rate in the recent period, thereby increasing the gap. Moreover, as already pointed out, women workers who work as casual labourers are able to get work for only part of the year–their estimated employment days was only 184.

Women agricultural labourers are also unemployed for more days a year than their male counterparts. The unemployment rate for agricultural labourers is quite high in rural areas by any standard; 16 per cent for men and 17 per cent for women for 2004-05 by the Current Daily Status criterion and this increased over 1993/94-2004/05.

Self Employed Workers

As noted earlier, women workers are increasingly engaged as self-employed in agriculture. There has been a steady increase in the numbers of both women and men farmers over all years since 1983 except 1999-00. The sharpest increase has taken place in the recent quinquennium when the share of women farmers increased to 41.8 per cent, the highest in 32 years. These results attest to the large role played by women farmers although they do not confirm a systematic trend towards feminization. Such a large presence of women farmers requires systematic public support to them, which is lacking mainly because women are not seen as principal producers in agriculture and because they do not have ownership or control over the assets on which they work. The poor support to women farmers has been highlighted in several studies and reports, notably Planning Commission and NCEUS. Srivastava et al., 2007, have shown that despite legislative changes few women have control over land. However, the Agricultural Census provides information on operational holdings, that is, agricultural holdings operated and controlled by men and women, whether or not they are owned by them. According to the Agricultural Census 2000-01, only 11.6 per cent of cultivated agricultural land holdings covering 9.1 per cent area were operated by women.

There is a systematic decline in the percentage of land holdings and area controlled by women as the size of holding increases. In the smallest size class the percentage of land holdings operated by women was 13.4 whereas the area operated by them was 12 per cent. In large holdings, the corresponding percentages declined to 5.7 and 5.6 respectively. These figures could partly be explained by the pattern of outmigration since it is in smaller holdings where male outmigration is also likely to be higher.

However, cultural and social factors are also very important in explaining the fact that a miniscule proportion of women have control on this critical resource. This is brought out by the regional pattern of women's control over land holdings. The percentage of such holdings was much higher in the more progressive Southern states and in some of the North-eastern states. In Kerala women operated 21 per cent of the land holdings and 18 per cent of area. In Andhra Pradesh the corresponding figures were 20 per cent and 17 per cent respectively while in Tamil Nadu they were 18.1 per cent and 15.1 respectively. In the absence of land titles, women farmers have much smaller access to institutional credit compared to male farmers, and receive a much lower degree of institutional support.

NON-AGRICULTURE

Casual Workers

Wages of casual workers estimated from the 2004-05 NSSO Survey show that female wages are lower than male wages across all industry groups. The relative male-female wage gap is larger in non-agriculture where female casual workers earn 65 per cent of male wages. In manufacturing, female wages are only 59 per cent of male wages. The low wages of female workers are principally due to the undervaluation of work and skills in activities in which women predominate. Thus the segmentation of women workers in certain types of activities largely determines the gender gap which exists.

A number of national and international studies have documented the sex-typing of occupations. In India, this has been noted in a number of industries such as knitwear and garments. These jobs provided limited opportunity for upward mobility. Such segregation can also be found in the services sector.

In the health and education sectors, women are concentrated at the lower end as paramedics, teachers in lower grades, or support staff. The hierarchy of jobs within manufacturing or services is then used to value the jobs where women are concentrated as low skilled workers even if it involves exceptional talent and years of informal training.

Self-employed Workers

As we have noted earlier, the self-employed workers are not a homogeneous group. They fall into three sub-groups. The first are the 'employers'. The second are the 'own account workers', and the third group is constituted by the 'helpers' who assisted the main family workers in an unpaid capacity. A significant percentage of self-employed women workers are classified as helpers *i.e.,* they are recognised only as auxiliary workers and this percentage is much larger than among male self-employed workers in nonagriculture among whom 15.2 per cent are classified as unpaid workers. Further, while one of the stated advantages of self-employment for women is that this work can be done based at home and women can work at their pace and convenience, this results in multiple disadvantages in the form of limited opportunities, seclusion, and lower earnings.

Female Proprietary Enterprises

The NSSO informal enterprises survey, 1999-2000, provides a profile of female and male proprietary enterprises. The survey found that about 12 per cent of proprietary enterprises were operated by women and these were mainly own account enterprises.

Approximately 10 per cent of the workers in proprietary enterprises were engaged in the female proprietary enterprises. A distinction is made between Own Account Enterprises employing no hired labour and Establishments which hire one or more labourers. In general, urban enterprises are larger in size, and for the same category, female proprietary enterprises are smaller than male proprietary enterprises.

In rural areas, female proprietary enterprises are very small in size, with an average fixed investment of less than ₹8000, while female establishments had a total fixed asset base of ₹123,786. The gross value added per worker was less than ₹000 per annum, while in the latter it was slightly more than ₹26,000 per year.

Among rural female OAEs, about 34 per cent of them have value of fixed assets of less than ₹1000, while only 7 per cent had value of assets greater than ₹25000. Not only are few women involved in running non-agricultural enterprises of any kind, the scale of operation of women operated units is distinctly very tiny particularly in rural areas. Compared to the National Minimum Wage, 89 per cent of female OAEs and 42 per cent of male OAEs gave lower imputed daily returns.

Home Workers

Nearly 81 per cent of rural female enterprises and 39.5 per cent of male enterprises operated from home in 1999-00 *i.e.* they were home based enterprises. About 40 per cent of these enterprises in rural areas work on sub-contracted basis *i.e.* their workers were homeworkers as defined by the ILO. Home-workers work at the lowest end of a value chain, usually dealing with petty contractors, on whom they depend for supply of work, raw material and sale of finished goods. This dependence on the contractor together with the isolation undermines their ability to bargain for higher piece-rates, timely payments or overtime pay. The annual gross value addition of the rural female home-workers is, on average, ₹5270, much lower than even the ₹ 9000 that accrues in female OAEs. The average value of fixed assets engaged by them is also very low at ₹3800. About 79 per cent of the women and 63 per cent of the male home workers were paid on a piece-rate basis. This wage has many hidden costs, including use of the house and electricity, delayed payments, and arbitrary cuts in wages on the pretext of poor quality..

Regular Workers

Female regular workers in rural areas form a very small part of the female workforce as also of the total proportion of regular workers in rural areas.They are mainly concentrated in education, manufacturing, private households, health and social work and public administration. Work in private household earns women the lowest wages of ₹39 per day, followed by employment in hotels and restaurants, manufacturing, and agriculture. While the sectors with the highest daily remuneration, such as electricity gas and water, transport; financial intermediation; and real estate employ very few women on a regular basis, among the sectors where a larger proportion of women take up employment, education and health sectors afford reasonable daily earnings. The daily earnings of women regular/salaried workers are more than twice as high as women casual workers.

However, within regular work, as with casual work, there is a large gap in male-female earnings across most sectors, ranging from a female-male earning ratio of 0.3 in mining to 0.87 in construction. Even in the social sectors, there is a large gap in earnings, with this ratio being as low as 0.59 in education and 0.69 in health and social work. Women workers in these sectors tend to be concentrated in the lower segments–as paramedics, support staff, contract teachers or teachers in low grades.

CORRELATES OF POVERTY AND VULNERABILITY FOR WOMEN WORKERS

So far, this paper has discussed various dimensions of employment of rural women without relating them to the poverty status of the women workers. We now briefly draw attention to the characteristics of women workers and poverty levels in rural India. We have used the official poverty line as a benchmark, but have categorised the population into six groups following the methodology adopted by NCEUS. Consumption characteristics and social development levels, of households have been divided as follows: 1. Extremely Poor: up to 0.75 PL; 2. Poor: Between 0.75Pl and PL; 3. Marginal Poor: Between PL and 1.25 PL; 4. Vulnerable: between 1.25 PL and 2 PL; 5. Middle: Between 2 PL and 4PL; 6. Higher Income: The four lower categories have together been characterised as "Poor and Vulnerable".While the percentage of casual workers declines rapidly with improving economic status, the percentage of regular workers is only high in the last category.

The Self-employed have a presence in all economic categories, but are more predominant as economic well being improves. In terms of industrial composition, it can be seen that while agricultural workers are present in all categories in a large proportion, their weight declines in the highest while that of tertiary sector workers increases. It can also be seen that workers with higher levels of education are almost entirely present in the higher economic categories. Since education plays a critical role, this has been analysed in greater detail below. One of the major attributes of women engaged in agriculture is their low level of educational attainment. With the ongoing commercialisation of agriculture, crop diversification, introduction of new technologies and the imperative for better information processing, education has to be reckoned as a key input in any attempt at overall development and modernization of agriculture. However, the grim picture is that about 86 per cent of female agricultural labourers and 74 per cent of female farmers are either illiterate or have education below the primary level. Shocking as it may seem, the average education of a female agricultural labourer was less than one year in 2004-05.

DETERMINANTS OF WOMEN'S WORKFORCE PARTICIPATION

In this part the determinants of participation of rural women in employment is analysed by use of regression analysis. In the absence of a single data set containing all the relevant variables, this paper first does a Logistic Regression based on unit records of the NSS Employment-Unemployment Survey of 2004-05; this is followed by a similar analysis using the unit data records of another large-scale survey, *viz.* the National Family Health Survey of 2005-06 which also has information on women's autonomy using certain indicators. As both these analyses confirm significant differences across states/regions, an analysis using state level variables is also carried out.

DETERMINANTS OF PARTICIPATION IN EMPLOYMENT USING NSS DATA

The analysis attempts an explanation not only of why women participate in the workforce, but also why they participate in specific types of employment. The independent variables used are: age group, marital status, education status, caste group, religion, presence of children under 5 years, land holding size category, monthly per capita consumption quintile, and region. As mentioned earlier, Logistic Regression is used since the model does not make distributional assumptions on the predictors, which can be both continuous and discrete.

Agriculture: Determinants of Work Participation

As one would expect, possession of land has a very important influence on a woman's participation in employment. Controlling for land, the household's consumption level has a negative influence. Among the individual characteristics, it is seen that compared to women in the age group 15-29, older women have a higher probability of participating in work and women in the age group 30-44 have the highest odds ratio. Compared to never married women, married, divorced and separated women have a higher probability of participating in work, with divorced or separated women having the highest odds ratio. Compared to illiterate women, women with higher levels of education have a lower probability of being in the workforce. The odds ratio declines with rising levels of education, recouping somewhat only for women who are diploma holders or graduates. Compared to scheduled tribes, all other caste groups have lower probability of participating in work, with higher castes having the lowest probability. Muslim women have a much lower probability of being in the workforce compared to Hindu women. Finally women in all other regions have significantly higher probability are being in the workforce compared to those in the eastern region.

Agriculture: Casual Workers

In this case, younger women workers have the highest probability of working as casual agricultural labourers. The marital status variable is not significant. Scheduled caste women workers have a significantly higher odds ratio of being an agricultural labourer and this probability declines steeply with rising levels of education, for Muslims and for women workers with young children. Casual agriculture wage status for workers is much less probable for women workers possessing larger holdings and in higher consumption quintiles.

Agriculture: Self-employed workers

The highest proportion of women workers are engaged as self-employed in agriculture. The probability of a woman worker being self-employed in agriculture is highest for the high age group and for currently married women. The odds ratio are lower for divorced or separated women indicating that these women no longer have access to land. The odds ratio declines with increasing levels for education and is the lowest for women workers who are graduates or diploma holders. SC women workers who have the lowest access to land also have the lowest probability of being self-employed in agriculture. Muslim women workers again are less likely to be engaged in farming. As one may expect the probability of engaging in agriculture increases sharply with bigger landholdings and also with higher levels of household consumption. Women workers n the Northern region have the highest probability of being engaged in agriculture as self-employed, while women workers in the Southern region have the lowest probability of being so engaged.

Non-agriculture: Determinants of Work Participation

Since female workers have largely remained confined to agriculture, the characteristics of workers who have moved out of agriculture are of great interest. Any type of worker in non-agriculture is taken up first. The probability of being a non-agricultural worker is highest for women in the age group 30-44 than for workers in the youngest age group and is lower for currently married women. It rises sharply with increasing levels of education. Compared to illiterate women workers, those with secondary education have an odds ratio of 4.787 while those with graduate or vocational education have an odds ratio exceeding 30. Compared to ST women workers, all other social groups have significantly higher odds ratios, the highest being for "other" caste women. Muslim workers are more than twice as likely to participate in non-agricultural work. The odds ratio declines with increasing size of land holding and is significantly higher than one for women workers belonging to the highest consumption quintile.

Non-agriculture: Wage workers

Non agricultural wage workers are younger and either unmarried or divorced women. The odds ratio is 0.58 for the highest age group and 0.61 for currently married women workers. The odds ratio steadily declines with higher levels of education. While there is no significant difference across social groups, Muslims have a significantly lower than 1 odds ratio. These ratios also decline dramatically with higher land holdings. The consumption level has a smaller influence on this variable but the odds ratio is significantly lower than one for the highest quintile. Compared to the reference region, the West and the North both have significantly lower odds ratios.

Non-agriculture: Self Employed Workers

The probability of being self-employed is higher among young women workers and those who have never married. The odds ratio is significantly lower among currently married and widowed women workers. Education of the worker increases the probability of taking up self-employment, but the highest odds ratio are for those with secondary or higher secondary level of education. All social groups have higher odds ratio compared to the reference group and for the Muslim women workers, the odds ratio is more than twice as high as Hindu workers. This is principally due to the hereditary involvement of these workers' households in artisanal activities. Odds ratio declines steadily with increasing possession of land and is significantly higher than one only for the second quintile in terms of household MPCE. Women workers in the Eastern region have the highest probability of being so employed.

Non-agriculture: Regular Workers

This is the smallest segment of workers among rural women. Compared to the reference groups, the odds ratio is higher for higher aged women and for widowed/separated women. It increases dramatically with increasingly levels of education. Among social groups it is significantly lower than 1 for OBC and upper caste women workers. The odds ratio falls with increasing size of holding and is significantly higher than one for the highest quintile. The regressions bring out a number of interesting relationships between individual, household and regional characteristics in rural India. First, possession of land is naturally a very strong determinant of the participation of women in work and particularly their employment as women farmers. Controlling for land, the household's consumption status raises the possibility of a woman worker being self-employed either in agriculture or nonagriculture, but reduces this possibility in all other cases. It may be noted that these cases would require the worker to be employed outside the home where cultural and social roles begin to play a bigger role. Muslim women not only have a significantly lower than one odds ratio overall, this also holds for all types of employment except non-agricultural selfemployment.

As far as social/caste groups are concerned, our reference is the Scheduled Tribes among whom access to land and common property resources is much higher than that for SCs which accounts for their high WPR, the odds ratio for this being the lowest among upper castes. For the same reason, SCs have the highest odds ratio for participating in agricultural wage employment, as one might expect. In non-agriculture, overall STs have the lowest probability of participation, followed by SCs, OBC and upper castes. The surprising result is that among workers, upper castes and OBCs have a lower likelihood of participation in regular work than SC/ST, controlling for all the other factors. Considering the three demographic variables, the last has the smallest influence of participation in any/all type of work. Currently married women have a lower likelihood of working outside of homes, while single women are likelier to participate in self-employment. Other than this widowed and separated women have a higher likelihood of participating in most types of work. Other than land, education appears to be the most important determinant of employment status. Participation in the workforce as well as participation in wage employment declines with level of education, while the likelihood of participation in non-agricultural work as a whole, as well in self-employment or regular work increases with rising levels of education. From these regressions, it is apparent that while the level of education may not positively influence a woman's participation in work, for women who are in the workforce, education is indicated as the most important determinant of better quality non-agricultural work. It must be emphasised again that we are examining the outcome of social, cultural and economic processes.

The potential availability of work is highest in rural areas for women whose households possess a measure of adequate landholdings. But even here, actual participation may be determined by socio-cultural factors as is evident from our results. The absence of education relegates women workers to wage work, whereas having education improves their chances of being in non-agricultural self-employment or regular work, with the latter mainly requiring higher education qualifications. Participation in wage work or non-agriculture also requires a greater measure of autonomy for women, confining the rest principally to self-employment in agriculture.

DETERMINANTS OF PARTICIPATION IN EMPLOYMENT USING NFHS, 2005-06 DATA

The National Family Health Survey has been carried out in India periodically since 1992-93. The latest round of results are available from the third round carried out in 2005-06. The NFHS collects detailed information on socioeconomic, reproductive and health characteristics of women in the age group 15-49, along with certain health and other characteristics of young children and the spouses of the women interviewed. Since the focus of the survey is on women in the reproductive age group, compared to the NSS, which covers the entire population, the NFHS gives the characteristics of a truncated age group of women.

The employment characteristics of these women are captured in the survey but not in the same manner or depth as the NSS. The survey enquires whether women are currently working or have worked in the last year. It also asks whether they work for family production or paid. The women workers are classified as per their occupational categories. Logistic regression is used to estimate the influence of several variables on participation in employment, by status and industry so that the types of employment participation considered are similar to those in the NSS analysis. But it should be noted that the NFHS does not distinguish between paid casual and regular/ salaried employment which are clubbed together. The main distinguishing feature of the NFHS, because of which this data set has been analysed in this paper, is that it collects information on women's autonomy using a number of indicators.

Among these indicators, it used a set of three indicators to capture women's freedom of mobility which in our view is central to their participation in the labour market. The three indicators of women's mobility are if they are allowed to go alone to the market/ health facility/ or outside the village or community. The variables are similar to those used in earlier analysis, but with the following significant differences. First, this data has a younger age cohort. Second, as mentioned earlier, employment has been measured differently in this survey.

Third, the NSS does not provide information on how many children a woman has, though it does give the number of children in a household. With NFHS data it is possible to identify the mothers with young children. Fourthly, this paper uses the synthetic wealth indicator given by NFHS which is built on a factor analytic score based on 33 assets. Finally, the NFHS does not allow us to estimate consumption expenditure as in the case of the NSSO and hence this variable has been dropped from the analysis. These results are similar to the earlier results in many basic ways and are not discussed here. Attention is drawn only to fresh findings. Three main conclusions emerge sharply from the analysis. First, the role of education is delineated more sharply among this age cohort of women.

Increasing levels of education increases the possibility of women being in non-agricultural vocations. This result holds separately, both for self-employment as well as for paid work. Second, women's autonomy, proxied here by their ability to make mobility decisions autonomously, significantly increases the probability of their participation in all types of employment, except agricultural self-employment. The reason for this is that whether it is in low paid work as casual labour or better paid work as regular workers, both take women out of the confines of the house and therefore require women to have freedom of mobility.

However, where women do not have this freedom and are constrained by social norms to the home, but still need to work, self employment provides the answer. Third, women with young children are most likely to be working as self employed in agriculture and least likely to be employed as paid workers or in non-agriculture. This suggests the urgent need to provide early child care and crèche facilities for rural women.

DETERMINANTS OF STATE LEVEL VARIATIONS IN EMPLOYMENT PARTICIPATION

The large state-wise and regional difference in rural female employment participation in India has been alluded to earlier. The logit regressions confirm these differences but the NSSO data set gives very limited measures of socio-cultural differences. We therefore explore the impact of additional variables, gleaned from other data sources such as the National Family Health Survey, the Agricultural Census, the Central Statistical Organisation, and the National

Bank for Rural Development on state-level variations in female employment. The total and sectoral workforce participation rates across twenty states in 2004-05. The WPRs by employment status and sector are also presented. Total WPRs are high in some of the Southern, Western and Hill states. They are the lowest in the Eastern states. There are important sectoral differences. For example, states such as Kerala, West Bengal and Orissa which have low total WPRs show a high participation of women in non-agriculture and the highest participation rate of women in regular work is in Kerala. The state level values of the other variables, as well the correlation between the variables.

It is anticipated that these differences could be a result of supply related characteristics such as:

- The percentage of SC/ST households in a state;
- Mean years of education of women,
- Variables which could proxy women's autonomy to undertake economic activity;
- Rural wages; or
- Employment demand.

Since our objective is to understand not only total work force participation rates, but also women's participation in specific types of work, especially in non-agriculture, these rates are regressed for 20 states across the variables, selecting only one variable. The 'best' fits are presented below. Some of the independent variables that were considered were found to be highly correlated, in particular with Mean Years of Education and were dropped from the analysis. Fewer numbers of variables have therefore been tested and used in the regression analysis. These are briefly discussed below.

- *Total WPR*: The share of SC/ST in the total population is highly significant variable. A one per cent increase in the share of SC/ST in the population would increase total WPR by one per cent. Share of women operated holdings in total is also marginally significant. The Mean Years of education of the population is not significant.
- *WPR in non-agriculture*: The Mean Years of Education of the female population and the density of Self-help Groups are both significant variables. Increase in Mean Years of Education would increase the WPR of women in non-agricultural vocations by 1.35.
- *WPR in non-farm self-employment*: The only variable significant in this case is the state Density of Self-help groups. The Mean Educational attainment of women in a state is not a significant determinant of state level variation of WPR in non-farm self-employment.
- *WPR in non-agricultural wage work*: Mean Years of education and Share of area operated by women are both significant variables. A one level increase in education would increase the WPR in non-agricultural wage work by 0.81. The coefficient of share of area operated by women is 0.21.

- *WPR in non-agricultural regular/salaried work*: Mean Years of education is a highly significant variable; one level increase in education would increase the WPR in regular/salaried work by 0.82. The share of area in holdings operated by women is also significant but only at 10 per cent level of significance. The coefficient of this variable is quite low.
- *Discussion*: The share of SC/ST in the population emerges as the only significant variable in explaining inter-state variation in total rural female WPR. However, interstate variations in WPR in non-agriculture as a whole, as well as participation in non-agricultural wage labour are determined by the average educational level of the female population and by variables which reflect women's economic autonomy and control over resources. However, education is not a significant variable in explaining the inter-state variations in participation by women in nonagricultural self-employment, but here also their autonomous participation in self-help groups is an important determinant. It has already been noted that the regression analysis has been able to incorporate demand side factors to a very limited extent. This probably accounts for the fact the adjusted Coefficient of Determinations are on the low side. Nevertheless, these results which focus on state level variation reinforce the results and bring out the role of education and women's autonomy in promoting women's employment outside agriculture.

CONCLUSION

While women workers in general constitute a marginalised category within the class of workers, rural women workers occupy a lower position compared to their urban counterparts, and the lowest layer among them is constituted by those belonging to the bottom strata of the society *i.e.* SCs and STs. Women's time use in economic activities that give them a return is limited but their participation in household activities that indirectly contribute to the economic output of the household far exceeds that of men. But women have lower work participation rates in SNA activities. For rural women these are higher than urban women but also closer to men. These rates are also higher for women belonging to SCs/STs than the other women.

A significant percentage of rural women workers are engaged in subsidiary status work. An important argument in this paper is that higher work participation rates per se do not indicate a higher level of welfare. Only when higher work participation rates are accompanied by higher educational capabilities and/or asset and income, higher work participation rates become meaningful from a welfare and, especially, income point of view. We show that rural women workers are concentrated in agriculture to a much larger extent than men.

On the other hand, a much smaller proportion among them work in nonagricultural jobs, particularly the more valued regular/salaried jobs. The conditions of work, especially of women wage worker, are quite dismal. Women workers are also subjected to various forms of discrimination including job-typing which gives them a lower wage compared to men. Among the women wage workers, a proportion of those who report regular employment also work in poor conditions, receiving low wages with long hours of work, no social security and very few holidays. The position of self-employed women in non-agriculture is also poor. Their capital base is low and consequently their value addition is also low. One third of them operate from their own homes.

The overall picture that emerges is one of greater disadvantage for women workers in general and those belonging to rural as well as SCs/STs in particular. Apart from inherited social disadvantages in a patriarchal structure, the other important contributory factors are a limited access to assets and other resources, and low level of education and skills. We show that women with low levels of education and autonomous mobility whose households operate land are concentrated in agriculture as self-employed. Poorer women who lack land but have some degree of mobility are concentrated in agricultural wage work which pays most poorly. All types of non-agricultural work require, on average, relatively more education and some degree of autonomy.

The more valued jobs require a greater quantum of these. We show that these variables also determine the variations in women's participation in the more valued jobs outside agriculture. The poor status of rural women in terms of their autonomy and control over assets, and low level of education and employable skills calls for interventions of a promotional nature from different entry points.

In this concluding part we draw attention to some of the major issues which emerge from our analysis:

- A higher level of education and employable skills for women workers is a sine qua nom for improving their levels of productivity and enabling them to move into nonagricultural vocations. The emphasis on universalising elementary education has undoubtedly narrowed the enrolment gap between men and women, but given the low levels of education and employable skills and the gap between men and women workers, initiatives should also focus on the exiting workforce. Further, as the results of this paper and the evidence from other studies shows, break point occurs when women and men acquire a higher secondary level of education, enabling them to enter higher quality jobs.
- Women's autonomy, measured here in terms of access to land and control over its operation, mobility, and willingness to join self-help groups affects their ability to access resources and improve

productivity, and also to move into non-agricultural vocations. Such autonomy responds to a complex set of social factors. But policy initiatives can move the frontier outwards and can improve women's access to knowledge, technology and resources, empowering them as economic agents. Fostering a group approach, drawing upon some of the existing experiences documented by FAO and Indian experiences can help to overcome many of the existing asymmetries.

- The bulk of women workers remain in agriculture as farmers and the most recent figures indicate an increase in their proportion among farmers. As shown by a Planning Commission Sub-group and by NCEUS, they are regarded as peripheral producers and are marginal recipients of benefits of government programmes and from development and credit institutions. There is a strong need for a gender sensitive agricultural strategy which strengthens the role of women workers in all aspects of agriculture.
- Labour market segmentation and discrimination has kept the returns to women workers low, in most cases well below the legal minimum. The analysis in this paper supports the creation of a body which can examine the issue of valuation of women's work in those activities in which women predominate in fixing minimum wages in casual wage work as well as home based work. This is in line with a recent proposal made by the National Commission for Enterprises in the Unorganised Sector which has asked for the creation of a Skill Certification Council. The Commission has also recommended a tri-partite dispute settlement framework which can help to enforce non-discriminatory practices in the informal labour market in India.
- Finally, rural women workers, especially agricultural labourers, have high rates of unemployment and underemployment among women workers. These workers also receive abysmally low wages for a variety of reasons. The National Rural Employment Guarantee Programme which has been initiated in 2006 and which has now been extended to all rural areas can play a major role in improving demand for women's labour, increasing reservation wages, and setting labour standards in rural areas. While some impact has already been felt in a number of areas, much more needs to be done to implement this scheme effectively and to increase opportunities for quality and decent work in rural areas. In our view this programme constitutes the axis around which the employment conditions of the poorest women workers can improve in rural India.

10

Groups and Power

SOCIAL GROUPS

A social group consists of two or more people who interact with one another and who recognize themselves as a distinct social unit. The definition is simple enough, but it has significant implications. Frequent interaction leads people to share values and beliefs. This similarity and the interaction cause them to identify with one another. Identification and attachment, in turn, stimulate more frequent and intense interaction. Each group maintains solidarity with all to other groups and other types of social systems. Groups are among the most stable and enduring of social units.

They are important both to their members and to the society at large. Through encouraging regular and predictable behaviour, groups form the foundation upon which society rests. Thus, a family, a village, a political party a trade union is all social groups. These, it should be noted are different from social classes, status groups or crowds, which not only lack structure but whose members are less aware or even unaware of the existence of the group. These have been called quasi-groups or groupings. Nevertheless, the distinction between social groups and quasi-groups is fluid and variable since quasi-groups very often give rise to social groups, as for example, social classes give rise to political parties.

PRIMARY GROUPS

If all groups are important to their members and to society, some groups are more important than others. Early in the twentieth century, Charles H. Cooley gave the name, primary groups, to those groups that he said are characterized by intimate face-to-face association and those are fundamental in the development and continued adjustment of their members. He identified three basic primary groups, the family, the child's play group, and the neighborhoods or community among adults. These groups, he said, are almost universal in all societies; they give to people their earliest and most complete experiences of social unity; they are instrumental in the development of the social life; and they promote the integration of their members in the larger society. Since Cooley wrote, over 65 years ago, life in the United States has become much more urban, complex, and impersonal, and the family play group and neighborhood have become less dominant features of the social order. Secondary groups, characterized by anonymous, impersonal, and instrumental relationships, have become much more numerous. People move frequently, often from one part of the country to another and they change from established relationships and promoting widespread loneliness. Young people, particularly, turn to drugs, seek communal living groups and adopt deviant lifestyles in attempts to find meaningful primary-group relationships. The social context has changed so much so that primary group relationship today is not as simple as they were in Cooley's time.

SECONDARY GROUPS

An understanding of the modern industrial society requires an understanding of the secondary groups. The social groups other than those of primary groups may be termed as secondary groups. They are a residual category. They are often called special interest groups.Maclver and Page refers to them as great associations.

They are of the opinion that secondary groups have become almost inevitable today. Their appearance is mainly due to the growing cultural complexity. Primary groups are found predominantly in societies where life is relatively simple. With the expansion in population and territory of a society however interests become diversified and other types of relationships which can be called secondary or impersonal become necessary. Interests become differentiated.

The services of experts are required. The new range of the interests demands a complex organization. Especially selected persons act on behalf of all and hence arises a hierarchy of officials called bureaucracy. These features characterize the rise of the modern state, the great corporation, the factory, the labor union, a university or a nationwide political party and so on. These are secondary groups.Ogburn and Nimkoff defines secondary groups as groups which provide experience lacking in intimacy. Frank D. Watson writes that the secondary group is larger and more formal,is specialized and direct in its contacts and relies more for unity and continuance upon the stability of its social organization than does the primary group.

Characteristics of Secondary Group

Dominance of Secondary Relations

Secondary groups are characterized by indirect, impersonal, contractual and non-inclusive relations. Relations are indirect because secondary groups are bigger in size and members may not stay together. Relations are contractual in the sense they are oriented towards certain interests

Largeness of the Size

Secondary groups are relatively larger in size. City, nation, political parties, trade unions and corporations, international associations are bigger in size. They may have thousands and lakhs of members. There may not be any limit to the membership in the case of some secondary groups.

Membership

Membership in the case of secondary groups is mainly voluntary. Individuals are at liberty to join or to go away from the groups. However there are some secondary groups like the state whose membership is almost involuntary.

No Physical Basis

Secondary groups are not characterized by physical proximity. Many secondary groups are not limited to any definite area. There are some secondary groups like the Rotary Club and Lions Club which are international in character. The members of such groups are scattered over a vast area. Specific ends or interest: Secondary groups are formed for the realization of some specific interests or ends. They are called special interest groups. Members are interested in the groups because they have specific ends to aim at. Indirect communication: Contacts and communications in the case of secondary groups are mostly indirect. Mass media of communication such as radio, telephone, television, newspaper, movies, magazines and post and telegraph are resorted to by the members to have communication. Communication may not be quick and effective even. Impersonal nature of social relationships in secondary groups is both the cause and the effect of indirect communication.

Nature of Group Control

Informal means of social control are less effective in regulating the relations of members. Moral control is only secondary. Formal means of social control such as law, legislation, police, court etc are made of to control the behaviour of members. The behaviour of the people is largely influenced and controlled by public opinion, propaganda, rule of law and political ideologies. Group structure: The secondary group has a formal structure. A formal authority is set up with designated powers and a clear-cut division of labor in which the function of each is specified in relation to the function of all. Secondary groups are mostly organized groups. Different statuses and roles that the members assume are specified. Distinctions based on caste, colour, religion, class, language etc are less rigid and there is greater tolerance towards other people or groups.

Limited Influence on Personality

Secondary groups are specialized in character. People involvement in them is also of limited significance. Member's attachment to them is also very much limited. Further people spend most of their time in primary groups than in secondary groups. Hence secondary groups have very limited influence on the personality of the members.

GROUP DYNAMICS

GROUP FORMATION

A group is able to share experiences, to provide feedback, to pool ideas, to generate insights, and provide an arena for analysis of experiences. The group provides a measure of support and reassurance. Moreover, as a group, learners may also plan collectively for change action. Group discussion is a very effective learning method.

Participation

Participation is a fundamental process within a group, because many of the other processes depend upon participation of the various members. Levels and degrees of participation vary.

Some members are active participants while others are more withdrawn and passive. In essence, participation means involvement, concern for the task, and direct or indirect contribution to the group goal. If members do not participate, the group ceases to exist.

Factors which affect member's participation:

- The content or task of the group—is it of interest, importance and relevance?
- The physical atmosphere—is it comfortable physically, socially and psychologically?
- The psychological atmosphere—is it accepting, non-threatening?
- Member's personal preoccupations—are there any distracting thoughts in their mind?
- The level of interaction and discussions—is adequate information provided for everyone to understand? —is it at a level everyone understands?
- Familiarity—between group members- do members know each other from before?

Communication

Communication within a group deals with the spoken and the unspoken, the verbal and the non-verbal, the explicit and the implied messages that are conveyed and exchanged relating to information and ideas, and feelings. Two-way communication implies a situation where not only the two parties talk to each other, but that they are listening to each other as well.

It helps in:

- Clarification of doubts, confusions and misconceptions
- Both parties understanding each other
- Receiving and giving of feedback

It indicates the degree of respect between the two parties.

Helpful hints for effective communication:

- Have a circular seating arrangement so that everyone can see and interact with everyone else
- If there are two facilitators, they should sit apart so that communication flow is not in one direction
- Respect individuals- let everyone call everyone else by name respectfully
- Encourage and support the quiet members to voice their opinions
- Try and persuade the people who speak too much to give others a chance
- Ensure that only one person speaks at a time or no one else will be heard
- Discourage sub groups from indulging in side talk

Problem Solving

Most groups find themselves unable to solve problems because they address the problem at a superficial level. After that they find themselves blocked because they cannot figure out why the problem occurred and how they can tackle it.

Therefore an effective problem solving procedure would be to:

- *Clearly define the problem*: Is it what appears on the surface or are there deep hidden aspects?
- Try to thoroughly explore and understand the causes behind the problem
- Collect additional information, from elsewhere if necessary, and analyse it to understand the problem further
- The group should suspend criticism and judgment for a while and try to combine each other's ideas or add on improvements. The objectives should be to generate as many ideas and suggestions as possible. This is called "brainstorming" in a group, when individuals try lateral thinking.

Leadership

Leadership involves focussing the efforts of the people towards a common goal and to enable them to work together as one. In general we designate one individual as a leader. This individual may be chosen from within or appointed from outside. Thus, one member may provide leadership with respect to achieving the goal while a different individual may be providing leadership in maintaining the group as a group. These roles can switch and change.

DEVELOPMENT OF GROUPS

The developmental process of small groups can be viewed in several ways. Firstly, it is useful to know the persons who compose a particular small group.

- People bring their past experiences
- People come with their personalities
- People also come with a particular set of expectations

The priorities and expectations of persons comprising a group can influence the manner in which the group develops over a period of time

Stages

Viewing the group as a whole we observe definite patterns of behaviour occurring within a group. These can be grouped into stages.

First Stage

The initial stage in the life of a group is concerned with forming a group. This stage is characterized by members seeking safety and protection, tentativeness of response, seeking superficial contact with others, demonstrating dependency on existing authority figures. Members at this stage either engage in busy type of activity or show apathy.

Second Stage

The second stage in this group is marked by the formation of dyads and triads. Members seek out familiar or similar individuals and begin a deeper sharing of self. Continued attention to the subgroup creates a differentiation in the group and tensions across the dyads/triads may appear. Pairing is a common phenomenon.

Third Stage

The third developmental stage is marked by a more serious concern about task performance. The dyads/triads begin to open up and seek out other members in the group. Efforts are made to establish various norms for task performance. Members begin to take greater responsibility for their own group and relationship while the authority figure becomes relaxed.

Fourth Stage

This is a stage of a fully functional group where members see themselves as a group and get involved in the task. Each person makes a contribution and the authority figure is also seen as a part of the group. Group norms are followed and collective pressure is exerted to ensure the effectiveness of the group. The group redefines its goals in the light of information from the outside environment and shows an autonomous will to pursue those goals. The long-term viability of the group is established and nurtured.

FACILITATING A GROUP

A group cannot automatically function effectively, it needs to be facilitated. Facilitation can be described as a conscious process of assisting a group to successfully achieve its task while functioning as a group. Facilitation can be performed by members themselves, or with the help of an outsider.

To facilitate effectively the facilitator needs to:

- Understand what is happening within the group
- Be aware of his/her own personality
- And know how to facilitate

Group Diagnosis

The process of finding out what is going on in a group may be called diagnosing. It is an essential skill of a facilitator. Diagnosis involves understanding the causes after looking for clues within the group and outside the group. Some examples follow to illustrate the point.

- *Problem*: Not everyone participates or shows interest and a few remain silent
- *Possible causes*: Perhaps the goal or task is not relevant to some of the participants. Some of the members may feel insecure or dominant on the basis of caste, class, education or gender.
- *Problem*: Some members ignore or disregard contributions from other members
- *Possible causes*: Members of the group may be nervous and unaware of others' needs.
- *Problem*: The group is not able to come to consensus or are unable to devise a plan to implement the decision.
- *Possible causes*: Perhaps the group lacks adequate information or skills to solve the problem. Perhaps the decision is threatening to some of the group members. Perhaps the group fears failure.

GROUP BEHAVIOUR

Group behaviour in sociology refers to the situations where people interact in large or small groups. The field of group dynamics deals with small groups that may reach consensus and act in a coordinated way. Groups of a large number of people in a given area may act simultaneously to achieve a goal that differs from what individuals would do acting alone. A large group is likely to show examples of group behaviour when people gathered in a given place and time act in a similar way—for example, joining a protest or march, participating in a fight or acting patriotically.

Special forms of large group behaviour are:

- Crowd "hysteria"
- *Spectators*: When a group of people gathered together on purpose to participate in an event like theatre play, cinema movie, football match, a concert, etc.
- *Public*: Exception to the rule that the group must occupy the same physical place. People watching same channel on television may react in the same way, as they are occupying the same type of place-in front of television-although they may physically be doing this all over the world.

Group behaviour differs from mass action's which refers to people behaving similarly on a more global scale, while group behaviour refers usually to people in one place. If the group behaviour is coordinated, then it is called group action. Swarm intelligence is a special case of group behaviour, referring to the interaction between a group of agents in order to fulfil a given task. This type of group dynamics has received much attention by the soft computing community in the form of the particle swarm optimization family of algorithms.

THE IMPORTANCE OF GROUP SIZE

The distinction made earlier between small primary groups and larger secondary groups reflects the importance of group size for the functioning of a group, the nature of its members' attachments, and the group's stability. If you have ever taken a very small class, say fewer than 15 students, you probably noticed that the class atmosphere differed markedly from that of a large lecture class you may have been in.

In the small class, you got to know the professor better, and the students in the room got to know each other better. Attendance in the small class was probably more regular than in the large lecture class. Over the years, sociologists and other scholars have studied the effects of group size on group dynamics. One of the first to do so was German sociologist Georg Simmel who discussed the effects of groups of different sizes. The smallest group, of course, is the two-person group, or dyaddyadA two-person group., such as a married couple or two people engaged to be married or at least dating steadily. In this smallest of groups, Simmel noted, relationships can be very intense emotionally but also very unstable and short lived: if one person ends the relationship, the dyad ends as well.

A triadtriadA three-person group., or three-person group, involves relationships that are still fairly intense, but it is also more stable than a dyad. A major reason for this, said Simmel, is that if two people in a triad have a dispute, the third member can help them reach some compromise that will satisfy all the triad members. The downside of a triad is that two of its members may become very close and increasingly disregard the third member. As one example, some overcrowded college dorms are forced to house students in triples, or three to a room. In such a situation, suppose that two of the roommates are night owls and like to stay up very late, while the third wants lights out by 11:00 p.m. If majority rules, as well it might, the third roommate will feel very dissatisfied and may decide to try to find other roommates. As groups become larger, the intensity of their interaction and bonding decreases, but their stability increases. The major reason for this is the sheer number of relationships that can exist in a larger group. For example, in a dyad only one relationship exists, that between the two members of the dyad. In a triad, three relationships exist: A-B, A-C, and B-C. In a four-person group, the number of relationships rises to six: A-B, A-C, A-D, B-C, B-D, and C-D. In a five-person group, 10 relationships exist, and in a six-person group, 15 exist.

As the number of possible relationships rises, the amount of time a group member can spend with any other group member must decline, and with this decline comes less intense interaction and weaker emotional bonds. But as group size increases, the group also becomes more stable because it is large enough to survive any one member's departure from the group. When you graduate from your college or university, any clubs, organizations, or sports teams to which you belong will continue despite your exit, no matter how important you were to the group, as the remaining members of the group and new recruits will carry on in your absence.

GROUP LEADERSHIP AND DECISION MAKING

Most groups have leaders. In the family, of course, the parents are the leaders, as much as their children sometimes might not like that. Even some close friendship groups have a leader or two who emerge over time. Virtually all secondary groups have leaders. These groups often have a charter, operations manual, or similar document that stipulates how leaders are appointed or elected and what their duties are. Sociologists commonly distinguish two types of leaders, instrumental and expressive.

An instrumental leaderinstrumental leaderA leader whose main focus is to achieve group goals and accomplish group tasks. is a leader whose main focus is to achieve group goals and accomplish group tasks. Often instrumental leaders try to carry out their role even if they alienate other members of the group. The second type is the expressive leaderexpressive leaderA leader whose main focus is to maintain and improve the quality of relationships among group members and more generally to ensure group harmony., whose main focus is to maintain and improve the quality of relationships among group members and more generally to ensure group harmony. Some groups may have both types of leaders. Related to the leader types is leadership *style*. Three such styles are commonly distinguished. The first, authoritarian leadershipauthoritarian leadership Leadership with a primary focus on achieving group goals and on rigorous compliance with group rules., involves a primary focus on achieving group goals and on rigorous compliance with group rules and penalties for noncompliance. Authoritarian leaders typically make decisions on their own and tell other group members what to do and how to do it. The second style, democratic leadershipdemocratic leadershipLeadership that involves extensive consultation with group members on decisions., involves extensive consultation with group members on decisions and less emphasis on rule compliance. Democratic leaders still make the final decision but do so only after carefully considering what other group members have said, and usually their decision will agree with the views of a majority of the members.

The final style is laissez-faire leadershiplaissez-faire leadershipLeadership that allows a group to function on its own.. Here the leader more or less sits back and lets the group function on its own and really exerts no leadership role. When a decision must be reached, laissez-faire leadership is less effective than the other two in helping a group get things done. Whether authoritarian or democratic leadership is better for a group depends on the group's priorities. If the group values task accomplishment more than anything else, including how well group members get along and how much they like their leader, then authoritarian leadership is preferable to democratic leadership, as it is better able to achieve group goals quickly and efficiently. But if group members place their highest priority on their satisfaction with decisions and decision making in the group, then they would want to have a lot of input in decisions. In this case, democratic leadership is preferable to authoritarian leadership.

Some small groups shun leadership and instead try to operate by *consensus*. In this model of decision making popularized by Quakers, no decision is made unless all group members agree with it. If even one member disagrees, the group keeps discussing the issue until it reaches a compromise that satisfies everyone. If the person disagreeing does not feel very strongly about the issue or does not wish to prolong the discussion, she or he may agree to "stand aside" and let the group make the decision despite the lack of total consensus.

But if this person refuses to stand aside, no decision may be possible. A major advantage of the consensus style of decision making is psychic. Because everyone has a chance to voice an opinion about a potential decision and no decisions are reached unless everyone agrees with them, group members will ordinarily feel good about the eventual decision and also about being in the group. The major disadvantage has to do with time and efficiency. When groups operate by consensus, their discussions may become long and tedious, as no voting is allowed and discussion must continue until everyone is satisfied with the outcome. This means the group may well be unable to make decisions quickly and efficiently. One final issue in leadership has to do with gender differences in leadership styles. Although the evidence indicates that women and men are equally capable of being good leaders, their leadership styles do tend to differ. Women are more likely to be democratic leaders, while men are more likely to be authoritarian leaders. Because of this difference, women leaders sometimes have trouble securing respect from their subordinates and are criticized for being too soft. Yet if they respond with a more masculine, or authoritarian, style, they may be charged with acting too much like a man and be criticized in ways a man would not be.

GROUPS, ROLES, AND CONFORMITY

We have seen in this and previous stages that groups are essential for social life, in large part because they play an important part in the socialization process and provide emotional and other support for their members. As sociologists have emphasized since the origins of the discipline during the 19th century, the influence of groups on individuals is essential for social stability.

This influence operates through many mechanisms, including the roles that group members are expected to play. Secondary groups such as business organizations are also fundamental to complex industrial societies such as our own. Social stability results because groups induce their members to conform to the norms, values, and attitudes of the groups themselves and of the larger society to which they belong.

As the stage-opening news story about teenage vandalism reminds us, however, conformity to the group, or peer pressure, has a downside if it means that people might adopt group norms, attitudes, or values that are bad for some reason to hold and may even result in harm to others. Conformity is thus a double-edged sword. Unfortunately, bad conformity happens all too often, as several social-psychological experiments, to which we now turn, remind us.

SOLOMON ASCH AND PERCEPTIONS OF LINE LENGTHS

Several decades ago Solomon Asch conducted one of the first of these experiments. Consider the pair of cards in Figure, "Examples of Cards Used in Asch's Experiment". One of the lines on the right card is identical in length to the single line in the left card. Which is it? If your vision is up to par, you undoubtedly answered Line B. Asch showed several students pairs of cards similar to the pair in Figure, "Examples of Cards Used in Asch's Experiment" to confirm that it was very clear which of the three lines was the same length as the single line. Next, he had students meet in groups of at least six members and told them he was testing their visual ability. One by one he asked each member of the group to identify which of the three lines was the same length as the single line. One by one each student gave a wrong answer. Finally, the last student had to answer, and about one-third of the time the final student in each group also gave the wrong answer that everyone else was giving.

Unknown to these final students, all the other students were confederates or accomplices, to use some experimental jargon, as Asch had told them to give a wrong answer on purpose. The final student in each group was thus a naive subject, and Asch's purpose was to see how often the naive subjects in all the groups would give the wrong answer that everyone else was giving, even though it was *very* clear it was a wrong answer. After each group ended its deliberations, Asch asked the naive subjects who gave the wrong answers why they did so. Some replied that they knew the answer was wrong but they did not want to look different from the other people in the group, even though they were strangers before the experiment began.

But other naive subjects said *they had begun to doubt their own visual perception*: they decided that if everyone else was giving a different answer, then somehow they were seeing the cards incorrectly. Asch's experiment indicated that groups induce conformity for at least two reasons. First, members feel pressured to conform so as not to alienate other members. Second, members may decide their own perceptions or views are wrong because they see other group members perceiving things differently and begin to doubt their own perceptive abilities. For either or both reasons, then, groups can, for better or worse, affect our judgments and our actions.

STANLEY MILGRAM AND ELECTRIC SHOCK

Although the type of influence Asch's experiment involved was benign, other experiments indicate that individuals can conform in a very harmful way. One such very famous experiment was conducted by Yale University psychologist Stanley Milgram, who designed it to address an important question that arose after World War II and the revelation of the murders of millions of people during the Nazi Holocaust. This question was, "How was the Holocaust possible?" Many people blamed the authoritarian nature of German culture and the so-called authoritarian personality that it inspired among German residents, who, it was thought, would be quite ready to obey rules and demands from authority figures. Milgram wanted to see whether Germans would indeed be more likely than Americans to obey unjust authority.

He devised a series of experiments and found that his American subjects were quite likely to give potentially lethal electric shocks to other people. During the experiment, a subject, or "teacher," would come into a laboratory and be told by a man wearing a white lab coat to sit down at a table housing a machine that sent electric shocks to a "learner." Depending on the type of experiment, this was either a person whom the teacher never saw and heard only over a loudspeaker, a person sitting in an adjoining room whom the teacher could see through a window and hear over the loudspeaker, or a person sitting right next to the teacher. The teacher was then told to read the learner a list of word pairs, such as mother-father, cat-dog, and sun-moon. At the end of the list, the teacher was then asked to read the first word of the first word pair—for example, "mother" in our list—and to read several possible matches. If the learner got the right answer, the teacher would move on to the next word pair, but if the learner gave the wrong answer, the teacher was to administer an electric shock to the learner. The initial shock was 15 volts, and each time a wrong answer was given, the shock would be increased, finally going up to 450 V, which was marked on the machine as "Danger: Severe Shock."

The learners often gave wrong answers and would cry out in pain as the voltage increased. In the 200-V range, they would scream, and in the 400-V range, they would say nothing at all. As far as the teachers knew, the learners had lapsed into unconsciousness from the electric shocks and even died. Before his study began, Milgram consulted several psychologists, who assured him that no sane person would be willing to administer lethal shock in his experiments. He thus was shocked to find that more than half the teachers went all the way to 450 V in the experiments, where they could only hear the learner over a loudspeaker and not see him. Even in the experiments where the learner was sitting next to the teacher, some teachers still went to 450 V by forcing a hand of the screaming, resisting, but tied-down learner onto a metal plate that completed the electric circuit. It turned out that the learners were not actually being shocked.

Instead the voice and screams heard through the loudspeaker were from a tape recorder, and the learner that some of the teachers saw was placed there by Milgram to pretend to be in agony. Milgram concluded that people are quite willing, however reluctantly, to obey authority even if it means inflicting great harm on others. If that could happen in his artificial experiment situation, he thought, then perhaps the Holocaust was not so incomprehensible after all, and it would be too simplistic to blame the Holocaust just on the authoritarianism of German culture. Instead, perhaps its roots lay in the very conformity to roles and group norms that makes society possible in the first place. The same processes that make society possible may also make tragedies like the Holocaust possible.

THE THIRD WAVE

In 1969, concern about the Holocaust prompted Ron Jones, a high school teacher from Palo Alto, California, to conduct a real-life experiment that reinforced Milgram's findings by creating a Nazi-like environment in the school in just a few short days. He began by telling his sophomore history class about the importance of discipline and self-control. He had his students sit at attention and repeatedly stand up and sit down in quiet unison and saw their pride as they accomplished this task efficiently.

All of a sudden everyone in the class seemed to be paying rapt attention to what was going on. The next day, Jones began his class by talking about the importance of community and of being a member of a team or a cause. He had his class say over and over, "Strength through discipline, strength through community." Then he showed them a new class salute, made by bringing the right hand near the right shoulder in a curled position. He called it the Third Wave salute, because a hand in this position resembled a wave about to topple over. Jones then told the students they had to salute each other outside the classroom, which they did so during the next few days. As word of what was happening in Jones's class spread, students from other classes asked if they could come into his classroom.

On the third day of the experiment, Jones gave membership cards to every student in his class, which had now gained several new members. He told them they had to turn in the name of any student who was disobeying the class's rules. He then talked to them about the importance of action and hard work, both of which enhanced discipline and community. Jones told his students to recruit new members and to prevent any student who was not a Third Wave member from entering the classroom.

During the rest of the day, students came to him with reports of other students not saluting the right way or of some students criticizing the experiment. Meanwhile, more than 200 students had joined the Third Wave. On the fourth day of the experiment, more than 80 students squeezed into Jones's classroom. Jones informed them that the Third Wave was in fact a new political movement in the United States that would bring discipline, order, and pride to the country and that his students were among the first in the movement. The next day, Jones said, the Third Wave's national leader, whose identity was still not public, would be announcing a grand plan for action on national television at noon.

At noon the next day, more than 200 students crowded into the school auditorium to see the television speech. When Jones gave them the Third Wave salute, they saluted back. They chanted, "Strength through discipline, strength through community," over and over, and then sat in silent anticipation as Jones turned on a large television in front of the auditorium. The television remained blank. Suddenly Jones turned on a movie projector and showed scenes from a Nazi rally and the Nazi death camps. As the crowd in the auditorium reacted with shocked silence, the teacher told them there was no Third Wave movement and that almost overnight they had developed a Nazi-like society by allowing their regard for discipline, community, and action to warp their better judgment.

Many students in the auditorium sobbed as they heard his words. The Third Wave experiment once again indicates that the normal group processes that make social life possible also can lead people to conform to standards—in this case fascism—that most of us would reject. It also helps us understand further how the Holocaust could have happened. As Jones told his students in the auditorium, "You thought that you were the elect. That you were better than those outside this room. You bargained your freedom for the comfort of discipline and superiority. You chose to accept the group's will and the big lie over your own conviction.... Yes, we would all have made good Germans."

ZIMBARDO'S PRISON EXPERIMENT

In 1971, Stanford University psychologist Philip Zimbardo conducted an experiment to see what accounts for the extreme behaviours often seen in prisons: does this behaviour stem from abnormal personalities of guards and prisoners or, instead, from the social structure of prisons, including the roles their members are expected to play? His experiment remains a compelling illustration of how roles and group processes can prompt extreme behaviour. Zimbardo advertised for male students to take part in a prison experiment and screened them out for histories of mental illness, violent behaviour, and drug use.

He then assigned them randomly to be either guards or prisoners in the experiment to ensure that any behavioral differences later seen between the two groups would have to stem from their different roles and not from any preexisting personality differences had they been allowed to volunteer. The guards were told that they needed to keep order. They carried no weapons but did dress in khaki uniforms and wore reflector sunglasses to make eye contact impossible. On the first day of the experiment, the guards had the prisoners, who wore gowns and stocking caps to remove their individuality, stand in front of their cells for the traditional prison "count." They made the prisoners stand for hours on end and verbally abused those who complained. A day later the prisoners refused to come out for the count, prompting the guards to respond by forcibly removing them from their cells and sometimes spraying them with an ice-cold fire extinguisher to expedite the process.

Some prisoners were put into solitary confinement. The guards also intensified their verbal abuse of the prisoners. By the third day of the experiment, the prisoners had become very passive. The guards, several of whom indicated before the experiment that they would have trouble taking their role seriously, now were quite serious. They continued their verbal abuse of the prisoners and became quite hostile if their orders were not followed exactly. What had begun as somewhat of a lark for both guards and prisoners had now become, as far as they were concerned, a real prison.

Shortly thereafter, first one prisoner and then a few more came down with symptoms of a nervous breakdown. Zimbardo and his assistants could not believe this was possible, as they had planned for the experiment to last for 2 weeks, but they allowed the prisoners to quit the experiment. When the first one was being "released," the guards had the prisoners chant over and over that this prisoner was a bad prisoner and that they would be punished for his weakness. When this prisoner heard the chants, he refused to leave the area because he felt so humiliated. The researchers had to remind him that this was only an experiment and that he was not a real prisoner. Zimbardo had to shut down the experiment after only 6 days. Zimbardo later observed that if psychologists had viewed the behaviours just described in a real prison, they would likely have attributed them to preexisting personality problems in both guards and prisoners. As already noted, however, his random assignment procedure invalidated this possibility.

Zimbardo thus concluded that the guards' and prisoners' behavioral problems must have stemmed from the social structure of the prison experience and the roles each group was expected to play. Zimbardo later wrote that these same processes help us understand "how good people turn evil," to cite the subtitle of his book, and thus help explain the torture and abuse committed by American forces at the Abu Ghraib prison in Iraq after the United States invaded and occupied that country in 2003. Once again we see how two of the building blocks of social life—groups and roles—contain within them the seeds of regrettable behaviour and attitudes.

As these examples suggest, sometimes people go along with the desires and views of a group against their better judgments, either because they do not want to appear different or because they have come to believe that the group's course of action may be the best one after all. Psychologist Irving Janis called this process group think group think The tendency of group members to remain silent and, against their better judgments, to go along with the desires and views of other group members. and noted it has often affected national and foreign policy decisions in the United States and elsewhere.

Group members often quickly agree on some course of action without thinking completely of alternatives. A well-known example here is the decision by President John F. Kennedy and his advisers in 1961 to take part in the invasion of the Bay of Pigs in Cuba. Although several advisers thought the plan ill advised, they kept quiet, and the invasion was an embarrassing failure. After most Americans decided that the decision to invade Iraq in 2003 was misguided, many commentators said that the decision resulted from "collective groupthink" and regretted that they themselves had succumbed to it.

Groupthink is also seen in jury decision making. Because of the pressures to reach a verdict quickly, some jurors may go along with a verdict even if they believe otherwise. In juries and other small groups, groupthink is less likely to occur if at least one person expresses a dissenting view. Once that happens, other dissenters feel more comfortable voicing their own objections.

FORMAL ORGANIZATIONS

Modern societies are filled with formal organizations formal organizationsLarge secondary groups that follow explicit rules and procedures to achieve specific goals and tasks., or large secondary groups that follow explicit rules and procedures to achieve specific goals and tasks. Max Weber, one of the founders of sociology, recognized long ago that as societies become more complex, their procedures for accomplishing tasks rely less on traditional customs and beliefs and more on *rational* methods of decision making. The development of formal organizations, he emphasized, allowed complex societies to accomplish their tasks in the most efficient way possible. Today we cannot imagine how any modern, complex society could run without formal organizations such as businesses and health-care institutions.

TYPES OF FORMAL ORGANIZATIONS

Sociologist Amitai Etzioni developed a popular typology of organizations based on how they induce people to join them and keep them as members once they do join. His three types are utilitarian, normative, and coercive organizations. Utilitarian organization sutilitarian organizations Organizations that people join to provide them an income or some other personal benefit. provide an income or some other personal benefit.

Business organizations, ranging from large corporations to small Mom-and-Pop grocery stores, are familiar examples of utilitarian organizations. Colleges and universities are utilitarian organizations not only for the people who work at them but also for their students, who certainly see education and a diploma as important tangible benefits they can gain from higher education. In contrast, normative organization allow people to pursue their moral goals and commitments.

Their members do not get paid and instead contribute their time or money because they like or admire what the organization does. The many examples of normative organizations include churches and synagogues, Boy and Girl Scouts, the Kiwanis Club and other civic groups, and groups with political objectives, such as the National Council of La Raza, the largest advocacy organization for Latino civil rights. Alexis de Tocqueville observed some 175 years ago that the United States was a nation of joiners, and contemporary research finds that Americans indeed rank above average among democratic nations in membership in voluntary associations. Some people end up in organizations involuntarily because they have violated the law or been judged to be mentally ill.

Prisons and state mental institutions are examples of such coercive organizationscoercive organizationsFormal organizations that people enter involuntarily., which, as total institutions seek to control all phases of their members' lives. Our chances of ending up in coercive organizations depend on various aspects of our social backgrounds.

For prisons one of these aspects is geographical. The distribution of imprisonment in the United States and shows the imprisonment rate for each of the four major census regions. This rate tends to be highest in the South and in the West. Do you think this pattern exists because crime rates are highest in these regions or instead because these regions are more likely than other parts of the United States to send convicted criminals to prisons?

BUREAUCRACIES: THE GOOD, THE BAD, AND THE UGLY

As discussed earlier, Max Weber emphasized that modern societies increasingly depend on formal organizations to accomplish key tasks. He particularly had in mind bureaucraciesbureaucracyA formal organization with certain organizational features designed to achieve goals in the most efficient way possible., or formal organizations with certain organizational features designed to achieve goals in the most efficient way possible. He said that the ideal type of bureaucracy is characterized by several features that together maximize the efficiency and effectiveness of organizational decision making and goal accomplishment:

- *Specialization*: By specialization Weber meant a division of labor in which specific people have certain tasks—and only those tasks—to do. Presumably they are most skilled at these tasks and less skilled at others. With such specialization, the people who are best suited to do various tasks are the ones who work on them, maximizing the ability of the organization to have these tasks accomplished.
- *Hierarchy*: Equality does not exist in a bureaucracy. Instead its structure resembles a pyramid, with a few positions at the top and many more lower down. The chain of command runs from the top to the bottom, with the persons occupying the positions at the top supervising those below them. The higher you are in the hierarchy, the fewer people to whom you have to report. Weber thought a hierarchical structure maximizes efficiency because it reduces decision-making time and puts the authority to make the most important decisions in the hands of the people at the top of the pyramid who presumably are the best qualified to make them.
- *Written rules and regulations*: For an organization to work efficiently, everyone must know what to do and when to do it. This means their actions must be predictable. To ensure predictability, their roles and the organization's operating procedures must be written in a manual or handbook, with everyone in the organization expected to be familiar with its rules. Much of the communication among members of bureaucracies is written in the form of memos and e-mail rather than being verbal. This written communication leaves a paper trail so that accountability for individual behaviour can later be determined.
- *Impartiality and impersonality*: The head of a small, nonbureaucratic organization might prefer to hire people she or he knows and promote them on the same basis. Weber thought that impartiality in hiring, promotion, and firing would be much better for a large organization, as it guarantees people will advance through a firm

based on their skills and knowledge, not on whom they know. Clients should also be treated impersonally, as an organization in the long run would be less effective if it gave favorable treatment to clients based on whom they know or on their nice personalities. As Weber recognized, the danger is that employees and clients alike become treated like numbers or cogs in a machine, with their individual needs and circumstances ignored in the name of organizational efficiency.

- *Record keeping*: As you probably know from personal experience, bureaucracies keep all kinds of records, especially in today's computer age. A small enterprise, say a Mom-and-Pop store, might keep track of its merchandise and the bills its customers owe with some notes scribbled here and there, even in the information technology age, but a large organization must have much more extensive record keeping to keep track of everything.

The Disadvantages of Bureaucracy

Taking all of these features into account, Weber thought bureaucracies were the most efficient and effective type of organization in a large, complex society. At the same time, he despaired over their impersonality, which he saw reflecting the growing dehumanization that accompanies growing societies. As social scientists have found since his time, bureaucracies have other problems that undermine their efficiency and effectiveness:

- *Impersonality and alienation*: The first problem is the one just mentioned: bureaucracies can be very alienating experiences for their employees and clients alike. A worker without any sick leave left who needs to take some time off to care for a sick child might find a supervisor saying no, because the rules prohibit it. A client who stands in a long line might find herself turned away when she gets to the front because she forgot to fill out every single box in a form. We all have stories of impersonal, alienating experiences in today's large bureaucracies.
- *Red tape*: A second disadvantage of bureaucracy is "red tape," or, as sociologist Robert Merton called it, bureaucratic ritualismbureaucratic ritualismIn a bureaucracy, a greater devotion to rules and regulations than to organizational goals (red tape)., a greater devotion to rules and regulations than to organizational goals. Bureaucracies often operate by slavish attention to even the pickiest of rules and regulations. If every "t" isn't crossed and every "i" isn't dotted, then someone gets into trouble, and perhaps a client is not served. Such bureaucratic ritualism contributes to the alienation already described.
- *Trained incapacity*: If an overabundance of rules and regulations and

overattention to them lead to bureaucratic ritualism, they also lead to an inability of people in an organization to think creatively and to act independently. In the late 1800s, Thorstein Veblen called this problem trained incapacity. When unforeseen problems arise, trained incapacity may prevent organizational members from being able to handle them.

- *Bureaucratic incompetence*: Two popular writers have humorously pointed to special problems in bureaucracies that undermine their effectiveness. The first of these, popularly known as Parkinson's law after its coiner, English historian C. Northcote Parkinson, says that work expands to fill the time available for it. To put it another way, the more time you have to do something, the longer it takes. The second problem is called the Peter Principle, also named after its founder, Canadian author Laurence J. Peter and says that people will eventually be promoted to their level of incompetence. In this way of thinking, someone who does a good job will get promoted and then get promoted again if she or he continues doing a good job. Eventually such people will be promoted to a job for which they are not well qualified, impeding organizational efficiency and effectiveness. Have you ever worked for someone who illustrated the Peter Principle?
- *Goal displacement and self-perpetuation*: Sometimes bureaucracies become so swollen with rules and personnel that they take on a life of their own and lose sight of the goals they were originally designed to achieve. People in the bureaucracy become more concerned with their job comfort and security than with helping the organization accomplish its objectives. To the extent this happens, the bureaucracy's efficiency and effectiveness are again weakened.

MICHELS'S IRON LAW OF OLIGARCHY

Several decades ago Robert Michels, a German activist and scholar, published his famous iron law of oligarchyiron law of oligarchyRobert Michels's prediction that large organizations inevitably develop an oligarchy, or the undemocratic rule of many people by just a few people, because their leaders monopolize knowledge and act to advance their own positions., by which he meant that large organizations inevitably develop an oligarchy, or the undemocratic rule of many people by just a few people.

He said this happens as leaders increasingly monopolize knowledge because they have more access than do other organizational members to information and technology. They begin to think they are better suited than other people to lead their organizations, and they also do their best to stay in their positions of power, which they find very appealing. This latter goal becomes more important than helping the organization achieve its objectives and than serving the interests of the workers further down the organizational pyramid. Drawing on our earlier discussion of group size, it is also true that as an organization becomes larger, it becomes very difficult to continue to involve all group members in decision making, which almost inevitably becomes monopolized by the relatively few people at the top of the organization.

Michels thought oligarchization happens not only in bureaucracies but also in a society's political structures and said that the inevitable tendency to oligarchy threatens democracy by concentrating political decision-making power in the hands of a few. As his use of the term *iron law* suggests, Michels thought the development of oligarchies was inevitable, and he was very pessimistic about democracy's future. Has our society as a whole lost some of its democracy in the ways Michels predicted? Some evidence supports his prediction.

For example, many large organizations, including corporations, labor unions, political parties, and colleges and universities, do resemble the types of oligarchies over which Michels despaired. In most of these, decision making is indeed concentrated in the hands of a few, who often do work, at least according to their critics, for their own interests as least as much as they do for the interests of the organization and its members. On the other hand, organizational and political leaders do not work always for themselves and often have the interests of their organizations and the public in mind. Michels's law might not be so ironclad after all, but it does remind us to be on the alert for the undemocratic processes he predicted.

GENDER, RACE, AND FORMAL ORGANIZATIONS

We previously outlined three types of organizations: utilitarian, normative, and coercive. What does the evidence indicate about the dynamics of gender and race in these organizations? We have already seen that women in utilitarian organizations such as businesses have made striking inroads but remain thwarted by a glass ceiling and the refusal of some subordinates to accept their authority. The workforce as a whole remains segregated by sex, as many women work in a relatively few occupations such as clerical and secretarial work. This fact contributes heavily to the lower pay that women receive compared to men.

Turning to race, effective federal and state laws against racial discrimination in the workplace arose in the aftermath of the Southern civil rights movement of the 1960s. Although these laws have helped greatly, people of colour are still worse off than whites in hiring, promotion, and salaries, affirmative action efforts notwithstanding. Much less research exists on gender and race in normative organizations. But we do know that many women are involved in many types of these voluntary associations, especially those having to do with children and education and related matters. These associations allow them to contribute to society and are a source of self-esteem and, more practically, networking. Many people of colour have also been involved in normative organizations, especially those serving various needs of their communities. One significant type of normative organization is the church, which has been extraordinarily important in the African-American community over the decades and was a key locus of civil rights activism in the South during the 1960s.

Turning to coercive organizations, we know much about prisons and the race and gender composition of their inmates. Men, African Americans, and Latinos are overrepresented in prisons and jails. This means that they constitute much higher percentages of all inmates than their numbers in the national population would suggest. Although men make up about 50% of the national population, for example, they account for more than 90% of all prisoners.

Similarly, although African Americans are about 13% of the population, they account for more than 40% of all prisoners. The corresponding percentages for Latinos are about 15% and almost 20%, respectively. Why these patterns exist is unclear. Do they reflect discrimination against African Americans, Latinos, and men, or do they reflect higher offending rates by these groups?

GROUPS, ORGANIZATIONS, AND SOCIAL CHANGE

VEHICLES FOR SOCIAL CHANGE

One individual can certainly make a difference, but it is much more common for any difference to be made by individuals acting together—that is, by a group. In this regard, it is very clear that groups of many types have been and will continue to be vehicles for social reform and social change of many kinds. Many of the rights and freedoms Americans enjoy today were the result of committed efforts by social reform groups and social movements of years past: the abolitionist movement, the woman suffrage movement and contemporary women's movement, the labor movement, the civil rights movement, the gay rights movement, and the environmental movement, to name just a few.

Their experience reflects the wisdom of anthropologist Margaret Mead's famous quote that we should "never doubt that a small group of thoughtful, committed citizens can change the world. Indeed, it is the only thing that ever has." In today's world, there are innumerable social service and social advocacy groups that are attempting to bring about changes to benefit a particular constituency or the greater society, and you might well belong to one of these groups on your campus or in your home community. All such groups, past, present, and future, are vehicles for social reform and social change, or at least have the potential for becoming such vehicles.

OBSTACLES TO SOCIAL CHANGE

Groups can bring about social reform and social change, but they can also thwart efforts to achieve a just society. For every social change and social reform effort that so many groups and organizations undertake, other groups and organizations try to block such efforts. Groups may be the building blocks of social reform and social change, but they are also the building blocks for the status quo. If the study of sociology can be said to be the study of group life, as noted earlier, the study of social reform and social change can also be said to be the study of what groups and organizations do to try to bring about social reform or to maintain the status quo.

CHANGING GROUPS AND ORGANIZATIONS FROM WITHIN

Groups and organizations are typically set in their ways and do not often change their dynamics, goals, or other key aspects. This is especially true of the formal organizations we call bureaucracies, which, as we saw, are so committed and even "stuck" to certain procedures that they become inefficient and even alienating. Groupthink can also set in and stifle creativity and keep group and organizational members from raising concerns about certain practices and/or goals. Whistle-blowingwhistle-blowingThe revealing by an employee of organizational practices that the employee believes to be illegal and/or immoral. is now the common term for raising such concerns, especially when the concern involves illegal and/or potentially harmful behaviour.

It is not easy to be a whistle-blower, and several individuals who have "blown the whistle" have been harassed, fired, or sued for doing so. In response to such reprisals, various federal and state laws have been passed to protect whistle-blowers. Still, it takes a certain amount of courage and no small amount of perseverance to be a whistle-blower. It is almost certain that some readers of this book will one day find themselves in a position where they, too, might have to decide whether to become a whistle-blower when they perceive some violation of the law and/or harmful behaviour to be occurring. If so, they will have great potential for changing a group or an organization from within while performing a social good for the larger society.

IMPORTANT POINTS

- Social groups are the building blocks of social life, and it is virtually impossible to imagine a society without groups and difficult to imagine individuals not being involved with many types of groups. They are distinguished from social categories and social aggregates by the degree of interaction among their members and the identification of their members with the group.
- Primary groups are small and involve strong emotional attachments, while secondary groups are larger and more impersonal. Some groups become in-groups and vie, sometimes hostilely, with people they

identify as belonging to out-groups. Reference groups provide standards by which we judge our attitudes and behaviour and can influence how we think and act.

- Social networks connect us through the people we know to other people they know. They are increasingly influential for successful employment but are also helpful for high-quality health care and other social advantages.
- The size of groups is a critical variable for their internal dynamics. Compared to large groups, small groups involve more intense emotional bonds but are also more unstable. These differences stem from the larger number of relationships that can exist in a larger group than in a smaller one.
- Instrumental and expressive leaders take different approaches in exercising leadership. Instrumental leaders focus more on solving tasks, even at the risk of alienating group members, while expressive leaders focus more on group relations. Of the three major styles of leadership—authoritarian, democratic, and laissez-faire—laissez-faire leadership seems the least effective in helping a group achieve its goals.
- Women and men are equally effective as leaders but exhibit different leadership styles. Women tend to be expressive leaders, while men tend to be more authoritarian leaders. Women leaders still face problems in securing the respect of the group members they seek to lead.
- Processes of group conformity are essential for any society and for the well-being of its many individuals but also can lead to reprehensible norms and values. People can be influenced by their group membership and the roles they're expected to play to engage in behaviours most of us would condemn. Laboratory experiments by Asch, Milgram, and Zimbardo illustrate how this can happen, while a real-life classroom experiment called the Third Wave dramatized how a fascist atmosphere could develop from everyday group processes.
- Formal organizations are commonly delineated according to the motivations of the people who join them. According to Etzioni's popular typology, three types of formal organizations exist: utilitarian, normative, and coercive.
- Max Weber outlined several characteristics of bureaucracy that he felt make them the most efficient and effective type of large formal organization possible. At the same time, other scholars have pointed to several disadvantages of bureaucracies that limit their efficiency and effectiveness and thus thwart organizational goals.
- Robert Michels hypothesized that the development of oligarchies in

formal organizations and political structures is inevitable. History shows that such "oligarchization" does occur but that society remains more democratic than Michels foresaw.

- Women and people of colour have long been involved in normative organizations and continue to expand their numbers in utilitarian organizations, but in the latter they lag behind white men in rank and salary. In a major type of coercive organization, prisons, people of colour and men are overrepresented. The stage closes with the question of whether the reason for this overrepresentation is the offending rates of these two groups or, instead, discrimination against them in criminal justice processing.

11

Time Management

INTRODUCTION

Time management refers to a range of skills, tools, and techniques used to manage time when accomplishing specific tasks, projects and goals. This set encompasses a wide scope of activities, and these include planning, allocating, setting goals, delegation, analysis of time spent, monitoring, organizing, scheduling, and prioritizing. Initially time management referred to just business or work activities, but eventually the term broadened to include personal activities as well. A time management system is a designed combination of processes, tools and techniques.

Some authors offered a categorization scheme for the hundreds of time management approaches that they reviewed:

- *First generation*: Reminders based on clocks and watches, but with computer implementation possible; can be used to alert a person when a task is to be done.
- *Second generation*: Planning and preparation based on calendar and appointment books; includes setting goals.
- *Third generation*: Planning, prioritizing, controlling activities on a daily basis. This approach implies spending some time in clarifying values and priorities.
- *Fourth generation*: Being efficient and proactive using any of the above tools; places goals and roles as the controlling element of the system and favours importance over urgency.

Some of the recent general arguments related to "time" and "management" point out that the term "time management" is misleading and that the concept should actually imply that it is "the management of our own activities, to make sure that they are accomplished within the available or allocated time, which is an unmanageable continuous resource".

Time management literature paraphrased:

- *"Achieve through Goal management Goal Focus"*: Motivational emphasis
- *"Get Organized"*: Paperwork and task triage
- *"Go with the Flow"*: Natural rhythms, Eastern philosophy

- "Master the Skills of Time Management"
- "*Protect Your Time*": Insulate, isolate, delegate
- "*Recover from Bad Time Habits*": Recovery from underlying psychological problems, *e.g.* procrastination
- "*Set gravitational goals*": That attract actions automatically
- "*Use Magical Tools to Get More Out of Your Time*": Depends on when written
- "*Work in Priority Order*": Set goals and prioritize

TIME MANAGEMENT AND RELATED CONCEPTS

Time management has been considered as subsets of different concepts such as:

- *Project management*: Time Management can be considered as a project management subset and is more commonly known as project planning and project scheduling. Time Management has also been identified as one of the core functions identified in project management.
- *Attention management*: Attention Management relates to the management of cognitive resources, and in particular the time that humans allocate their mind to conduct some activities.
- Personal knowledge management.

PERSONAL TIME MANAGEMENT

Time management strategies are often associated with the recommendation to set goals. These goals are recorded and may be broken down into a project, an action plan, or a simple task list. For individual tasks or for goals, an importance rating may be established, deadlines may be set, and priorities assigned.

This process results in a plan with a task list or a schedule or calendar of activities. Authors may recommend a daily, weekly, monthly or other planning periods, usually fixed, but sometimes variable. Different planning periods may be associated with different scope of planning or review. Authors may or may not emphasize reviews of performance against plan. Routine and recurring tasks may or may not be integrated into the time management plan and, if integrated, the integration can be accomplished in various ways.

Task List

A task list is a list of tasks to be completed, such as chores or steps towards completing a project. It is an inventory tool which serves as an alternative or supplement to memory. Task lists are used in self-management, grocery lists, business management, project management, and software development. It may involve more than one list. When you accomplish one of the items on a task list, you *check* it off or *cross* it off. The traditional method is to write these on a piece of paper with a pen or pencil, usually on a note pad or clip-board. Numerous digital equivalents are now available, including PIM applications and most PDA's. There are also several web-based task list applications, many of which are free.

Task List Organization

Task lists are often tiered. The simplest tiered system includes a general to-do list to record all the tasks the person needs to accomplish, and a daily to-do list which is created each day by transferring tasks from the general to-do list.

Task lists are often prioritized:

- An early advocate of "ABC" prioritization was Alan Lakein. In his system "A" items were the most important, "B" next most important, "C" least important.
- A particular method of applying the *ABC method* assigns "A" to tasks to be done within a day, "B" a week, and "C" a month.
- To prioritize a daily task list, one either records the tasks in the order of highest priority, or assigns them a number after they are listed which indicates in which order to execute the tasks. The latter method is generally faster, allowing the tasks to be recorded more quickly.

Alternatives to Prioritizing

A completely different approach which argues against prioritising altogether was put forward by British author Mark Forster in his book "Do It Tomorrow and Other Secrets of Time Management". This is based on the idea of operating "closed" to-do lists, instead of the traditional "open" to-do list. He argues that the traditional never-ending to-do lists virtually guarantees that some of your work will be left undone.

This approach advocates getting all your work done, every day, and if you are unable to achieve it helps you diagnose where you are going wrong and what needs to change. Recently, Forster developed the "Autofocus Time Management System", which further systematizes working a to-do list as a series of closed sublists and emphasizes intuitive choices.

Software Applications

Modern task list applications may have built-in task hierarchy, may support multiple methods of filtering and ordering the list of tasks, and may allow one to associate arbitrarily long notes for each task. In contrast to the concept of allowing the person to use multiple filtering methods, at least one new software product additionally contains a mode where the software will attempt to dynamically determine the best tasks for any given moment. Many of the software products for time management support multiple users. It allows the person to give tasks to other users and use the software for communication. Task list applications may be thought of as lightweight personal information manager or project management software.

Resistors

- *Fear of change*: Change can be daunting and one may be afraid to change what's proven to work in the past.
- *Uncertainty*: Even with the change being inevitable, one may be hesitant as being not sure where to start. Uncertainty about when or how to begin making a change can be significant.
- *Time pressure*: To save time, one has to invest time, and this time investment may be a cause of concern. Fearing that changing may involve more work at the start—and thus, in the very short term, make things worse—is a common resistor.

Attention Deficit Disorder

Excessive and chronic inability to manage time effectively may be a result of Attention Deficit Disorder. Diagnostic criteria include: A sense of underachievement, difficulty getting organized, trouble getting started, many projects going simultaneously and trouble with follow-through.

- *Prefrontal cortex*: The prefrontal cortex is the most evolved part of the brain. It controls the functions of attention span, impulse control, organization, learning from experience and self-monitoring, among others. Some authors argue that changing the way the prefrontal cortex works is possible and offers a solution.

Drivers

- *Increased effectiveness*: One may feel the need to make more time so as to be more effective in performing the job and carrying out responsibilities.
- *Performance improvement*: Time management is an issue that often arises during performance appraisals or review meetings.
- *Personal development*: One may view changing the approach to time management as a personal development issue and reap the benefit of handling time differently at work and at home.
- *Increased responsibilities*: A change in time-management approach may become necessary as a result of a promotion or additional responsibilities. Since there is more work to do, and still the same amount of time to do it in, the approach must change.
- *The end result*: Working towards the end goal. example completing an assignment.
- *Crossing task of the list*: The feeling you get when you have completed a task then you cross it off your list, and being able to see what has been completed

Caveats

Dwelling on the Lists:

- According to Sandberg, task lists "aren't the key to productivity [that] they're cracked up to be". He reports an estimated "30% of listers spend more time managing their lists than [they do] completing what's on them".

- This could be caused by procrastination by prolonging the planning activity. This is akin to analysis paralysis. As with any activity, there's a point of diminishing returns.

Rigid Adherence:

- Hendrickson asserts that rigid adherence to task lists can create a "tyranny of the to-do list" that forces one to "waste time on unimportant activities".
- Again, the point of diminishing returns applies here too, but towards the size of the task. Some level of detail must be taken for granted for a task system to work. Rather than put "clean the kitchen", "clean the bedroom", and "clean the bathroom", it is more efficient to put "housekeeping" and save time spent writing and reduce the system's administrative load. The risk of consolidating tasks, however, is that "housekeeping" in this example may prove overwhelming or nebulously defined, which will either increase the risk of procrastination, or a mismanaged project.
- Listing routine tasks wastes time. If you are in the habit of brushing your teeth every day, then there is no reason to put it down on the task list. The same goes for getting out of bed, fixing meals, etc. If you need to track routine tasks, then a standard list or chart may be useful, to avoid the procedure of manually listing these items over and over.
- To remain flexible, a task system must allow for disaster. A disaster occurs constantly whether it is personal or business-related. A company must have a cushion of time ready for a disaster. Even if it is a small disaster, if no one made time for this situation, it can blow up bigger, causing the company to bankruptcy just because of poor time management.
- To avoid getting stuck in a wasteful pattern, the task system should also include regular planning and system-evaluation sessions, to weed out inefficiencies and ensure the user is headed in the direction he or she truly desires.
- If some time is not regularly spent on achieving long-range goals, the individual may get stuck in a perpetual holding pattern on short-term plans, like staying at a particular job much longer than originally planned.

Techniques for Setting Priorities

- *ABC Analysis*: A technique that has been used in business management for a long time is the categorization of large data into groups. These groups are often marked A, B, and C—hence the name.

Activities are ranked upon these general criteria:

- A – Tasks that are perceived as being urgent and important.
- B – Tasks that are important but not urgent.
- C – Tasks that are neither urgent nor important.

Each group is then rank-ordered in priority. To further refine priority, some individuals choose to then force-rank all "B" items as either "A" or "C". ABC analysis can incorporate more than three groups. ABC analysis is frequently combined with Pareto analysis.

- *Pareto Analysis*: This is the idea that 80% of tasks can be completed in 20% of the disposable time. The remaining 20% of tasks will take up 80% of the time. This principle is used to sort tasks into two parts. According to this form of Pareto analysis it is recommended that tasks that fall into the first category be assigned a higher priority. The 80-20-rule can also be applied to increase productivity: it is assumed that 80% of the productivity can be achieved by doing 20% of the tasks. If productivity is the aim of time management, then these tasks should be prioritized higher. It depends on the method adopted to complete the task. There is always a simpler and easy way to complete the task. If one uses a complex way, it will be time consuming. So, one should always try to find out the alternate ways to complete each task.
- *Fit*: Essentially, fit is the congruence of the requirements of a task with the available resources at the time. Often people are constrained by externally controlled schedules, locations, etc., and "fit" allows us to maximize our productivity given those constraints. For example, if one encounters a gap of 15 minutes in their schedule, it is typically more efficient to complete a task that would require 15 minutes, than to complete a task that can be done in 5 minutes, or to start a task that would take 4 weeks. This concept also applies to time of the day: free time at 7am is probably less usefully applied to the goal of learning the drums, and more productively a time to read a book. Lastly, fit can be applied to location: free time at home would be used differently from free time at work, in town, etc.
- *POSEC method*: POSEC is an acronym for *Prioritize by Organizing, Streamlining, Economizing and Contributing*. The method dictates a template which emphasizes an average individual's immediate sense of emotional and monetary security. It suggests that by attending to one's personal responsibilities first, an individual is better positioned to shoulder collective responsibilities. Inherent in the acronym is a hierarchy of self-realization which mirrors Abraham Maslow's "Hierarchy of needs".

- *Prioritize*: Your time and define your life by goals.
- *Organizing*: Things you have to accomplish regularly to be successful.
- *Streamlining*: Things you may not like to do, but must do.
- *Economizing*: Things you should do or may even like to do, but they're not pressingly urgent.
- *Contributing*: By paying attention to the few remaining things that make a difference.

- *The Eisenhower Method*: All tasks are evaluated using the criteria important/unimportant and urgent/not urgent and put in according quadrants. Tasks in unimportant/not urgent are dropped, tasks in important/urgent are done immediately and personally, tasks in unimportant/urgent are delegated and tasks in important/not urgent get an end date and are done personally. This method is said to have been used by US President Dwight D. Eisenhower, and is outlined in a quote attributed to him: *What is important is seldom urgent and what is urgent is seldom important.*

PROJECT MANAGEMENT

Project Management is a well-established approach to managing and controlling the introduction of new initiatives or organizational changes. Projects are finite in length, usually one-time pieces of work involving a number of activities that must be completed within a given time frame, and often on a fixed budget. Common examples of projects are construction of a building, introduction of a new product, installation of a new piece of machinery in a manufacturing plant, creation of a new software tool, or the design and launch of a new advertising campaign. While the very simplest projects can be managed easily by applying common sense and just getting on with things, projects that are more complex need a great deal of planning, and benefit from a formal, disciplined management approach.

From making sure that activities will actually meet the specified need, to devising a workable schedule, developing systems for reporting progress, and managing requests for changes–all of these issues require thoughtful consideration. Managing projects well requires a great deal of time, skill, and finesse. There are many sides to project management and this is what makes it so interesting and demanding. Project managers are expected to take an uncertain event and make a certain promise to deliver. They are also expected to do this within a specified time and within a limited budget.

ATTENTION MANAGEMENT

Attention management refers to models and tools for supporting the management of attention at the individual or at the collective level and at the short term of at a longer terms.

APPROACHES FOR ATTENTION SUPPORT

Different researches have been conducted in using ICT for supporting attention, and in particular models have been elaborated for supporting attention.

Supporting the management of attention objective is to bring a certain number of solution to:

- People perception cognitive limitations, such as the limited capacity of the human short term memory or the theoretical cognitive limit to the number of people with whom one can maintain stable social relationships.
- Information overload
- Social interaction overload
- Interruption
- Multitasking

Tools can been designed for supporting attention:

- At the organizational level, by supporting organisation processes
- At the collective level
- At the individual level, for instance using attentive user interfaces.
- At the individual level by helping people to assess and analyse their attention related practices.

These tools are often adaptive hypermedia, and often rely on the profiling the user in order determine how to better support people attention.

PROJECTS

A certain number of projects have been conducted to investigate how to use ICT to support attention such as:

- AtGentive Attentive Agents for Collaborative Learners.
- Sake-Semantic-enabled Agile Knowledge-based e-Government
- Suitor

PERSONAL KNOWLEDGE MANAGEMENT

Personal knowledge management refers to a collection of processes that an individual carries out to gather, classify, store, search, retrieve, and share knowledge in his/her daily activities and how these processes support work activities. It is a response to the idea that knowledge workers increasingly need to be responsible for their own growth and learning and represents a bottom-up approach to knowledge management, as opposed to more traditional, top-down KM. Although as early as 1998 Davenport wrote on the importance to worker productivity of understanding individual knowledge processes, the term *personal knowledge management* appears to be relatively new.

Its origin can be traced in a working paper by Frand and Hixon. PKM integrates personal information management, focused on individual skills, with knowledge management in addition to input from a variety of disciplines such as cognitive psychology, management, and philosophy. From an organizational perspective, understanding of the field has developed in light of expanding knowledge about human cognitive capabilities and the permeability of organizational boundaries. From a metacognitive perspective, it compares various modalities within human cognition as to their competence and efficacy. It is an underresearched area.

PKM MODELS

Dorsey identified information retrieval, assessment and evaluation, organization, analysis, presentation, security, and collaboration as essential to PKM. Wright's model involves four interrelated domains: analytical, information, social, and learning. The analytical domain involves competencies such as interpretation, envisioning, application, creation, and contextualization.

The information dimension comprises the sourcing, assessment, organization, aggregation, and communication of information. The social dimension involves finding and collaborating with people, development of both close networks and extended networks, and dialogue. The learning dimension entails expanding pattern recognition and sensemaking capabilities, reflection, development of new knowledge, improvement of skills, and extension to others.

This model stresses the importance of both bonding and bridging networks. In Nonaka and Takeuchi's SECI model of knowledge creation, knowledge can be tacit or explicit, with the interaction of the two resulting in new knowledge. Smedley has developed a PKM model based on Nonaka and colleagues' model in which an expert provides direction and a community of practice provides support for personal knowledge creation. Trust is central to knowledge sharing in this model.

Personal knowledge management can also be viewed along two main dimensions, personal knowledge and personal management. Zhang has developed a model of PKM in relation to organizational knowledge management that considers two axes of knowledge properties and management perspectives, either organizational or personal. These aspects of organizational and personal knowledge are interconnected through the OAPI process, whereby organizational knowledge is personalized and individualized and personal knowledge is aggregated and operationalized as organizational knowledge.

CRITICISMS OF PKM

Not everyone agrees that the focus on the individual is a good thing, or that PKM is anything more than a new wrapper around personal information management. Dave Snowden has asserted that most individuals cannot manage their knowledge in the traditional sense of "managing" and has advocated thinking in terms of sensemaking rather than PKM. Most notably, some argue that knowledge is never an individual product-that it emerges through connections, dialog and social interaction. However, in Wright's model, PKM involves the application to problem solving of analytical, information, social, and learning dimensions, which are interrelated, and so is inherently social.

An aim of PKM is "helping individuals to be more effective in personal, organisational and social environments", often through the use of technology such as networking software. It has been argued, however, that equation of PKM with technology has limited the value and utility of the concept.

PKM SKILLS

Skills associated with personal knowledge management:

- *Collaboration skills*: Coordination, synchronization, experimentation, cooperation, and design.
- *Communication skills*: Perception, intuition, expression, visualization, and interpretation.
- *Creative skills*: Imagination, pattern recognition, appreciation, innovation, inference. Understanding of complex adaptive systems.
- *Information literacy*: Understanding what information is important and how to find unknown information.
- *Manage learning*: Manage how and when the individual learns.
- *Networking with others*: Knowing what your network of people knows. Knowing who might have additional knowledge and resources to help you
- *Organizational skills*: Personal librarianship. Personal categorization and taxonomies.
- *Reflection*: Continuous improvement on how the individual operates.
- Researching, canvassing, paying attention, interviewing and observational 'cultural anthropology' skills

PKM TOOLS

Some organizations are now introducing PKM 'systems' with some or all of four components:

- *Just-in-time Canvassing*: Templates and e-mail canvassing lists that enable people to identify and connect with the appropriate experts and expertise quickly and effectively
- *Knowledge harvesting*: Software tools that automatically collect appropriate knowledge residing on subject matter experts' hard drives
- *Content management tools*: Taxonomy processes and desktop search tools that enable employees to subscribe to, find, organize, and publish information that resides on their desktops
- *Personal Productivity Improvement*: Knowledge fairs and one-on-one

training sessions to help each employee make more effective personal use of the knowledge, learning, and technology resources available in the context of their work

PKM has also been linked to these tools:

- Social bookmarking and enterprise social bookmarking
- Knowledge logs
- E-mail, calendars, task managers
- Online Web Assistants
- Wikis
  - Desktop wikis
  - Personal wikis
  - Semantic Wikis

Other useful tools include Open Space Technology, cultural anthropology, stories and narrative, mindmaps, concept maps and eco-language, and single frames and similar visualization techniques. Individuals use these tools to capture and ideas, expertise, experience, opinions, or thoughts, and this 'voicing' will encourage cognitive diversity and promote free exchanges away from a centralized policed knowledge repository. The goal is to facilitate knowledge sharing and personal content management.

BEATING PROCRASTINATION

If you've found yourself putting off important tasks over and over again, you're not alone. In fact, many people procrastinate to some degree–but some are so chronically affected by procrastination that it stops them fulfilling their potential and disrupts their careers. The key to controlling this destructive habit is to recognize when you start procrastinating, understand why it happens and take active steps to manage your time and outcomes better.

WHAT IS PROCRASTINATION?

In a nutshell, you procrastinate when you put off things that you should be focusing on right now, usually in favour of doing something that is more enjoyable or that you're more comfortable doing. According to psychologist Professor Clarry Lay, a prominent writer on procrastination, procrastination occurs when there's "a temporal gap between intended behaviour and enacted behaviour." That is, procrastination is occurring when there's a significant time period between when people intend to do a job, and when they actually do it.

HOW TO OVERCOME PROCRASTINATION

Follow these steps to deal with and control procrastination:

Step 1: Recognize that you're Procrastinating

If you're honest with yourself, you probably know when you're procrastinating. But to be sure, take our Are You a Procrastinator? self test.

Here are some useful indicators that will help you know when you're procrastinating:

- Filling your day with low priority tasks from your To Do List.
- Reading e-mails several times without starting work on them or deciding what you're going to do with them.
- Sitting down to start a high-priority task, and almost immediately going off to make a cup of coffee.
- Leaving an item on your To Do list for a long time, even though you know it's important.
- Regularly saying "Yes" to unimportant tasks that others ask you to do, and filling your time with these instead of getting on with the important tasks already on your list.
- Waiting for the "right mood" or the "right time" to tackle the important task at hand.

Step 2: Work Out why you're Procrastinating

Why you procrastinate can depend on both you and the task. But it's important to understand which of the two is relevant in a given situation, so that you can select the best approach for overcoming your reluctance to get going. One reason for procrastination is that people find a particular job unpleasant, and try to avoid it because of that. Most jobs have unpleasant or boring aspects to them, and often the best way of dealing with these is to get them over and done with quickly, so that you can focus on the more enjoyable aspects of the job.

Another cause is that people are disorganized. Organized people manage to fend of the temptation to procrastinate, because they will have things like prioritized to-do lists and schedules which emphasize how important the piece work is, and identify precisely when it's due. They'll also have planned how long a task will take to do, and will have worked back from that point to identify when they need to get started in order to avoid it being late. Organized people are also better placed to avoid procrastination, because they know how to break the work down into manageable "next steps". Even if you're organized, you can feel overwhelmed by the task.

You may doubt that you have the skills or resources you think you need, so you seek comfort in doing tasks you know you're capable of completing. Unfortunately, the big task isn't going to go away–truly important tasks rarely do. You may also fear success as much as failure. For example, you may think that success will lead to you being swamped with more requests to do this type of task, or that you'll be pushed to take on things that you feel are beyond you.

Surprisingly, perfectionists are often procrastinators, as they can tend to think "I don't have the right skills or resources to do this perfectly now, so I won't do it at all." One final major cause of procrastination is having underdeveloped decision-making skills. If you simply can't decide what to do, you're likely to put off taking action in case you do the wrong thing.

Step 3: Adopt Anti-Procrastination Strategies

Procrastination is a habit–a deeply ingrained pattern of behaviour. That means that you won't just break it overnight. Habits only stop being habits when you have persistently stopped practising them, so use as many approaches as possible to maximize your chances of beating procrastination. Some tips will work better for some people than for others, and for some tasks than others. And, sometimes, you may simply need to try a fresh approach to beat the "procrastination peril"!

These general tips will help motivate you to get moving:

- Make up your own rewards. For example, promise yourself a piece of tasty flapjack at lunchtime if you've completed a certain task. And make sure you notice how good it feels to finish things!
- Ask someone else to check up on you. Peer pressure works! This is the principle behind slimming and other self-help groups, and it is widely recognized as a highly effective approach.
- Identify the unpleasant consequences of NOT doing the task.
- Work out the cost of your time to your employer. As your employers are paying you to do the things that they think are important, you're not delivering value for money if you're not doing those things. Shame yourself into getting going!
- Aim to "eat an elephant beetle" first thing, every day!

If you're pocrastinating because you're disorganized, here's how to get organized!

- Keep a To-Do list so that you can't "conveniently" forget about unpleasant or overwhelming tasks.
- Use an Urgent/Important Matrix to help prioritize your to-do list so that you can't try to kid yourself that it would be acceptable to put off doing something on the grounds that it's unimportant, or that you have many urgent things which ought to be done first when, in reality, you're procrastinating.
- Become a master of scheduling and project planning, so that you know when to start those all-important projects.
- Set yourself time-bound goals: that way, you'll have no time for procrastination!
- Focus on one task at a time.

If you're putting off starting a project because you find it overwhelming, you need to take a different approach.

Here are some tips:

- Break the project into a set of smaller, more manageable tasks. You may find it helpful to create an action plan.
- Start with some quick, small tasks if you can, even if these aren't

the logical first actions. You'll feel that you're achieving things, and so perhaps the whole project won't be so overwhelming after all.

If you're procrastinating because you find the task unpleasant:

- Many procrastinators overestimate the unplea-santness of a task. So give it a try! You may find that it's not as bad as you thought!
- Hold the unpleasant consequences of not doing the work at the front of your mind.
- Reward yourself for doing the task.

Finally, if you're procrastinating because you can't decide what action to take, and are putting off making a decision because you're nervous about making the wrong choice, see our decision-making part. This teaches a range of powerful and effective decision-making techniques. Remember: the longer you can spend without procrastinating, the greater your chances of breaking this destructive habit for good!

KEY POINTS

To have a good chance of conquering procrastination, you need to spot straight away that you're doing it. Then, you need to identify why you're procrastinating and taken appropriate steps to overcome the block. Part of the solution is to develop good time management, organizational and personal effectiveness habits, such as those described in Make Time for Success! This helps you establish the right priorities, and manage your time in such a way that you make the most of the opportunities open to you.

ACTIVITY LOGS

How long do you spend each day on unimportant things; Things that don't really contribute to your success at work? Do you KNOW how much time you've spent reading junk mail, talking to colleagues, making coffee and eating lunch? And how often have you thought, "I could achieve so much more if I just had another half hour each day." And are you aware of when in the day you check your e-mail, write important articles or do your long-term planning? Most people find they function at different levels of effectiveness at different times of day as their energy levels fluctuate.

Your effectiveness may vary depending on the amount of sugar in your blood, the length of time since you last took a break, routine distractions, stress, discomfort, or a range of other factors. Activity logs help you to analyse how you actually spend your time. The first time you use an activity log you may be shocked to see the amount of time that you waste! Memory is a very poor guide when it comes to this, as it can be too easy to forget time spent on non-core tasks. Keeping an Activity Log for several days helps you to understand how you spend your time, and when you perform at your best. Without modifying your behaviour any further than you have to, note down the things you do as you do them on this template. Every time you change activities, whether opening mail, working, making coffee, gossiping with colleagues or whatever, note down the time of the change. As well as recording activities, note how you feel, whether alert, flat, tired, energetic, etc.

Do this periodically throughout the day. You may decide to integrate your activity log with a stress diary. Once you have logged your time for a few days, analyse your daily activity log. You may be alarmed to see the amount of time you spend doing low value jobs! You may also see that you are energetic in some parts of the day, and flat in other parts. A lot of this can depend on the rest breaks you take, the times and amounts you eat, and quality of your nutrition. The activity log gives you some basis for experimenting with these variables.

Your analysis should help you to free up extra time in your day by applying one of the following actions to most activities:

- Eliminate jobs that your employer shouldn't be paying you to do. These may include tasks that someone else in the organization should be doing, possibly at a lower pay rate, or personal activities such as sending non-work e-mails.
- Schedule your most challenging tasks for the times of day when your energy is highest. That way your work will be better and it should take you less time.
- Try to minimize the number of times a day you switch between types of task. For example, read and reply to e-mails in blocks once in the morning and once in the afternoon only.
- Reduce the amount of time spent on legitimate personal activities such as making coffee.

Activity logs are useful tools for auditing the way that you use your time. They can also help you to track changes in your energy, alertness and effectiveness throughout the day. By analyzing your activity log you will be able to identify and eliminate time-wasting or low-yield jobs. You will also know the times of day at which you are most effective, so that you can carry out your most important tasks during these times.

TO-DO LISTS

Do you frequently feel overwhelmed by the amount of work you have to do? Do you face a constant barrage of looming deadlines? Or do you sometimes just forget to do something important, so that people have to chase you to get work done? All of these are symptoms of not keeping a proper "To-Do List". To-Do Lists are prioritized lists of all the tasks that you need to carry out. They list everything that you have to do, with the most important tasks at the top of the list, and the least important tasks at the bottom. While this sounds a simple thing to do, it's when people start to use To-Do Lists properly that they often make their first personal productivity/ time management breakthrough, and start to make a real success of their careers.

By keeping a To-Do List, you make sure that you capture all of the tasks you have to complete in one place. This is essential if you're not going to forget things. And by prioritizing work, you plan the order in which you'll do things, so you can tell what needs your immediate attention, and what you can quietly forget about until much, much later.

This is essential if you're going to beat work overload. Without To-Do Lists, you'll seem dizzy, unfocused and unreliable to the people around you. With To-Do Lists, you'll be much better organized, and will seem much more reliable. This is very important!

PREPARING A TO-DO LIST

Start by writing down all of the tasks that you need to complete, and if they are large, break them down into their component elements. If these still seem large, break them down again. Do this until you have listed everything that you have to do, and until tasks are will take no more than 1-2 hours to complete. This may be a huge and intimidating list, but our next step makes it manageable! Next, run through these jobs allocating priorities from A to F. If too many tasks have a high priority, run through the list again and demote the less important ones. Once you have done this, rewrite the list in priority order. You will then have a precise plan that you can use to eliminate the problems you face. You will be able to tackle these in order of importance or urgency. This allows you to separate important jobs from the many time-consuming trivial ones.

USING YOUR TO-DO LISTS

Different people use To-Do Lists in different ways in different situations: if you are in a sales-type role, a good way of motivating yourself is to keep your list relatively short and aim to complete it every day. In an operational role, or if tasks are large or dependent on too many other people, then it may be better to keep one list and 'chip away' at it. It may be that you carry unimportant jobs from one To-Do List to the next. You may not be able to complete some very low priority jobs for several months. Only worry about this if you need to–if you are running up against a deadline for them, raise their priority. If you have not used To-Do Lists before, try them now: They are one of the keys to being really productive and efficient.

KEY POINTS

Prioritized To-Do Lists are fundamentally important to efficient work.

If you use To-Do Lists, you will ensure that:

- You remember to carry out all necessary tasks
- You tackle the most important jobs first, and do not waste time on trivial tasks.
- You do not get stressed by a large number of unimportant jobs.

To draw up a Prioritized To-Do List, download our template and use it to list all the tasks you must carry out. Mark the importance of the task next to it, with a priority from A to F. Redraft the list into this order of importance. Now carry out the jobs at the top of the list first. These are the most important, most beneficial tasks to complete.

ACTION PROGRAMMES

To-Do Lists are great for managing a small number of tasks. The problem is that, for most of us, our To-Do List is not really a planned, focused action list. Rather, it is a sort of a catch-all for a lot of things that are unresolved and not yet translated into outcomes. Specific entries, such as "Call Tina," exist along with vaguer aspirations, such as "Get started on house painting project." Often, the real actionable details of what the list-maker has "to do" are actually missing. What this means is that you tend to do the specific tasks, and fail to make progress with the big, important projects. And even if you do get beyond the quick actions, having a complete project as a "to do" can lead you to focus all of your attention on it. This makes multi-tasking difficult.

This can be a serious problem in a job where you need to make progress on many different projects at the same time-and this is exactly the situation most senior managers find themselves in. This is where Action Programmes are useful. Action Programmes are "industrial strength" versions of To-Do Lists. Because they incorporate short-, medium- and long-term goals, they allow you to plan your time, without forgotten commitments coming in to blow your schedule apart. Because priorities are properly thought through, you'll be focusing on the things that matter, and not frittering your time away on low value activities. And because they support delegation, they help you get into the habit of delegating jobs where you can. All of this lets you save time-and get away on time-whilst also significantly increasing your effectiveness and productivity.

HOW TO USE THE TOOL

Follow this four-step procedure to create your Action Programme:

Step 1. Collection

First, make a list inventory of all the things in your world that require resolution. Try to collect and write down everything-urgent or not, big or small, personal or professional-that you feel is incomplete and needs action from you to get completed. To an extent, this collection is taking place automatically. E-mail requests are getting stored in your e-mail account, memos demanding attention are being delivered to your in-tray, mail is reaching your mailbox and messages asking for action are accumulating on your voice mail. But there is other stuff-stuff that is idling in your head, projects you want to run, things you intend to deal with lying at the bottom of the drawer, ideas written down on stray bits of paper-that need to be gathered and put in place too. Bring all of these actions and projects together and inventory them in one place. And-this is really important-make sure that your personal goals are brought onto this list.

Step 2. Pruning

Now, process the list you made in step 1, by looking carefully at each item. Decide whether you should, actually, take action on it. A lot of what comes our way has no real relevance to us, or is really not important in the scale of things. If that is the case, then delete these things from your inventory.

Step 3. Organizing and Prioritizing

This comes in three parts. First of all, review your inventory of items. For any which are separate, individual actions that make up part of a larger project, group these individual actions together into their projects. For example, at home, you may want to improve your bathroom, and repaint your living room: these can go into a "Home Renovation" project.

At work, you may be providing input into the requirements for a new computer system, and may be expected to test and then train your team on this system at a point in the future: all of these go into a "computer system" project. What you'll find is that once you start, items will almost seem to "organize themselves" into coherent projects. You also need to make sure that your personal goals are included as individual projects. Second, review these projects, and allocate a priority to them depending on their importance. Clearly, your personal goals are exceptionally important projects! Third, insert your projects into a formatted Action Programme.

The Action Programme is split up into three parts:

- A "Next Action List," which shows the small next actions that you will take to move your projects forward.
- A "Delegated Actions List," which shows projects and actions have delegated to other people.
- A "Project Catalog" that shows all of the projects you are engaged in and the small individual tasks that you have identified so far that contribute to them.

The great news is that, by this stage, you've already created the largest part of this: the Project Catalog! This is the list of prioritized projects and activities that you've just completed. Typically, the Project Catalog is at the back of the Action Programme, as it's often only referred to during a weekly review process.

Next, create the Delegated Actions List by working through your Project Catalog, and identifying tasks that you've delegated. Record these under the name of the person who you've delegated the activity to, along with the checkpoints you've agreed. Typically, the Delegated Actions List sits in front of the Project Catalog in your Action Programme document, as it's referred to quite often. Finally, create your Next Action List by working through the projects to which you've given the highest priority-the projects that you want and need to move forward on straight away-and extracting the small, logical next actions for these projects. Now review the Next Action List. If it is too cluttered, move some of the less urgent/important jobs back into the project catalog. If it is thin and under-challenging, pull up some more Next Actions from the Project Catalog. Also, it makes sense to prioritize the items in the Next Action List so you know what to focus on.

Step 4. "Working" your Action Programme

An Action Programme is typically fairly long. But you don't have to run through the entire Programme every day! Usually, you'll only be dealing with the top page or pages. Some activities may be day-specific or time-specific. Depending of the way you work, these can be either maintained as the top page of your Action Programme or marked on your calendar. In effect, these pages are just a new form of your old To-Do List. It is just that only specific short actions are outlined here, while the major projects to which the actions belong are stored in your Project Catalog. What you must do, however, is review your Action Programme periodically, for example, every week. Delete or archive items you've completed, move items from the Project Catalog to the front pages as you make progress on your project, and add any new actions that have come your way.

PRIORITIZATION

Prioritization is the essential skill you need to make the very best use of your own efforts, and those of your team. It is particularly important when time is limited and demands are seemingly unlimited. It helps you to spend your time wisely, freeing you and your team up from less important tasks that can be attended to later–or quietly dropped. With good prioritization you can bring order to chaos, massively reduce stress, and move forwards successfully. Without it, you'll flounder around, drowning in competing demands.

SIMPLE PRIORITIZATION

At a simple level, you can prioritize based on time constraints, on the potential profitability or benefit of the task you're facing, or on the pressure you're under to complete a job:

- Prioritization based on project value or profitability is probably the most commonly-used and rational basis for prioritization. Whether this is based on a subjective guess at value or a sophisticated financial evaluation, it often gives the most efficient results.
- Time constraints are important where other people are depending

on you to complete a task, and particularly where this task is on the critical path of an important project. Here, a small amount of your own effort can go a very long way.

- And it's a brave person who resists his or her boss's pressure to complete a task, when that pressure is reasonable and legitimate.

PRIORITIZATION TOOLS

While these simple approaches to prioritization suit many situations, there are plenty of special cases where you'll need other prioritization and time management tools if you're going to be truly effective. While these simple approaches to prioritization suit many situations, there are plenty of special cases where you'll need other tools if you're going to be truly effective.

We look at some of these below:

- *Paired Comparison Analysis*: Paired Comparison Analysis is most useful where decision criteria are vague, subjective or inconsistent. It helps you prioritize options by asking you to compare each item on a list with all other items on the list individually. By deciding in each case which of the two is most important, you can consolidate results to get a prioritized list.
- *Grid Analysis*: Grid Analysis helps you prioritize a list of tasks where you need to take many different factors into consideration.
- *The Action Priority Matrix*: This quick and simple diagramming technique asks you to plot the value of the task against the effort it will consume. By doing this you can quickly spot the "quick wins" which will give you the greatest rewards in the shortest possible time, and avoid the "hard slogs" which soak up time for little eventual reward. This is an ingenious approach for making highly efficient prioritization decisions.
- *The Urgent/Important Matrix*: Similar to the Action Priority Matrix, this technique asks you to think about whether tasks are urgent or important. Frequently, seemingly urgent tasks actually aren't that important. And often, really important activities just aren't that urgent. This approach helps you cut through this.
- *The Ansoff and Boston Matrices*: These give you quick "rules of thumb" for prioritizing the opportunities open to you. The Ansoff Matrix helps you evaluate and prioritize opportunities by risk. The Boston Matrix does a similar job, helping you prioritize opportunities based on the attractiveness of a market and your ability to take advantage of it.
- *Pareto Analysis*: Where you're facing a flurry of problems needing to be solved, Pareto Analysis helps you identify the most important changes to make. It firstly asks you to group together the different types of problem you face, and then asks you to count the number

of cases of each type of problem. By prioritizing the most common type of problem, you can focus your efforts on resolving it. This clears time to focus on the next set of problems, and so on.

- *Nominal Group Technique*: Nominal Group Technique is a useful technique for prioritizing issues and projects within a group, giving everyone fair input into the prioritization process. This is particularly useful where consensus is important, and where a robust group decision needs to be made. Using this tool, each group participant "nominates" his or her priority issues, and then ranks them on a scale, of say 1 to 10. The score for each issue is then added up, with issues then prioritized based on scores. The obvious fairness of this approach makes it particularly useful where prioritization is based on subjective criteria, and where people's "buy in" to the prioritization decision is needed.

EFFECTIVE SCHEDULING

So far in this part of Mind Tools, we have looked at your priorities and your goals–these define what you aspire to do with your time. Scheduling is where these aspirations meet reality. Scheduling is the process by which you look at the time available to you, and plan how you will use it to achieve the goals you have identified.

By using a schedule properly, you can:

- Understand what you can realistically achieve with your time;
- Plan to make the best use of the time available;
- Leave enough time for things you absolutely must do;
- Preserve contingency time to handle 'the unexpected'; and
- Minimize stress by avoiding over-commitment to others.

A well thought-through schedule allows you to manage your commitments, while still leaving you time to do the things that are important to you. It is therefore your most important weapon for beating work overload.

HOW TO USE THE TOOL

Scheduling is best done on a regular basis, for example at the start of every week.

Go through the following steps in preparing your schedule:

- Start by identifying the time you want to make available for your work. This will depend on the design of your job and on your personal goals in life.
- Next, block in the actions you absolutely must take to do a good job. These will often be the things you are assessed against.
- For example, if you manage people, then you must make time available for coaching, supervision, and dealing with issues that arise. Similarly, you must allow time to communicate with your boss and key people around you.

- Review your To Do List, and schedule in the high-priority, urgent activities, as well as the essential maintenance tasks that cannot be delegated and cannot be avoided.
- Next, block in appropriate contingency time. You will learn how much of this you need by experience. Normally, the more unpredictable your job, the more contingency time you need. The reality of many people's work is of constant interruption: Studies show some managers getting an average of as little as six minutes uninterrupted work done at a time.
- Obviously, you cannot tell when interruptions will occur. However, by leaving space in your schedule, you give yourself the flexibility to rearrange your schedule to react effectively to urgent issues.
- What you now have left is your "discretionary time": the time available to deliver your priorities and achieve your goals. Review your Prioritized To Do List and personal goals, evaluate the time needed to achieve these actions, and schedule them in.

By the time you reach step 5, you may find that you have little or no discretionary time available. If this is the case, then revisit the assumptions you used in the first four steps. Question whether things are absolutely necessary, whether they can be delegated, or whether they can be done in an abbreviated way.

Remember that one of the most important ways people learn to achieve success is by maximizing the 'leverage' they can achieve with their time. They increase the amount of work they can manage by delegating work to other people, spending money outsourcing key tasks, or using technology to automate as much of their work as possible. This frees them up to achieve their goals.

Also, use this as an opportunity to review your To Do List and Personal Goals. Have you set goals that just aren't achievable with the time you have available? Are you taking on too many additional duties? Or are you treating things as being more important than they really are? If your discretionary time is still limited, then you may need to renegotiate your workload. With a well-thought through schedule as evidence, you may find this surprisingly easy.

KEY POINTS

Scheduling is the process by which you plan your use of time. By scheduling effectively, you can reduce stress and maximize your effectiveness. This makes it one of the most important time management skills you can use. Before you can schedule efficiently, you need an effective scheduling system. This can be a diary, calendar, paper-based organizer, PDA or a software package like MS Outlook. The best solution depends entirely on your circumstances. Scheduling is then a five-step process.

1. Identify the time you have available.
2. Block in the essential tasks you must carry out to succeed in your job.
3. Schedule in high priority urgent tasks and vital "house-keeping" activities.
4. Block in appropriate contingency time to handle unpredictable interruptions.
5. In the time that remains, schedule the activities that address your priorities and personal goals.

If you have little or no discretionary time left by the time you reach step five, then revisit the assumptions you have made in steps one to four.

GOAL SETTING

The ability to set goals is at the very core of personal productivity, career success, and effective leadership; and the resources on this page help you learn how to do this.

PERSONAL GOAL SETTING

Why is personal goal setting so important in personal time management? From the time management perspective, your life is a sequence of big and small choices and decisions. It is those choices that you really manage, not the flow of time.

Personal goal setting is the wisdom that comes out of a lot of practical experience and psychology research to help you direct your conscious and subconscious decisions towards success, building up your motivation to achieve your personal or business goals.

LOCKE'S GOAL SETTING THEORY

Edwin Locke's theory of goal setting has many practical applications, in and outside of the business environment. A professor at the University of Maryland, Locke's theory defines characteristics that encourage success. While the theory rings of psychology, its applications in the business world have been profound and enduring.

The Influence of Ryan

Locke's goal-setting theory was created on the premise, originally set forth by professor Thomas A. Ryan, that "conscious goals affect action." As quoted in Locke's "Building a Practically Useful Theory of Goal Setting and Task Motivation," Ryan argued that human behaviour is affected by conscious purposes, plans, intentions, tasks and the like.

Basic Definition

Locke's theory operates on the premise that individuals create goals by making careful decisions to do so and are compelled towards those goals by virtue of the goal having been set. Basically, Locke's theory states that if an individual sets goals, he will be motivated to achieve those goals by virtue of having set them. Several elements must exist in order for the goal-setting effect to take place.

Goals must be clear, challenging and attainable, and there must be some method of receiving feedback. Locke finds that the goal itself is not the motivator, but rather the perceived difference between what was actually attained and what had been planned for.

Goal Difficulty and Performance

Locke, and professors Steve Motowidlo and Phil Bobko found that "higher expectancies lead to higher levels of performance," which is in accordance with Vroom's valence-instrumentality-expectancy theory. Somewhat contradictorily, they also showed that when expectations are low but goal level is high, performance would be high also.

Goal Mechanisms

Goals serve four primary functions:

- By specifying a goal, one must direct focus towards that goal and away from activities unrelated to that goal.
- The setting of a goal is a behaviour-stimulating act. According to Locke, "high goals lead to greater effort than low goals."
- Goals have a positive effect on persistence. However, there is an inverse relationship between time and intensity.
- Goals subconsciously direct the person towards discovering better ways of doing things, be they calculations or physical acts.

Goal Moderators

Locke's theory states that, in order for a goal to be successful, the person must be committed to it wholly and possess self-efficacy. This self-efficacy must be boosted initially by the fact that the person was assigned the task and thus believed to be capable of its completion.

He also found that "for goals to be effective, people need summary feedback that reveals progress in relation to their goals. If they do not know how they are doing, it is difficult or impossible for them to adjust the level or direction of their effort or to adjust their performance strategies to match what the goal requires." Task complexity also moderates the effects of goals because more complex goals require the review of more complex strategies than lower difficulty goals.

Lastly, more complex goals require proximal goals rather than a singular distal goal. Basically, the complex goals should be broken down into several smaller goals. The setting of proximal goals also promotes progress feedback.

Limitations

As noted by Locke, his goal-setting theory has several limitations:

- Goal conflict. Sometimes an individual has several goals, some of which may be in conflict. When this occurs, performance will suffer.
- Goals and risk. More difficult goals/deadlines can spur riskier behaviours and strategies.
- Personality. Goal success is largely effected by self-efficacy. Also, personality plays a large role in goal determination and approach.
- Goals and subconscious motivation. Subconscious motivators affect people regularly, but how these subconscious motivators affect goal performance has not been studied.

GOLDEN RULES OF GOAL SETTING

If you want to succeed, you need to set goals. Without goals you lack focus and direction. Goal setting not only allows you to take control of your life's direction; it also provides you a benchmark for determining whether you are actually succeeding. Think about it: Having a million dollars in the bank is only proof of success if one of your goals is to amass riches. If your goal is to practice acts of charity, then keeping the money for yourself is suddenly contrary to how you would define success. To accomplish your goals, however, you need to know how to set them. You can't simply say, "I want." and expect it to happen. Goal setting is a process that starts with careful consideration of what you want to achieve, and ends with a lot of hard work to actually do it. In between there are some very well defined steps that transcend the specifics of each goal. Knowing these steps will allow you to formulate goals that you can accomplish.

The Five Golden Rules

Rule No. 1

Set Goals that Motivate You When you set goals for yourself, it is important that they motivate you: This means making sure it is something that's important to you and there is value in achieving it. If you have little interest in the outcome, or it is irrelevant given the larger picture, then the chances of you putting in the work to make it happen are slim. Motivation is key to achieving goals.

Set goals that relate to the high priorities in your life. Without this type of focus you can end up with far too many goals, leaving you too little time to devote to each one. Goal achievement requires commitment, so to maximize the likelihood of success, you need to feel a sense of urgency and have an "I must do this" attitude. When you don't have this "must do" factor, you risk putting off what you need to do to make the goal a reality. This in turn leaves you feeling disappointed and frustrated with yourself, both of which are demotivating. And you can end up in a very destructive "I can't do anything or be successful at anything" frame of mind.

Rule No. 2: Set Smart Goals

You have probably heard of "SMART goals" already. But do you always apply the rule? The simple fact is that for any goal to be achieved it must be designed to be SMART.

There are many variations on what SMART stands for, but the essence is this-Goals should be:

- Specific
- Measurable
- Attainable
- Relevant
- Time Bound
  - *Set Specific Goals*: You goal must be clear and well defined. Vague or generalized goals are not achievable because they don't provide sufficient direction. Remember, you need goals to show you the way. How useful would a map of the United States be if there were only state borders marked on it and you were trying to get from Miami to Los Angeles? Do you even know which state you are starting from let alone which one you're headed to? Make it as easy as you can to get where you want to go by defining precisely where it is you want to end up.
  - *Set Measurable Goals*: Include precise amounts, dates, etc in your goals so you can measure your degree of success. If your goal is simply defined as "To reduce expenses" how will you know when you are successful? In one month's time if you have a 1% reduction or in two year's time when you have a 10% reduction? Without a way to measure your success you miss out on the celebration that comes with knowing you actually achieved something.
  - *Set Attainable Goals*: Make sure that it's possible to achieve the goals you set. If you set a goal that you have no hope of achieving you will only demoralize yourself and erode your confidence. However, resist the urge to set goals that are too easy. Accomplishing a goal that you didn't have to work very hard for can be an anticlimax at best, and can also make you fear setting future goals that carry a risk of non-achievement. By setting realistic yet challenging goals you hit the balance you need. These are the types of goals that require you to "raise the bar" and they bring the greatest personal satisfaction.
  - *Set Relevant Goals*: Goals should be relevant to the direction you want your life and career to take. By keeping goals aligned with

this, you'll develop the focus you need to get ahead and do what you want. Set widely scattered and inconsistent goals, and you'll fritter your time-and your life-away.

- *Set Time-Bound Goals*: You goals must have a deadline. This again, is so that you know when to celebrate your success. When you are working on a deadline, your sense of urgency increases and achievement will come that much quicker.

Rule No. 3: Set Goals in Writing

The physical act of writing down a goal makes it real and tangible. You have no excuse for forgetting about it. As you write, use the word "will" instead of "would like to" or "might". For example, "I will reduce my operating expenses by 10% this year." Not, "I would like to reduce my operating expenses by 10% this year." The first goal statement has power and you can "see" yourself reducing expenses, the second lacks passion and gives you an out if you get sidetracked. Post your goals in visible places to remind yourself everyday of what it is you intend to do. Put them on your walls, desk, computer monitor, bathroom mirror or refrigerator as a constant reminder. You can even post them in the Mind Tools Career Excellence Club forum and share them with other members, for added motivation.

Rule No. 4: Make an Action Plan

This step is often missed in the process of goal setting. You get so focused on the outcome that you forget to plan all of the steps that are needed along the way. By writing out the individual steps, and then crossing each one off as you complete it, you'll realise that you are making progress towards your ultimate goal. This is especially important if your goal is big and demanding, or long-term.

Rule No. 5: Stick With It!

Remember, goal setting is an ongoing activity not just a means to an end. Build in reminders to keep you on track and remember to review your goals continuously. Your end destination may remain quite similar over the long term but the action plan you set for yourself along the way can change significantly. Make sure the relevance, value, and necessity remain high.

Key Points

Goal setting is much more than simply saying you want something to happen. Unless you clearly define exactly what you want and understand why you want it the first place, your odds of success are considerably reduced. By following the Five Golden Rules of Goal Setting you can set goals with confidence and enjoy the satisfaction that comes along with knowing you achieved what you set out to do. What will you decide to accomplish today?

BACKWARD GOAL-SETTING

If your goal is to become an account executive within the next five years, where do you start your planning process? Or if your team needs to redesign the company's organizational structure, where do you begin? In planning, most of us would usually start building our plan from start to finish. What do you have to do first, second, third, and so on? What milestones do you have to reach before you can continue on with the next step in the plan? By what date does each step need to be completed? This is a solid form of Personal Goal Setting that works very well. When combined with the Golden Rules of Goal Setting, you have a motivating formula that can help you actively move yourself forward.

A New Approach

However, there's another, simple but lesser-used method of goal setting that can be equally as powerful. It can show you other ways to achieve the same result, and it can help you deal with the necessary unknowns of goal setting that can so often cause you to give up on your plan entirely. It's called backward planning, backward goal-setting, or backward design, and it's used quite often in education and training.

The idea is to start with your ultimate objective, your end goal, and then work backward from there to develop your plan. By starting at the end and looking back, you can mentally prepare yourself for success, map out the specific milestones you need to reach, and identify where in your plan you have to be particularly energetic or creative to achieve the desired results. It's much like a good presentation, when the presenter tells you where he's headed right at the beginning. Then, as the presentation unfolds, it's easy for you to follow the concepts and think critically about what's being said. If you have to figure out the main points as they come, your energy is often used up by just trying to keep up.

The Backward Planning Process

Here's how it works:

- Write down your ultimate goal. What specifically do you want to achieve, and by what date?
  - *Example*: "By January 1, 2013, I will be the key accounts director for Crunchy Chips International."
- Then ask yourself what milestone you need to accomplish just before that, in order to achieve your ultimate goal. What specifically do you have to do, and by when, so that you're in a position to reach your final objective?
  - *Example*: "By September 30, 2011, I will successfully complete the executive training programme offered by Crunchy Chips International."

- Then work backward some more. What do you need to complete before that second-to-last goal?
  - *Example*: "By March 1, 2011, I will submit my application for the executive training programme, outlining my successes as a key accounts manager, and I will be accepted into the programme."
- Work back again. What do you need to do to make sure the previous goal is reached?
  - *Example*: "By January 1, 2011, I will complete my second year as a key accounts manager with Crunchy Chips International, and I will earn the prestigious Key Accounts Manager of the Year award."
- Continue to work back, in the same way, until you identify the very first milestone that you need to accomplish.
  - *Example*: "By January 1, 2010, I will complete my first year as a key accounts manager with Crunchy Chips International, and I will be rewarded for my performance by gaining responsibility for clients purchasing over $10 million per year." "By January 1, 2009, I will be promoted to key accounts manager with Crunchy Chips International, and I will have responsibility for clients purchasing over $1 million per quarter."

When you read a backward plan, it doesn't look much different from a traditional forward plan. However, creating a backward plan is very different. You need to force yourself to think from a completely new perspective, to help you see things that you might miss if you use a traditional chronological process.

This can also help you avoid spending time on unnecessary or unproductive activities along the way. Furthermore, it highlights points of tension within the plan, showing where you'll need to be particularly creative to make the next step successfully.

KEY POINTS

On the surface, backward planning doesn't seem much different from traditional goal-setting processes. You start with a basic vision, and then you ask yourself what needs to be done to achieve that vision. You can read your plan from the beginning to the end, or from the end back to the beginning. Backward planning, however, is more than reversing the direction of your traditional plan.

It's about adopting a different perspective and, perhaps, identifying different milestones as a result. It's a great supplement to traditional planning, and it gives you a much fuller appreciation for what it may take to achieve success. After all, the more alternatives you have, the better your final plan will likely be.

LEVERAGE

To lift a heavy object, you have a choice: use leverage or not. You can try to lift the object directly–risking injury–or you can use a lever, such as a jack or a long plank of wood, to transfer some of the weight, and then lift the object that way. Which approach is wiser? Will you succeed without using leverage? Maybe. But you can lift so much more with leverage, and do it so much more easily! So what has this got to do with your life and career?

The answer is "a lot". By applying the concept of leverage to business and career success, you can, with a little thought, accomplish very much more than you can without it. Without leverage, you may work very hard, but your rewards are limited by the hours you put in. With leverage, you can break this connection and, in time, achieve very much more.

LEVERS OF SUCCESS

So how can you apply leverage to your career? And how can you achieve much more, while–if you choose to–reducing the number of hours that you work?

To do this, you'll need to learn how to use the leverage of:

- Time.
- Resources.
- Knowledge and education.
- Technology.

Time Leverage

Using the leverage of time is the most fundamental strategy for success. There are only so many hours in a day that you can work. If you use only your own time, you can achieve only so much. If you leverage other people's time, you can increase productivity to an extraordinary extent.

To leverage your own time:

Practice effective time management. Eliminate unnecessary activities, and focus your effort on the things that really matter.

As part of this, learn how to prioritize, so that you focus your energy on the activities that give the greatest return for the time invested.

Use goal setting to think about what matters to you in the long term, set clear targets, and motivate yourself to achieve those targets.

To leverage other people's time:

- Learn how to delegate work to other people.
- Train and empower others.
- Bring in experts and consultants to cover skill or knowledge gaps.
- Outsource non-core tasks to people with the experience to do them more efficiently.

Providing that you do things properly, the time and money that you invest in leveraging other people's time is usually well spent. Remember, though, that you'll almost always have to "pay" up front in some way in order to reap the longer-term benefits of using leverage.

Resource Leverage

You can also exert leverage by getting the most from your assets, and taking full advantage of your personal strengths. You have a wide range of skills, talents, experiences, thoughts, and ideas. These can, and should, be used in the best combination. What relevant skills and strengths do you have that others don't?

How can you use these to best effect, and how can you improve them so that they're truly remarkable? What relevant assets do you have that others don't? Can you use these to create leverage? Do you have connections that others don't have? Or financial resources? Or some other asset that you can use to greater effect? A good way of thinking about this is to conduct a personal SWOT analysis, focusing on identifying strengths and assets, and expanding from these to identify the opportunities they give you.

Knowledge and Education Leverage

Another significant lever of success is applied knowledge. Combined with education and action, this can generate tremendous leverage. Learning by experience is slow and painful. If you can find more formal ways of learning, you'll progress much more quickly. What's more, if you select a good course, you'll have a solid foundation to your knowledge, and one that doesn't have high-risk gaps.

This is why people working in life-or-death areas need long and thorough training. After all, would you want to be operated on by an unqualified surgeon? While few of us operate in quite such immediately critical areas, by determining what you need to know, and then acquiring that knowledge, you can avoid many years of slow, painful trial and error learning. In the same way, it's inefficient if many people in an organization have to learn how to do their work by trial and error. A much better way is for organizations to capture the knowledge gained by the first few in some way and pass it on to others.

This is the core of the "knowledge management" concept. Premium Members of the Career Excellence Club can hear more about this in our Book Insight on The Complete Idiot's Guide to Knowledge Management. The keys to successfully leveraging knowledge and education are: firstly, knowing what you need to learn; secondly knowing to what level you need to learn it; thirdly, being very focused and selective in your choices; and fourthly, in taking the time to earn the qualifications you need. Even then, having more education or more knowledge isn't necessarily a point of leverage. These become advantages only when they can be directly applied to your career goals and aspirations—and when they're used actively and intelligently to do something useful.

Technology Leverage

Finding technology leverage is all about thinking about how you work, and using technology to automate as much of this as you can. At a simple level, you might find that all you need to keep you in touch with home and work is a laptop computer.

Alternatively, a personal digital assistant can help you maintain a single, convenient, properly-backed-up time management system. Cell phones that access e-mail and browse the web are handy tools for making the best of your downtime during working hours or while traveling. If you're a slow typist, voice recognition software can help you dictate documents and save time. Tools like Google Desktop Search can help you manage and find documents in such a way that you no longer need to file digital documents. And Google itself provides a great, quick way of finding relevant information online. At a more sophisticated level, you may find that you can use simple desktop databases like Microsoft Access to automate simple work processes. If you do a lot of routine data processing you can find that this saves you a great deal of time. More than this, you only need to set up a process once with a tool like this-afterwards the process will be executed the same way each time, by whomever initiates the process Businesses can choose from a wide array of software solutions.

Some of these can automate or simplify tasks that are otherwise very time-consuming. Customer relationship management databases can bring tremendous benefits for sales and customer service organizations, as can point-of-sale inventory systems for organizations that need to track and manage inventory. Websites and web-based catalogs can give clients easy access to up-to-date product information, and help them place orders simply and easily. And blogs and e-mail-based newsletters help people stay in contact with thousands of people quickly and easily. All of these use technology to provide tremendous leverage.

KEY POINTS

Using leverage is the art and science of getting much more done with the same, or less, effort. At a simple level, this can free up your time to concentrate on things with the highest priority. At a more sophisticated level, it helps you achieve at a much higher level. When you invest time and resources to leverage technology-as well as to leverage time, resources, and knowledge —you have a recipe for unprecedented success. Use what you and others have to your advantage, and see how far it will take you.

Index

N

O

P

R

S

T

U

V